Preparing for Digital Law Practice

David Whelan

LAW LIBRARY DIRECTOR & ASSISTANT PROFESSOR

UNIVERSITY OF ILLINOIS CHICAGO SCHOOL OF LAW

CAROLINA ACADEMIC PRESS

Durham, North Carolina

Library of Congress Cataloging-in-Publication Data

Names: Whelan, David P. author
Title: Preparing for digital law practice / David Whelan.
Description: Durham : Carolina Academic Press, 2026. |
Includes bibliographical references and index.
Identifiers: LCCN 2026005030 | ISBN 9781531034252 paperback |
ISBN 9781531034269 ebook
Subjects: LCSH: Practice of law--Automation | Practice of law--
Data processing | Legal research--Data processing |
Legal ethics--Technological innovations | Artificial intelligence--
Law and legislation | Records--Management
Classification: LCC K120 .W455 2026
LC record available at https://lccn.loc.gov/2026005030

Carolina Academic Press
700 Kent Street
Durham, North Carolina 27701
(919) 489-7486
www.cap-press.com

Printed in the United States of America

This book is dedicated to the memory of L. Ray Bishop,
a lawyer and mentor who kindled the
law practice technology flame in me and who remains a beacon for me
and to Leila, Gillian, Gareth, Oliver, and Sirius

Contents

Introduction

This book is for law students and will introduce them to a wide variety of contexts in which they will experience or interact with technology during their law practice. While much of the information is applicable to lawyers in private practice, it is written to help a law student, about to graduate, to understand the technology they will see in law practice and understand *why* it is used in the way it is.

It is particularly important for law students to start to understand that technology use in law practice comes with professional ethics obligations as well as something more basic: law practice technology has to serve some purpose. The legal profession has been scrutinized for decades and sometimes referred to as laggards or luddites for failing to quickly adopt the latest technology as each wave crashed against the door of the law practice. There is some truth to the vision that a lawyer who went to sleep in 2005 and woke up in 2025 would (except perhaps for the Apple iPhone, cloud computing, and generative artificial intelligence) recognize most of the technology that they had to use to successfully represent clients. Even the brand names and products are largely the same.

This consistency is a reflection of how lawyers use technology and how the very practice of law has not changed substantially over the decades that the personal computer, and later the mobile phone and tablet, has been a part of the law office. That is why this coursebook will start with a client matter and you will follow it through the many paths it might follow—including a non-engagement letter but always to a closed file—in its lifecycle in your law practice.

When you see how technology supports the law practice, it is easier to see how you can use it yourself. We have used technologies like books and pens for centuries and the shift to silicon-based tools only means we may have to adapt more rapidly to the change they bring. At heart, though, the same fundamentals are at play: a lawyer must act competently and represent their client within the scope of their professional obligations. As you work through each chapter, you will have the opportunity to consider what selections you might make in order to comply and still be an effective legal practitioner.

The practice of law is an individual one. You may end up at a firm or clerking for judges or working in a clinic. At the end of the day, though, the professional obligation is yours alone. You will want to ensure that the technology you choose, even amongst the technology your organization may provide you, enables you to fulfill that obligation. Hopefully, this book will help you to start to think about those choices as you prepare to join the bar.

Acknowledgments

This is a book that has existed in my head for more than a decade. It would be impossible to name everyone who impacted this project. This is my third book, but the first would never have been written without Lilly Ghizas at Canada Law Book. That encouragement was a pebble starting a rockslide. I am so grateful to Meg Mitchell and the team at Carolina Academic Press for their support. Meg particularly helped me navigate a new process, and her feedback as I fine-tuned my approach was critical to this book seeing the light of day.

Any errors in this book are my own, but I am grateful to my erstwhile colleague and collaborator, Phil Brown at the Law Society of Ontario, for reading through the manuscript and providing feedback. We have discussed many of these issues in his podcast series and on educational programs we contributed to. This text is a product of my own hands—no artificial intelligence included!—but, while I enjoy writing, I dread the mechanics related to preparation of the manuscript. I owe my son, Gareth Whelan, a huge debt for reviewing and conforming the text's citations. His attention to detail and his expertise at organizing information found holes that I had missed in my own revisions. It made the preparation of the text that much easier and enjoyable for me.

Preparing for Digital Law Practice

Chapter 1

A Look at Practice Technology

Application of Technology Over Time

Technology is a foundation of law practice. It is a mistake, however, to think that law practice technology emerged with the silicon transistor and micro computing processor. Lawyers have used technology for centuries to make their delivery of legal services more efficient and to support their professional competence.

We ignore the book and the pen as technology at our own peril. This perspective—that lawyers began using technology 40 or 50 years ago with the advent of the personal computer—subordinates the practice of law to the latest technology fad. This book will aim to reset that perspective.

Lawyers have been practicing law using a tried-and-true set of processes since long before the Microsoft Corporation was a gleam in Bill Gates' eye. These processes provide a framework to practice law onto which the latest technology is layered. The law student or lawyer who understands this interplay between the process and the tool will be able to adapt to the never-ending change of technology that will occur over the decades of law practice in their future. You are not preparing just for your first year after graduating law school; you may be thinking about, selecting, and adopting technology for the next fifty years.

We replace the pen with a word processor and migrate from paper documents to emails and other digital objects. Sometimes we return those objects to a print format to satisfy a court or other purpose. We even make some of our digital objects look like they are pieces of paper. But the purpose, the why, remains the same.

We can put this another way: lawyers' processes for decades if not centuries have not changed. A lawyer will be drafting documents and managing their availability for years if not their entire career. Lawyers have had to communicate with clients, to represent them in negotiations or in court, and to manage their retainers and to bill them for the work the lawyer has performed. They have had to file documents with courts and make persuasive arguments with visuals and discovered evidence in a wide range of formats.

Unsurprisingly, lawyers have, over time, considered that there may be ways to practice law more efficiently and in ways that generate more revenue. The American Bar Association's Special Committee on Economics of Law Practice distributed a pamphlet to all ABA members in 1958 exhorting them to:

> Periodically examine their own practice through cost analyses of types of practice, maintenance of time records, computation of fees and maintenance of simple accounting records.[1]

By the 1960s, the ABA had upgraded the Special Committee to a Standing Committee. It was joined by a Special Committee on Electronic Data Retrieval. At a panel discussion in 1961, there were some very specific needs for the modern lawyer:

1) The biggest and of most immediate interest to lawyers [of the use of electronics], and a use for which a number of systems are already operational, is storage and retrieval.
2) Also of great interest are mathematical calculations that lawyers perform continually and often with great difficulty in view of the many individual factors they have to take into account. A specific example is the use of computers to handle the mathematical aspects of estate planning.
3) A third use is to assist in predicting or guiding judicial behavior.[2]

It would be many more years before most lawyers were using computers to manage these law practice challenges. They would continue to find those core issues—storage and retrieval—to be key challenges even as technological

1. *Report of the Special Committee on Economics of Law Practice*, 83 ANN. REP. A.B.A. 439 (1958).

2. *Proceedings of the Special Committee on Electronic Data Retrieval, August 7, 1962*, 3 MOD. USES LOGIC L. 244 (1962).

change accelerated. Already, though, in 1963, the computer's place in the law practice was being identified:

> There appear to be definite areas of the attorney's work in which the computer will affect his present practice.... The computer will simplify the preparation of paper work for the lawyer's clients who are required by statutes, regulations and contracts to prepare formal reports, e.g. income tax. It will assist in the preparation of pre-trial factual information and in handling large-scale evidence in the "Big Cases."[3]

Soon, the Special Committee on Electronic Data Retrieval would be upgraded to a Standing Committee on Law and Technology. These committees evolved, becoming the precursors to the Law Practice Management Section and today's Law Practice Division. Like small rivulets of water snaking out across the professional landscape, then combining and growing, law practice technology has changed incrementally as new tools were found to improve old processes. These lawyers were clear, though, that, in order to use technology, the lawyer first had to understand what it was they were trying to accomplish. The recipe needed to exist before the cake could be baked.

The Shift to Law Practice Management

Today's law practice technology—or #LegalTech—is built upon decades of thinking about how lawyers can apply better tools to familiar processes. This is one explanation for why the adoption of new technology by the legal profession has appeared to be so much slower than the pace of technological change. The creation of newer tools does not necessarily create an improvement or efficiency that will benefit the practicing lawyer. Additionally, the U.S. legal profession is a collection of over 1 million individuals. Each individual will come to law practice in a different way, adopting and using processes in a personalized manner, one which can make it challenging for a new, generic technology to be quickly adopted by a large group.

One of the focuses of this text will be the cost to acquire and maintain new technologies. It is not just the price tag of the device or software, whether it is bought and owned or just leased in the cloud. There is a cost to adapt a

3. Thomas H. Wilson, *Can Lawyers Use Computers?*, 7 So. Tex. L.J. 35 (1963).

current, functioning process to align with the new technology. There is a cost to train the lawyer and their staff on how to use the technology. There is also the cost to train them so they use it in a way that ensures compliance with the lawyer's obligations around confidentiality and professional conduct. This will impact not only the lawyer and the lawyer's staff, but also the relationships with the people you will rely on who provide outside services to your law firm.

There is a tension between the continual change in available technology and the friction caused by the need to carefully and ethically adapt to that change. When a lawyer prepares to make a change in their practice, to apply a new technology, they should do so with an understanding of the risk and the impact it might have on those obligations. While we immediately think of confidentiality and lawyer-client privilege, a lawyer's duty goes much deeper and is impacted far more widely by practice technology.

Let's look at two relatively recent technology advances that significantly rattled the legal profession. Both of these continue to impact operational choices by law firms in the United States, despite being increasingly mature technologies. When a lawyer is considering adopting new technology, the existence of an analogous technology—just as with an analogous case on one of your research memos—can make this assessment easier.

Cloud Technology

We take cloud computing as a normal part of law practice now, but it caused a great deal of consternation for lawyers when it emerged. Like many other emerging technologies, it seemed to create confusion about what a lawyer could do with it, ethically. Lawyers looked to their regulators, who were themselves not well informed or prepared to address the new technology, to no avail. We will look at it in more detail later, but cloud computing essentially took your data storage or your application that had, up to that moment, lived on a computer in your law office and moved it out onto a computer on the internet.

A lawyer who moved their client files, calendar, emails, and other communication out onto someone else's servers might have felt very much ill at ease. Where was client data being stored and how was it being secured? Who could access the data in addition to the lawyer, even if only to ensure it was being backed up? What happened if the cloud service went out of business and the lawyer needed to recover the data or migrate it to a new service?

Or the lawyer might have been entirely comfortable, feeling confident because they were already using the same cloud tools for their personal information. Or they may not even have realized that, by making certain choices to use websites for their law practice, they were working in the cloud. Cloud technology was adopted very quickly by consumers, who used applications like Google Mail or Microsoft's SkyDrive (a Microsoft OneDrive precursor) without too much concern about where the files lived and who maintained them. As you will discover, it is not uncommon for a solo or small law firm legal professional to use the same technologies in their personal and professional lives. A lawyer adopting cloud computing in their personal life may not have considered the ethical implications of using the same technology in their law practice.

Some lawyers insisted on keeping everything on computers controlled by the law firm and within the physical confines of the firm's property: on-premises or "on prem." But even that was a bit of a blurred line. A law firm with multiple offices almost certainly used some network to transmit information from office to office, and file and email servers in that law firm may not be in the same geographic location. A solo lawyer sending an email attachment to a client may not be able to control whether that client is using cloud technology, even if the lawyer does not.

Over time, lawyers have adapted to these concerns. Not surprisingly perhaps, it may be because there was precedent for the technology. We put files on a hard drive or computer in our office. Now we put them on someone else's hard drive or computer. There are analogies we can draw that help us understand how the technology is supposed to perform. Not at a technical level, because a lawyer's technology competence need not be the same as that of a computer systems administrator, data scientist, or software developer. But analogies help lawyers assess when they can adopt a similar technology and when they need to investigate it more.

It would be incorrect to say that all lawyers embrace cloud computing. Many large law firms still use internal services and technologies and some solo and small law practices cannot use the cloud without putting their clients at risk. But in the intervening 20 years, lawyers have found a way to balance what they need to do with what cloud technology provides.

Artificial Intelligence

At the other end of the spectrum is technology like generative artificial intelligence. Artificial intelligence has been used by lawyers for a few decades, often through their information systems. Legal publishing websites like Westlaw and LexisNexis have used natural language processing, a type of artificial intelligence. So have law library catalogs or a Google search: "did you mean" prompts are a form of artificial intelligence.

Generative AI does not have an analog, though. It is fundamentally unknowable because each time a lawyer interacts with it, the outcome may be different. That is how it works: it generates. Unlike cloud computing, though, which was relatable technology provided in a new way, AI is new technology provided in a relatable way. We ask a question, and it mimics a response. We call our interactions with it "conversations" as if there was a sentient creature on the other end.

A lawyer who uses generative AI may find efficiencies in drafting documents, performing legal research, or even some of the computational and automation solutions that lawyers of the 1960s contemplated. Artificial intelligence is different from automation, though. Automation is a repeatable, knowable process. If it works, you can see the result. If it fails, you can see that it has failed and make modifications until it works. AI is not transparent in that way. It creates greater risk and requires greater effort by the lawyer to affirm that it is not undermining professional obligations.

This lack of analogy has caused hundreds of lawyers to mistake what they thought it was doing with what it was actually doing. The lawyers adopted the technology without fully understanding that it was not, in fact, something they were familiar with. It has become commonplace to see lawyers sanctioned, fined, and disciplined—and not only in the United States but in other common law jurisdictions as well where the same technology vendors support the legal profession—for misusing generative artificial intelligence in court filings and proceedings. It raises concerns about what lawyers are doing in transactional work where, like an AI-generated will or trust, the impact of the technology may not be known for years, perhaps even after the life of the lawyer who used it.

There is a balance to be struck, then, by the lawyer using generative AI. Each efficiency will be balanced with the need to verify and validate the outcome, something they may not have had to do before they applied AI to their process. You will need to consider the long-term impact of using generative AI.

The focus at the moment is on generative artificial intelligence but we are already starting to see the same label creep that we saw with cloud computing when it was an emerging technology. We went from cloud computing to very specific market differentiations, for example between Software-as-a-Service and Platform-as-a-Service, both cloud-based offerings. Artificial intelligence is increasingly referring to *agentic* AI, or artificial intelligence agents that can act more autonomously as opposed to merely generating responsive content. This suggests that we will be moving from chat bots, where lawyers interacted with systems to get outcomes, to something more akin to a robot, who will take automated steps based on their own learning. Lawyers will need to not only validate the steps that the artificial intelligence is taking but engage in supervision of the steps they are performing. This blurring of the automation and artificial intelligence line will most likely, as with generative AI, occur within law practice technology systems, and that will be where most lawyers will experience it.

Professional Ethics and Technology Acquisition

Every consumer of technology will make a cost-benefit analysis about the technology they use. These decisions are going to impact more than a lawyer's pocketbook. What technology a lawyer acquires access to, and how they use it, will be measured against their professional ethical obligations.

The most obvious of these are a lawyer's duties under their rules of professional conduct. In addition, lawyers who file documents with courts or who engage in certain business practices may have other ethical requirements. One common example is compliance with procedural rules like Federal Rule of Civil Procedure 11, where a lawyer makes a representation to a court that the filing is supported by evidence and warranted:

> (b) Representations to the Court. By presenting to the court a pleading, written motion, or other paper—whether by signing, filing, submitting, or later advocating it—an attorney or unrepresented party certifies that to the best of the person's knowledge, information, and belief, formed after an inquiry reasonable under the circumstances:
>
> (1) it is not being presented for any improper purpose, such as to harass, cause unnecessary delay, or needlessly increase the cost of litigation;
>
> (2) the claims, defenses, and other legal contentions are warranted by existing law or by a nonfrivolous argument for extending, modifying, or reversing existing law or for establishing new law;
>
> (3) the factual contentions have evidentiary support or, if specifically so identified, will likely have evidentiary support after a reasonable opportunity for further investigation or discovery; and

> (4) the denials of factual contentions are warranted on the evidence or, if specifically so identified, are reasonably based on belief or a lack of information.[4]

Missteps and noncompliance can lead to sanctions, professional discipline, and potentially disbarment. As noted above in relation to artificial intelligence, lawyers who are filing court documents citing to or relying on language with fictitious, AI-generated confabulations are in violation of the "existing" law part of the rule.

Some technology acquisitions will incorporate common criteria. A lawyer would use the same criteria buying a piece of furniture or a new appliance. These criteria will include:

- Cost to use or acquire
- Whether they own the product or are leasing or subscribing to it
- How well it solves the problem they have identified
- How reliable or well-respected the product manufacturer or developer is
- What its life span is: how long hardware will last, how long software will continue to work, how long information or resources in a subscription will be accessible, how long objects created with it will be retrievable and reusable
- How it works and integrates with their other systems

For example, in a survey of large law firm technology purchasers, the top three criteria for laptop purchases were weight, durability and service, and battery life.[5] These are very likely the same criteria you used when you were preparing to get a laptop for law school.

A lawyer needs to go beyond these typical consumer concerns, though. Professional obligations impute duties to a lawyer to take reasonable precautions to protect information and to engage in oversight of others, including third parties:

- How it is secured, to meet the lawyer's duty of confidentiality
- What its uptime or availability is, to meet the lawyer's duty of timeliness and responsiveness to their client as well as to be able to work

---

4. Fed. R. Civ. P. 11(b).

5. Int'l Legal Tech. Ass'n, 2024 Technology Survey Executive Summary 7 (2024).

without losing files or data or equipment that might impede or otherwise negatively impact a client matter, or cause a lawyer to lose information that belongs to the client

- If third parties have access to the information or resource, how does the lawyer manage their duty of supervision
- Whether the output of the technology is truthful and accurate, so that a document or communication is an expression of the lawyer's expertise and reflects the client's need

Lawyers have had to be competent advisors for a very long time. It was only in this century that the agencies who regulate lawyer professional conduct decided that they needed to be specific about technology competence. In 2012, the American Bar Association amended Rule 1.1—Competence—to add a comment that discussed technology:

> To maintain the requisite knowledge and skill, a lawyer should keep abreast of changes in the law and its practice, including the benefits and risks associated with relevant technology, engage in continuing study and education and comply with all continuing legal education requirements to which the lawyer is subject.[6]

There is a difference of opinion over whether this commentary to the competence rule has any practical relevance. I do not think it does, and lawyers who are meeting the overall rule standard of "reasonable competence" would be expected to extend that reasonableness to their use of the tools in their practice.

As I alluded to above, the Comment is reactive to a silicon-personal computer mindset and does not reflect that lawyers have been using technology for centuries. The biggest difference is that the tools, the technologies, change more quickly, and there is more choice in outcomes than there was before. A lawyer who is analyzing the costs and benefits in a reasonable manner with their professional obligations in mind and then using the technology in the way it is intended, should be well within the competence rule, with or without the Comment.

---

6. A.B.A. Model Rules of Professional Conduct, r. 1.1, cmt. 8 (Am. Bar Ass'n 2025). Lawyers are not bound by the ABA's model rules. However, around 40 American jurisdictions have adopted the Comment. In 2019, the Canadian Federation of Law Societies of Canada, the provincial and territorial regulators across Canada, adopted a similar comment to their competence rule. Model Code of Professional Conduct, r. 3.1-2, cmt. 4A (Fed'n of L. Soc. of Can. 2024). The language mimics the ABA Model Rule comment and uses the same "benefits and risks" language. The FLSC Model Rule has been adopted in every province and territory in Canada.

What is reasonable? I once presented a seminar to lawyers in Montana, and we discussed internet-based resources, cloud computing, and how a lawyer can secure their systems against outside attackers. "How do I protect my client files on the internet from the NSA?" one lawyer asked me. The National Security Agency is the United States' leading cryptographic and hacking agency.[7] I do not think that having to secure client information so that an entity like the NSA cannot access it is reasonable. In fact, the risk is far more likely that they are unreasonably failing to maintain their systems in a manner that would minimize the risk of attack.

It is reasonable that the lawyer understand the risks associated with using technology resources and whether those risks are reasonable. An encrypted web browser connection to an encrypted cloud host with your client files, where you are using passwords and multifactor authentication is reasonable. It would be unreasonable to upload a client file to an open web generative AI application, since your client's file may be exposed to other people. It might also be unreasonable to fail to put a PIN on your phone, used to access client emails and data, and that you then lose in the seat cushion of a rideshare car. Reasonableness will be more stable than the technology choices that are available.

The Many Faces of Lawyer Technology

The size of a law practice will impact the types of technology it will be able to select from and use. This is a function of economics and the costs of developing and maintaining software. It is worth touching on this point now although, in later chapters, the impact on choices will become clearer. A law practice where money is no object might have more technology options, but, depending on the law firm's size, they may not be better than the ones that are readily available and priced with their law firm's size and needs in mind.

Fundamentally, the entire legal profession runs on consumer software: software that is available and used by everyone. Lawyers may use business versions of this software or hardware but the software itself is not designed for lawyers. It will be used by architects, engineers, bakers, shipping companies, teachers, and others. The challenge for lawyers, then, is how to use it to fulfill

7. The NSA's mission, according to their website, is to "[lead] the U.S. Government in cryptology that encompasses both signals intelligence (SIGINT) insights and cybersecurity products and services and enables computer network operations to gain a decisive advantage for the nation and our allies."

the specific processes of a law firm—including drafting documents for court, e-filing, long-term client file retention, and so on—when the technology is not specifically designed for a lawyer.

The most common software applications in law firms are from Microsoft. Most law firms of any size will run on a version of Windows. They will use the Microsoft Office suite—Word, Excel, and PowerPoint primarily—and they are likely to use Microsoft Outlook for their email software. Law students who are familiar with Google Workspace apps or who use an Apple Macintosh computer may be able to continue to use those applications in law practice, especially if they are solos. But they will be outliers and will find that some law-specific processes, like creating a Table of Authorities for an appellate brief, cannot be done efficiently with any products that were not developed with lawyers in mind which, surprisingly, Microsoft Word was.

The Hourglass and the Legal Vertical

There is also a law-specific technology and services market. In sales parlance, the legal profession is a vertical market. This results in software and hardware vendors and service providers creating products specifically geared to lawyers: Westlaw and LexisNexis legal research products may be among the most well-known. Both products' parent companies make many other information platforms for vertical markets that do not include lawyers. The existence of the legal vertical can encourage vendors from other verticals, commonly from accounting or health due to overlapping professional or security concerns, to attempt to market their products to lawyers. These attempts to cross over are frequently unsuccessful because, while lawyers may share professional ethics with accountants or confidentiality with HIPAA-regulated industries, what lawyers do is fundamentally different.[8]

The legal vertical is a small market compared to consumer technology. The American Bar Associations estimates there are about 1.3 million lawyers in the United States, while the U.S. Bureau of Labor Statistics estimates about two-thirds as many.[9] The legal profession is highly fractured, though, with

8. HIPAA is the Health Insurance Portability and Accountability Act, and it has specific requirements that govern patient record privacy that can be similar to a lawyer's duty to maintain client confidentiality.

9. The American Bar Association estimate is based on a 2024 survey they conducted based on lawyer licensing data from U.S. states. AM. BAR ASS'N, *Profile of the Legal*

those lawyers spread widely across private law practices, government roles, non-profit and quasi-non-governmental jobs, and jobs that are not traditional legal roles at all. After all, what does it mean to be a lawyer?

This means that products developed for the legal profession's vertical market are often tailored to a specific market segment and usually aimed narrowly at the more affluent end of the market, the largest law firms. It is easier to market to a few hundred law firms who have large technology budgets, infrastructure, and identifiable decision-makers—and to make the repeated contacts and follow ups required to create a sale—than to identify potential customers out of hundreds of thousands of solo lawyers and persuading them to purchase your product. Let's talk about this market a bit.

Solos and small firms—defined variously as those from one lawyer to as many as 50 but more usually up to 10—have dominated the profession and are likely to do so for the foreseeable future. These are very, very small businesses. Solo and small lawyer practices account for roughly 70 to 75% of the lawyers in private practice in North America.[10]

Law firms with more than 10 lawyers fall into a variety of labeled groups. The largest law firms, who have consistently accounted for about 10–15% of the profession, may have thousands of lawyers, but even so, the largest U.S. law firm has fewer than 5,000 lawyers. Large law firms are slotted into a lea-

---

Profession 2024, AM. BAR ASS'N. (last visited July 9, 2025), https://www.americanbar.org/news/profile-legal-profession/demographics/ [https://archive.is/36hGP]. The United States Bureau of Labor Statistics sets the number much lower, at fewer than 900,000, with 18% of those in government roles. BUREAU OF LAB. STAT., DEP'T. OF LAB., *Occupational Outlook Handbook: Lawyers,* U.S. BUREAU OF LAB. STAT. (last visited July 9, 2025), https://www.bls.gov/ooh/legal/lawyers.htm [https://archive.ph/emEw2].

10. The legal profession does a poor job of gathering data about itself. The American Bar Foundation has conducted periodic research and found, between 1991 and 2005, solo practitioners made up about 49% of the profession. In 2005, about 20% of lawyers were in firms from 2 to 10 lawyers. Lawyers in firms of 101 or more lawyers accounted for 16% of the profession. As of 2023, the top 200 law firms (as measured by American Lawyer Media) accounted for just under 150,000 lawyers, or about 11% of the 1.33 million lawyers estimated by the American Bar Association to be in the profession in 2023. Canadian regulators track law firm size in a similar fashion—although solos and solo practices are treated as different because of their legal status—and their much more regular and recent data tracks with U.S. firm size distributions. See, for example, FED'N OF L. SOC. OF CAN., FEDERATION STATISTICS REPORT 10 (2023). AM. LAW., THE 2024 AM LAW 100 (2024); AM. LAW., THE 2024 AM LAW 200 (2024); AM. BAR ASS'N, 2023 PROFILE OF THE LEGAL PROFESSION 19 (2024), https://www.americanbar.org/content/dam/aba/administrative/news/2023/potlp-2023.pdf.

derboard by American Lawyer Media each year, designating the top 100 the Am Law 100, the next group being the Am Law 200.

The group of law firms between 10 and 100 is variously referred to as small law firms or midsize law firms. After the 2008 financial crisis, there was a contraction in this area, with some mid-size law firms being absorbed into larger law firms. Others broke apart into smaller law firms. The *National Law Journal* has surveyed the largest firms for decades, and its survey reflects more of this mid-sized firm range. The top firm in 1978 had 434 lawyers. The survey expanded to the top 350 law firms by 2014 and, as of 2024, was the NLJ 500. The largest firm in 2024 had over 4,561 lawyers, and the firm ranked 350th had 115 lawyers.[11]

You can picture the private practice legal profession as a bottom-heavy hourglass. Solo practitioners make up the base while the tapered middle consists of an undulating mass of small and mid-sized firms, topped off by what are, in the legal profession, the behemoths. The legal vertical largely excludes those lawyers who are not in private practice, if only because they often work in environments, like courts or regulatory agencies, where the entity belongs to a different vertical market and has different technology needs. You will find some crossovers—for example, you may have experienced a law firm practice management application in one of your experiential classes or clinics, even though those are not designed with law students in mind—but for the most part each vertical market has its own specific software needs.

It is helpful to understand this distribution because law firms are not, even at the high end, very large businesses. Technology, though, is sold in segments including consumer, small-to-medium business (SMB), and enterprise.[12] While a manufacturing enterprise may have 100,000 employees, in the

11. 2024 NLJ 500 data table, American Lawyer Media. The survey does not report firm size for law firms ranked 351–500. The firm ranked in the 500th place reports on its website that it has 70 lawyers. Copeland Stair Valz & Lovell, *About Us*, Copeland Stair Valz & Lovell (last visited Aug. 16, 2025), https://csvl.law/who-we-are/.

12. Another term for this segment of the market is "small/medium enterprise" or SME. This is not always a matter of marketing semantics. The United States Small Business Administration has a specific determination for law firms that are small. While some industries are measured by the number of individuals, lawyers are measured by gross revenue. Lawyer offices are classified under the North American Industrial Classification System (NAICS) with the code 541110. The US SBA sizing tool uses the amount of $15,500,000 to distinguish between small businesses and those too large to apply for government contracts as a small business. Small Bus. Admin., *Size Standards Tool*, U.S. Small Bus. Admin. (last visited Aug. 16, 2025), https://www.sba.gov/federal-contracting/contracting-guide/size-standards/size-standards-tool.

legal vertical, the term is still used when talking about technology sold to a 100-lawyer law firm. A firm of that size will have another few hundred support staff in addition to the lawyers. The marketing or sales segments are overlaid onto the smaller legal market because different sized firms will be able to take on technologies of varying complexity. A solo will have the ability to choose from both consumer and business products although they may bypass enterprise offerings, due to lack of need as much as cost and complexity.

A large law firm may use enterprise versions of Microsoft Office or Microsoft SharePoint just like any other professional services firm, university, or manufacturer of a similar size. They may have adopted an enterprise practice management application or customer relationship management platform. These are applications and implementations that a solo lawyer would not be likely to use due to their complexity and cost to maintain. But that is not to suggest that a solo or small law firm practitioner cannot use similar technology. Law practices of all sizes have the same business needs and processes but the degree of complexity, and the resources to support it, is what varies by law firm size. In fact, a solo lawyer might choose a less expensive version of Microsoft Office or Microsoft Windows—a home-oriented version for example instead of a business one—or make other choices that a larger firm would not. A solo practitioner may not use Microsoft SharePoint for file sharing and document organization but can implement many of the same processes with a personal Microsoft OneDrive account or with a cloud-based document management service. They may use ConstantContact or MailChimp for their email marketing, neither of which would provide them with a complete customer relationship management experience but would still help them with their marketing and customer interactions.

A solo practitioner or small law firm may also be more nimble, perhaps without even meaning to be. In order to scale to maximize revenue and reach, many consumer technology applications have shifted to or been born in the cloud. Even as recently as 2021, 35% of law firms responding to the ILTA technology survey had a technology acquisition philosophy that was either not yet comfortable with or only considering cloud.[13] That number dropped to 15% in 2024, but solo and small law firms are likely to have adopted cloud-based technology, whether law-specific or not, far earlier. They may not have had the resources to opt-out of cloud technology—like an internal information tech-

13. Int'l Legal Tech. Ass'n, 2024 Technology Survey Executive Summary 11 (2024).

nology (IT) team or space to house a large number of server computers—that the larger law firms were able to lean on.

There are some similarities across firm size, though. By default, a solo practitioner adopts a set of standards when they choose their own technology. It may not be coherent or planned but, if you add staff or hire a second lawyer, they will most likely be asked to adapt to those initial choices. A law firm or law school will also try to adopt a standard set of software, with law schools often emulating law firms rather than what their colleagues elsewhere on campus are providing to their students and faculty. Standards can simplify decision making and purchasing, as well as replacement and technical support. They may also constrain some choices on future technology adoption.

Even at large law firms, though, standards have some flexibility. As more law firms move to cloud computing, standardizing on and mandating specific hardware or software for items like personal phones became harder to justify. Nowadays, you are as likely to see a lawyer with a mobile device of their own choosing as you are to find a device that was provisioned by the law firm for the lawyer's use. The standardization has moved from requiring a specific device, also known as an endpoint, to requiring standardized endpoint security applications that can run on almost any device. It is a way to balance the need for confidentiality for the law practice and ease of use (and reduction in friction) for the lawyer and staff, who are unlikely to want to carry two phones, one personal and one for the office.

Law firms of every size have also standardized on a hardware environment that uses a mixture of clients, or endpoints, and connects them to the law firm's servers. Those servers are large computers running an operating system like Microsoft Windows. Traditionally, they were physical computers that contained storage and ran specific applications. Increasingly, these servers may be in the cloud or may be virtualized. A virtual server resembles the software components of a traditional server: an operating system and applications. Unlike a traditional server, though, a virtual server is not limited to a specific hardware configuration. In fact, a physical computer can host multiple virtual servers all at once where before a law firm might have needed one physical computer for each server instance. Virtualized servers can also be located in the cloud, enabling solo practitioners and small law firms to benefit from the technology advancement and shift away from the need for multiplying physical computers.

The physical servers may be located within the law firm's offices or in a secure remote location or they may be operated by a cloud technology provider.

The cloud computing environment will be the most common whether the lawyer is a solo using Google Workspace in the cloud and Microsoft OneDrive for file storage or a large law firm lawyer using Office 365 in a mixed cloud and on-premises environment. The standardized hardware will come from a small number of providers to help the information technology team to manage problems that arise. A solo lawyer has standardized by the mere fact that they only have one device. Even a small law firm will want to try to buy products from the same vendor to minimize technical support challenges and improve interoperability and parts replacement.

The areas where the greatest differences will be seen are in the complexity of the technology, growing more complex the larger the law firm, and in law-specific technology. We will explore these differences throughout this book so that, when the opportunity arises, you will be able to look for options and make decisions about whether a technology fits your particular style of practice and the processes you have implemented.

Chapter 1 Exercises

A. Inventory your own current technology choices. How many applications are you running on your own computer (that you could access without the internet and fully utilize) and how many applications do you regularly use for law school that are only cloud-based? Make a table—capturing product name, publisher or developer, version, and whether it's local ("on-premises") or based in the cloud—and write a reflection on why you think you have made those choices. Are you using technology that is mandated for you, installed by default, recommended by a friend, or are you making your own choices to adopt a technology?

B. Technology selection can be a very personal choice. Let's take an example that will be universal for law students: note-taking. Research supports the idea that handwriting can help with comprehension and retention of ideas and may be preferable to note-taking on a laptop.[14] A lawyer might write on paper with a pen or they might write on a digital tablet using a pen-like device to record the markings. They may also decide to use audio

14. Jonathan Lambert, *Why Writing by Hand Beats Typing for Thinking and Learning*, National Public Radio (May 11, 2024, 7:00 AM), https://www.npr.org/sections/health-shots/2024/05/11/1250529661/handwriting-cursive-typing-schools-learning-brain.

recording or typing for accessibility reasons. Most law students, whether initially or entirely, will record their notes into a laptop. Think about your own preferences around taking notes.

a. If you were to choose an ideal method of keeping notes, what would it incorporate? What are things specific to you that might focus your selection?
b. How would you go about identifying products that would help you implement your process?
c. How would you estimate the expenses and budget for the technology?
d. How would you store and share your notes? How would you make them portable, so you can archive them or share them with someone else?

C. One aspect of technology adoption that remains underutilized in law firms is training.[15] When you think about the technology you are using, which devices or software applications have you taken a class or watched videos to learn how to use better? Which technology do you wish you knew how to use better? Write down the technology and then write down what you wish you could do better with it or understood more about it. For each technology, research your training options, which might include paid courses from the vendor, free courses through services like Microsoft Lynda, or your public library's online subscriptions.

---

15. For example, a Thomson Reuters survey of professionals found that 79% of law firms and corporate legal departments had either no plans for generative AI training or did not know if they had plans. THOMSON REUTERS INST., 2024 GENERATIVE AI IN PROFESSIONAL SERVICES REPORT: PERCEPTIONS, USAGE & IMPACT ON THE FUTURE OF WORK 24 (2024).

Chapter 2

Planning

The first question to consider when thinking about law practice technology is whether a technology is needed at all. This may seem like a negative approach, but it is important to put the need for a solution in front of the acquisition of a solution. A frequently made mistake in technology purchases and implementation—in law firms and every other place—is to identify a technology before fully understanding the problem it is meant to solve. When you are trying out a new app or you purchase a new technology for your personal use, this sort of planning may matter less. Sometimes you just want to have the latest technology, not because you have a need but because it fulfills some other purpose: prestige, confidence, competitiveness. When it comes to your law practice technology, though, it is important to spend some time planning for your technology. Your professional ethical obligations will be closely tied to how you use the technology and how it is used—intentionally or inadvertently, allowed or unauthorized—by others. Now is also a good time to start to think about the costs you will incur and how you will manage those. This will be a shift from purchasing technology as an individual to thinking strategically, like the business that a law practice is.

The first thing you will want to do is apply technology only when you have a problem you are trying to solve. The adoption of technology comes with a number of costs that you may not have considered or experienced in your personal technology acquisition:

- The monetary cost to acquire it. This is nearly universal, unless the technology is free or free-to-you.
- The monetary cost to maintain it. In some cases, the monetary cost is low in actual dollars, but there is a time cost involved in you or some-

one else fixing and updating technology. With consumer technology, you may decide to throw old technology away rather than maintain it, but that will require budgeting for regular replacements.

- The opportunity cost from the lost time you and your staff will spend learning and adopting the new technology. That is time that cannot be billed to clients and may not generate any revenue for the firm. If the technology continues to eat away at your revenue-generating time, you may find that whatever efficiency or solution it was meant to provide has created new issues to resolve.
- The unplanned costs due to breakages and outages, which will involve money and time, whether yours or that of someone you hire to assist you or, in the case of an outage where you are unable to practice law, both.

A law firm is many things, but, at its heart, it is a business, and it will need to be profitable to be successful. This means that technology should be selected when it can improve your legal services delivery and expand the firm's resources. This means that, as you assess when to bring technology into your law practice, you should be considering whether the adoption of a new technology creates a risk of diminishing your firm's resources: lost time, lost billing, lost revenue, lost clients. Law practice technology should always be additive, making improvements so that your law practice goals are easier to achieve.

This is not just a money question. Technology can enable the generation of more revenue, but that is too narrow a perspective. Technology also addresses the question of time. Technology can make a law practice more efficient, enabling the lawyer or staff to deal with more legal issues. Or that improved efficiency, as measured by the time you have saved by applying new technology, can lead to you and your staff being able to better manage being away from work, improving your overall quality of life.

The time you spend planning your technology acquisition and use is all part of this investment. The planning process itself does not have to take a long time. It can be quite rapid, and, in many cases, it has to be relatively quick because there is a problem you are trying to solve. The technology acquisition and selection process will probably be simpler for a solo practitioner than at a large law firm merely because the decision-making is self-contained, and the lawyer may know what they are or are not capable of adopting easily. At the same time, a larger law firm is probably paying a technology professional to engage in most, if not all, of the decision-making so that the lawyers can continue to generate revenue. A solo lawyer or small firm practitioner often will not have this resource, and technology decision-making will require lost revenue as the lawyer is taken away from client matters. This pressure can lead towards a need to make a much more rapid decision on technology and can lead solo and small law firms into making relatively impulsive purchases of consumer technology. Solos and small law firms lack the friction that larger law firms will experience when they consider enterprise software costs, large implementations, and the impacts any technology change will have on the tens or hundreds of lawyers generating revenue for the firm.

Identify Your Budget

This is a good time to talk about your law firm's technology budget. Everyone budgets, whether they mean to or not. You may spend the money you have with intention, having planned out a purchase and saved up for it. Or you may spend it without that forethought in response to an emergency or because the expenditure is so minor as to not be worth planning for. Law firm technology budgeting can be similarly varied.

Firms know that salaries, building lease payments, research costs, and other overhead costs are a part of doing business. They design their fees and fee agreements and other, alternative revenue strategies around these costs. If you are not bringing in enough money to cover your overhead, and pay yourself an income, you will need to rethink your revenue planning. In order to create your fee structure, you will need to know what your costs are so that you can charge clients enough that you are able to cover those costs and hopefully have something left over. A starting point is to create a budget for these expenses (including yourself and your staff or other lawyers, when you have them).

Yet a surprising number of law firms fail to budget adequately for technology. This is surprising because it would be next to impossible to run a law firm without technology now. Any technology failure is likely to lead to a revenue loss for the law firm, often a loss that will far exceed the cost of the underlying technology and the time to plan the budget. If your fee structure or revenue stream is not accounting for these losses—lost revenue through lost time for billing or unexpected expenses due to replacement costs and technical support—then, at the end of the year, you may end up in a worse financial situation than you had planned.

Only about half of solo practitioners and small law firms have a budget for technology.[1] When you consider the central importance of technology—email to communicate with clients, a phone, internet access via an internet service provider (ISP), the ability to electronically file or to word process a document—it is always surprising to me that the number of lawyers or law firms with a technology budget is not at or almost 100%. This lack of technology budget planning may reflect that, for the vast majority of lawyers, technology purchases are essentially consumer purchases and not business purchases. They may be made in the same way as personal consumer technology choices, driven as much by desire or advertising or impulse rather than with a specific, strategic business purpose in mind. They may also be made only in an emergency mode: if it ain't broke, do not fix it. Either way, it is a risky strategy for a business to adopt when it comes to technology purchasing and maintenance.

The budget plays a specific role in a law practice's technology approach. It acts to document the costs that the law firm incurs each year in hardware and other technology equipment and software purchases and licenses. This is increasingly true as lawyers rely on cloud-based systems and are essentially licensing their software on an annual basis rather than owning anything. The existence of a budget reflects an awareness by the law firm that, if there is a technology failure or change, there will be a financial cost to remedy it. It can also act as a reminder to plan for the future and for technologies that may emerge in the near future that you have not yet heard of or imagined (like artificial intelligence).

Technology Budgets, Generally

There are two over-arching considerations when it comes to creating your technology budget. One is operational, and the other is project focused. Your operational costs are your day-to-day technology expenses: your internet connection, your Microsoft 365 license, and so on. Depending on your approach to budgeting, it may also include your legal research databases and other on-

1. Am. Bar Ass'n, 2023 Legal Technology Survey Report: Technology Basics 12 (2024). 51% of solos and 52% of law firms with two to nine lawyers have technology budgets. Large law firm respondents indicated only 79% of their firms have technology budgets, while around 18% said they did not know. I think it is unlikely that a large law firm does not have a technology budget, and this reflects a lack of awareness about the budget rather than lack of existence of a technology budget.

line services you license. Your operational costs are the expenses you will incur to run your law practice business operation.

An operational budget will include the actual costs that you are obligated to pay to enable your law practice to operate. For example, like electricity, internet access is largely a utility cost. You know the amount you will owe on a monthly or annual basis, and that is added to your budget. Your operational technology budget should include some amount for maintenance: the replacement of a broken mouse, the upgrade to a larger monitor. This maintenance amount does not need to be a large amount, but it should allow you to quickly acquire a replacement piece of technology, almost certainly a piece of hardware, so that you lose as little time away from your law practice as possible. You might think about this amount in relation to your most expensive or most important piece of equipment. For example, your maintenance budget may be equivalent to the cost of a replacement laptop or desktop computer. That way, your plan will be able to absorb the need to buy a replacement. Remember that a budget is just a budget; it is not a commitment to spend the money. The budget merely provides you with a guideline for how much your expenses might be, so that you can then devise your fee schedule to ensure that your income is equal to or greater than your expenses.

Your budget should also contemplate the renewal of your technology. This is a somewhat individual choice, but there are industry standards that can guide your renewal or replacement timeline choices. In general, you can expect a laptop to last three to five years.[2] A desktop computer will be designed for four to eight years of use.[3] Monitors may be more durable and are often scheduled for replacement, in a business environment, every five or six years.[4] Some lawyers will budget for the full amount in the year that they are going

2. Before the COVID-19 pandemic, desktop use in law firms tended to outweigh laptop use. That has been changing since the pandemic, most probably caused by professional services organizations considering hybrid working arrangements. The 2023 American Bar Association Legal Technology Survey found that more than 98% of large law firm lawyers were using a laptop. Only about 37% of solos and 41% of lawyers in firms of two to nine lawyers were using laptops. AM. BAR ASS'N, 2023 LEGAL TECHNOLOGY SURVEY REPORT: LAW OFFICE TECHNOLOGY 12 (2024).

3. A typical desktop computer will be cheaper to acquire and cheaper to maintain over its lifecycle, which may explain the longevity. While very small form factor desktop computers may create constraints, typical desktop cases can be opened and parts exchanged more readily than in many laptops.

4. Gartner Consulting issues a regular PC life span report, as do computer hardware manufacturers. Educational organizations, due to financial reasons, tend to renew on a longer timeline than commercial entities.

to make the technology purchase, but that can lead to greater fluctuations in revenue need. Another approach is to budget for a portion of the purchase and, year to year, put that money aside so that you have the full amount when the purchase is needed. You may have experienced this approach if your bank uses "savings buckets" to help you segment your savings to be earmarked for a given goal or purchase.

In contrast to an operations budget, you will make a project-focused technology budget only when you decide that you need to make a more substantial change to your law practice technology. For example, you may want to move from a desktop-based accounting package to a cloud-based accounting platform. This could involve a new ongoing license to the online accounting package as well as the expense of having a consultant or accountant help you migrate your desktop-based data to the cloud application. Or your firm may decide to migrate from one practice management platform to another, which can require a substantial amount of data migration as well as linkages to documents and the maintenance of critical date information for client matters. You may decide that there is too much variation in the types of hardware—desktops, laptops, monitors, tablets—in the firm and that you want to standardize on a single set of equipment to improve the ability to support it, requiring a large bulk purchase of a bunch of devices all at once. It could be something as simple as the Windows operating system installed on your computer approaching the end of its life, a point at which it no longer received updates, including security patches, and the need to move all law firm computers to a newer version of Windows. Whatever the project is, it may require planning and a larger amount of money than you would normally plan for in your day-to-day expenses, but the expense will be tied to a specific, known goal.

Unlike operations budgets, project-based budgets may not be contemplated in your fee structure and revenue plans unless you have ensured you are making a profit. In most cases, a project budget will require new, unencumbered money because it is a one-off expense. In many cases, this can mean that other budgets are cut in order to free up funds for the project. You may experience this too: a project is necessary, but your revenue is not sufficient to support it. This may mean your operations technology budget gets pared back to accommodate the project. The most important thing is that you have a budget so that you can see where your money is allocated when these sorts of issues arise, and they are almost certain to arise over the decades of your law practice.

Where to Begin Your Budget

The best place to begin your budget is to start with what you know. Identify the expenses you know you will have and work out from there. This is often referred to as zero-based budgeting—you start your budget from zero and add each expense to reach your overall budget amount—and is a simple budget approach. Once you have identified the known items, you can consider how you will plan for unknown expenses.

Unfortunately, with technology purchases, there can be a fair number of surprises in any given year. It may be as simple as a tool that comes on the market—think Apple iPhone to lawyers in 2007, or OpenAI's ChatGPT for lawyers in 2023—that you want to be able to have the flexibility to adopt. Or it could be a reliable piece of your technology that suddenly stops working, like your primary computer, and that needs to be replaced so that you can continue to serve your clients.

Your planning and your budget can go a long way toward minimizing those surprises. A good place to look at your technology expenses is to see what you have *actually* spent in recent years. As you come to the end of your law school career, you may want to start keeping track of those expenses of what you spend on technology now so that, when you enter law practice, you have a sense of what you have been spending on those items and what you might need to earn to cover them:

- Monthly or annual internet service.
- Monthly or annual telephone service.
- Hardware purchases you made during the year: new laptop, new mouse, new monitor, new headphones, new virtual meeting camera, new USB drive, etc.
- Software purchases you made during the year. This one will be hard for law students because so much is available for free or provided for free by your law school. Look at the apps you use regularly (Microsoft Word, Google Drive) and consider the annual cost that they require to maintain access.

One thing to consider and talk to your providers about is whether there are any discounts for annual payments—one and done—that might save you money over 12 monthly payments. When you start practicing law, many of the business-oriented platforms will have annual discounts to lock you in to their product. In some cases, the only option will be a one-year license, which can be as good for you, helping you to know what your expense will be, as it is for the platform knowing that it will be profitable.

Then you can consider the technology that you are not yet investing in as a law student. Some of these may be applications you are getting for free—like Microsoft 365 or Google Workspace—from your law school, or they may be technology that you have not yet adopted or really investigated. These might include:

- How do you backup and ensure you have a copy of your important data (external hard drive, online backup or disaster recovery tool)? Where do you keep your law school writing assignments and your class notes so that you will have them for the bar exam?
- How do you manage your online banking and finances, payment of bills and receipt of payments from others, and how would you do that differently in a professional setting? We'll get to accounting and the specific requirements that lawyers have but, for example, you may have Venmo or Zelle for payments (or being paid). Are these systems integrated with any accounting or other apps that you are using?
- How do you retain data over a long period of time?
- How do you ensure your devices are secured, with passwords or passkeys or multi-factor authentication, and how are those methods backed up and secured? What would happen if you were hit by a car and your mom or dad needed to pay your rent from your bank account or turn off your monthly delivery of avocados from Amazon so the boxes do not pile up while you are in the hospital?[5] How would you give them access to your passwords or your user accounts?

This approach of using prior year actual costs to create a future year budget is a standard budgetary approach. It is not always exact because costs change, often rising from year to year, but many organizations find actual expenses from a prior year give a good baseline for what future expenses will be. Another way to approach this sort of very basic budgeting is to identify what you are willing to pay for each item at the end of its lifespan, and build your budget based on

5. Jason Buechel, *How paper towels, avocados, and bananas became some of Amazon's most frequently purchased items*, Amazon Worldwide (June 4, 2025), https://www.aboutamazon.com/news/retail/amazon-grocery-sales-growth-paper-towels-produce-essentials, [http://web.archive.org/web/20250616223953/https://www.aboutamazon.com/news/retail/amazon-grocery-sales-growth-paper-towels-produce-essentials].

that. For example, let's say you want to plan to buy a laptop and a phone every three years. A laptop can range in price from $250 to $3,000, depending on the capabilities. A phone can be just as costly depending on your preferences.[6] You will need to find a price point that is comfortable for you and then spread that out over the time period that you are planning for, based on the life expectancy of the technology.

My personal price points are relatively low, but they would work for a solo practitioner or even a small firm lawyer. I try to replace a laptop every four years, and I typically have a budget for that laptop of about $1,000. I try to replace my phone every three years, and my price point is $200. If I'm buying a business desktop, I'll be looking in the $800 range, without a monitor. I usually set a budget for a monitor—and I buy dual monitors, although I only replace them as they fail—at about $200.

This means that, if I was to budget for everything—a laptop, desktop, and phone, and a one-time replacement for a monitor, it would work out to:

	Year 1	*Year 2*	*Year 3*	*Year 4*
Laptop	$250	$250	$250	**$250**
Desktop	$200	$200	$200	**$200**
Phone	$75	$75	**$50**	$75
Monitor	$50	$50	$50	**$50**
Total	$575	$575	$550	$575

In the table above, the bold amounts are the year in which the expense would be made. It also assumes a certain amount of fiscal discipline to put aside money as you go. This leaves out any software licenses that are on top, but it gives you a good idea of how simple a technology budget can be when you are thinking about your expenses ahead of time. This assumes, of course, that in Year 1 you have just acquired everything you need or, in the case of the desktop and monitor, within a year or two of purchase.

You may wonder what amount of money is enough. In fact, those are the amounts that I have used for nearly twenty years of technology purchases,

6. You may get your mobile device for free with your mobile plan because you maintain a contract with your telecom provider. If that's the case, you can use your contract as your ongoing technology expense and its conditions for how often and when you can replace your device.

both for personal purchases as well as a guideline for corporate purchases. There is always new technology coming to market, and it usually costs more than older technology and pushes the price of older technology down. This means that no matter what price point you land on for your device, you will almost always find technology at your price point, and it will be newer than the technology you last bought two or three years ago for the same amount.

There will be a wide range of opinions on what is enough and what is too much. In my experience, lawyers tend to pay more than they should for hardware and software, and even for services like website hosting and domain name maintenance. Most solo practitioners who budget for technology plan for expenses between $0 and $9,999 a year for software.[7] Small law firms, those with two to nine lawyers, tend to plan within the same range although they tend to skew towards the top end of that range, as opposed to solos who may budget less than $500 per year for software. Solo practitioners and small firm lawyers tend to plan for no more than $5,000 a year in hardware costs, with most solos under $3,000, and most small law firms over $1,000.[8]

There is a certain consistency in both hardware and software prices. They operate as many other commodities do. You can purchase higher end technology, without question, but you do not need to in order to practice competently and efficiently. At some point, paying more for what is marketed as *cutting-edge* technology may not yield sufficient financial returns to justify the inflated expense. If you set your price point *before* you start to seek out and acquire new technology, it provides a bit of a constraint on your acquisitiveness. It is a bit like when you are looking for housing: you know what you can afford for a lease, and that will dissuade you from applying for a new renovation in a chic building if you cannot afford it (although you might still go in for a quick tour).

For one thing, setting a price point and a budget for technology will make the process simpler merely by reducing the number of options. A slightly lower price point or a slightly longer renewal period to keep your license costs down can mean that you may will most likely be purchasing technology after it has been on the market for some time. This can reduce some of the risk of being an early adopter and the opportunity costs involved with a technology learning curve that draws you away from generating revenue. For most lawyers, purchasing or licensing technology a year or so behind the curve will

7. Am. Bar Ass'n, 2023 Legal Technology Survey Report: Law Office Technology 17 (2024).

8. *Id.* at 18.

afford a good balance between deploying modern technology and doing so at a manageable cost.

Project Costs

A project budget is generally simpler to manage because it is almost entirely a known quantity: what you are doing, why, and what the scope is. This does not mean that the project necessarily has to be a simple one but rather that you are often dealing with a relatively contained set of expenses. You may hire a consultant who will install a new upgrade or a new piece of technology. A law firm may need to pay someone to export files from one system and then re-organize or format them for importing into a new system.

Projects can often be planned for in advance. Once you have your goal in mind, you can identify potential software or hardware vendors. You can get quotes for services or parts or maintenance. You can find consultants who can help you if it is a complicated project that you or your staff cannot—or should not—attempt on your own.

Do you need to do a request for proposal (RFP) or a request for information (RFI)? While RFPs are frequently used by corporations hiring law firms—resulting in what is often described, unfortunately, as beauty contests or beauty pageants—I would expect that they are rarely used in smaller law firms or sole practices when it comes to technology. If your organization is not required to seek multiple bids or proposals because of a legal obligation or compliance reason, it may not go through either process. In particular, when you are looking at legal technology specifically, there are not many products to choose from, and it can be hard to meet even the traditional "three quotes" approach to comparison shopping.

You may not be required to do an RFP for a technology project in your law practice, but it cannot hurt to use some of the same process. One value of the RFP process is that it requires you to formulate your requirements so that the respondents can make an informed proposal. You should know the scope of your project before you start talking to any consultant or vendor about selecting a product or choosing an implementation path. The RFP process also suggests that you are open to speaking to multiple providers to reach your goal. This approach makes sense even outside of the RFP process, and it can help you to avoid being overly focused on a single product or provider for reasons that are outside the needs of the project. I have worked at two organizations that had chosen their email applications because "the CEO liked" the product or disliked the competitor product. An RFP or RFP-like approach can help to remove some of the personality-related issues that can infect a technology acquisition.

How do you create a project budget, though, if you have never tried to implement this type of technology? You start by defining the problem. Once you have defined what you need, you can start to research and ask for information about how to fill that need. A process for defining the problem is included below.

People Costs

It is a mistake to acquire technology without thinking about how it is going to be used and by whom. At the very least, consider who needs to be trained and how they will acquire that training. You should then identify the cost of this training—and the time that will be spent on training that will not be billed, reducing revenue—and include it in your budget. This is not only an investment in your people and yourself, but you are also improving the chances that you will maximize the value of the technology you have selected.

Practice Pointer

If you take no other training during legal career, get some professional training in how to use the Microsoft Office products. You do not need to become certified, but most lawyers lack anywhere near the amount of understanding of how Microsoft Word, PowerPoint, Excel, and Outlook can be leveraged for a more efficient law practice. There is a huge amount of automation capability built into office suites (of which Microsoft Office is just one) that, unfortunately, seems to go untapped by lawyers. Microsoft offers a wide variety of online courses, but I would recommend going to an in-person, sit down, hands-on training session in Microsoft Word or Excel at the very least. It will be money well spent, and the training will last the lifetime of your law practice.

In addition to training, plan for downtime whenever you have a new technology acquisition. Technology outages, even planned ones, have a cost associated with them. You may not be able to quantify that cost exactly enough to be able to put it in the budget, but it still exists as a potential revenue impact.

For example, let's say your law practice is growing, and you are adding a staff person or two. Now, instead of connecting your PC directly to the internet, you need to buy network hardware. The installation of that hardware may require a consultant. It will definitely involve some loss of internet access while the hardware installation interrupts your connectivity. These costs can be minimized—you can schedule offline tasks for the outage or you can participate in an in-person meeting, where the internet is not required—but they are part of the technology acquisition.

Many law firms do not have their own technology staff. According to the ABA's surveys, only about 10% of solos turn to an internal technical support person *first* when they have a problem.[9] In contrast, solos and many small and mid-sized law firms (up to about 50 lawyers) rely on consultants for technology assistance.[10] Some lawyers may tap into friends and family for technical support—again, blurring that line between personal or consumer technology and business technology—or engage in self-help with varying degrees of success. As a law student, you will have had years of schooling where you have been asked to use and perhaps self-support your own technology. You should not be surprised that you will find similar expectations or needs when you enter law practice.

There are a wide variety of technology support options available that allow a law firm to grow without necessarily hiring dedicated technology staff. These include on-call consultants, specialists brought in on a specific project, or even a round-the-clock virtual help desk service. Each one will have its own costs, but you can account for them in your technology budget.[11] If anything, there seem to be more services where you can bring on the exact amount of support you need, for the time you need it, without necessarily having to make a long-term commitment to hiring staff or engaging consultants.

Keep in mind that these outside support services will probably have access to your clients' confidential and private information. You have a professional responsibility to have oversight over how this information is accessed by third

9. Am. Bar Ass'n, 2023 Legal Technology Survey Report: Technology Basics 27, question 22 (2024).

10. *Id.*

11. The technology support burden will fall on someone. It will fall on you if you are a solo and do not have a plan for support. In many small law firms, the burden falls on paralegals and other staff who were hired to do tasks *other than* information technology. The ABA survey reports that lawyers turn to their non-technical support staff about 10% of the time in solo practices and as much as 17% of the time in law firms with two to nine lawyers. *Id.*

parties. There are well-known instances of technology support, like Best Buy's Geek Squad, being used to report to state actors on the contents of computers provided to them.[12] When you decide to select someone outside your law practice to support your technology, you will want to document what they are and are not allowed to do with your practice information and data.

Define the Problem

Every technology acquisition or enhancement should be matched to solving a problem for your law practice. You should start by defining exactly what it is you are trying to do. Some of these questions will be so clear—I need a way to send and receive email—that we do not even think about the need. We find out how to sign up for an email account, and we log in to our email account, via a web browser or through an email software application, and we send and receive messages.

Other questions will require more deliberation and exploration to understand the problem and potential solutions: I want to improve my client intake so that I can send an engagement letter out faster. Or I want to improve my response time to clients. Or I want to receive fewer calls after 5pm. Or I want to be able to retrieve my email more efficiently. What is "improve"? How do you measure "faster" or "more efficiently" or "fewer"? You will want to have some inkling, if not exactitude, about what you are trying to accomplish.

For example, it is common in technology licenses or support agreements to have what is known as a service level agreement (SLA). This agreement sets out the parameters of what you can expect as far as service, and you can often negotiate—or use as a selection criterion as to whether to hire a provider—these service levels. Not surprisingly, a more responsive service will cost

12. Laura Walmsley, *FBI Used Paid Informants on Best Buy's Geek Squad to Flag Child Pornography*, NATIONAL PUBLIC RADIO (Mar. 7, 2018, 6:00 PM), https://www.npr.org/sections/thetwo-way/2018/03/07/591698708/fbi-used-paid-informants-on-best-buys-geek-squad-to-flag-child-pornography [http://web.archive.org/web/20250518002711/https://www.npr.org/sections/thetwo-way/2018/03/07/591698708/fbi-used-paid-informants-on-best-buys-geek-squad-to-flag-child-pornography].

It would not be hard to imagine a lawyer involved in a child pornography case or one involving sexting to have images that would trigger a report by an FBI informant. Far more likely, though, is that your clients' files will be reviewed despite there being no child porn on your computer, and you are not going to be able to control what that knowledge of your client files is used for.

more money. Some organizations refer to the "Five 9s" for high availability service, service that is available 99.999% of the time.[13] You will need to determine whether you can accept a lower level of service for a lower price; it is a risk-balancing choice.

Some providers will offer compensation for any failure to meet the service level agreement. You might be promised a 24-hour response or 99.9% uptime on your internet service and experience a two-day outage (which is about a 97.5% uptime). Your agreement with the provider will determine if the outage qualifies for compensation and what that compensation is. The reality is that the compensation for most consumer or even small business systems is likely to be less than your lost revenue for your law practice. Even if you are able to afford high-availability service, you will want to consider what your backup plans are so that your law practice remains resilient even during outages. For example, you may decide that your mobile phone's data plan is your internet backup, since you can create a hotspot with it.

As you define your problem—I need my internet access to be more reliable, which means I want it to be available at least 99% of the time—you can start to find service providers or companies that can meet those requirements. A 99% uptime requirement immediately eliminates all of the providers who only promise 98%, making your selection a bit easier. Or you may find that your requirement sets the cost too high and you can start to engage in the balancing of what you really need versus what is available given your resources.

In each of these cases, you will want to understand the steps involved in your current process. Even if it is not a great process, you will have some sort of process unless you are doing something for the very first time. In those cases, you are often still able to identify a process—what you think the process will be, what you have observed or been informed by others the process is—to base your planning on. Thinking about the steps involved in your process can often help you to identify ways to improve the process: why am I doing X and not doing Y?

13. Definition of Five Nines. *High Availability*, WIKIPEDIA (last visited Aug. 16, 2025), https://en.wikipedia.org/wiki/High_availability#Percentage_calculation.

Practice Pointer

Process thinking is not set-and-forget. You will become better at using technology, lawyering, and at running a law practice business. As your expertise grows, you should revisit how you use technology and see if your expertise puts your process or choices in a different light. Put some time on your calendar each year to think about where you might make changes. Even better, start a task list with the process pain points that you experience. When time allows, look at that list and choose something to improve.

Some of our processes are so basic or ingrained we may not think about them. Think about how you use your web browser in relation to law school. When you start your web browser, do you start at the same page every time? Do you have to type in a new website URL location or click a bookmark to go to the page you need? How often does your process immediately involve opening the web browser and clicking that bookmark? Would you save time by making that bookmarked page your web browser's home page, so it opens automatically each time you open a browser tab or window? Even these little processes can benefit from a bit of thinking and can hide efficiencies that, cumulatively, can make a positive impact on your productivity.

It is not uncommon for people to jump over this planning stage and go directly to the new technology acquisition: I want to be more efficient doing X; therefore I need to acquire Y to be more efficient. This is risky in any but the simplest process change because you may not really know why you are inefficient and, therefore, may not be able to adequately assess how to make an improvement. It also means that you may miss the opportunity to ask two fundamental questions:

- Does my current technology allow me to make that improvement, using a feature I have as yet not used or used in this way, and that I might learn how to use with training?
- Do I need technology at all to make this change? Or do I need to make a process change without technology? For example, you may want to reduce the number of calls you receive from clients after 6pm to zero. You can do that without technology. First, communicate to

clients what their expectations will be (and are reasonable for the practice area you are in). Then practice turning off your device or your notifications or otherwise alter your habits so that, even should a call be made, you are still achieving your goal of zero calls after 6pm.

Practice Pointer

When you are called to the bar, you will have the professional obligation to respond to and inform your client promptly.[14] You can reduce the need for your client to contact you if you are regularly, proactively providing information to them. Unless you work in an area where client emergencies are common, you should be able to create reasonable boundaries around your communication. That can mean spending more time during your work hours to ensure that your outside-of-work hours are free of client contacts. Sometimes we look for technology to help us manage problems that are, in fact, caused by poor communication or other broken processes. Technology will not necessarily fix those problems or help you meet your professional obligation. Think about how you practice—without technology—so that the technology is an enhancer.

Let's start first by identifying the problem in need of resolution. It may not be clear to see how you identify the problem. The most common indication that there is a problem is that something has failed to work or it is not working in the way you'd like. You may hear yourself saying "I wish my computer would ..." or "I wish I could ... better." You might have missed a deadline you'd set yourself or, worse, a court deadline or undertaking. An important email may have arrived but ended up in your spam folder for a few days before you realized it, making it appear that you are unresponsive to the sender.

It does not always have to be something that failed. It could also be something much more mundane, like needing to do more without adding staff or without a particular set of skills or expertise. This might be things like adding content to a website on a regular basis or reducing the number of steps that it takes to schedule an event.

14. A.B.A. Model Rules of Professional Conduct, r. 1.4 (Am. Bar Ass'n 2025).

Whatever the case may be, you need to look at what the current steps are. If you have a missed appointment, then look at how appointments are created and by whom. Is there an approval process to ensure that conflicting appointments are avoided or that the person to whom the appointment is assigned confirms they are aware of it?

If it is a missed assignment, how are those assigned and by whom? For the person who receives an assignment, how are they able to prioritize the assignments they have received: are they given a priority list, for example, or do they have to make their own priority list, which may open the door to a misunderstanding of priorities. In the worst case, are assignments prioritized not so much by importance but by the assigner's hierarchy or status in the law firm, creating the potential for low-priority, high-status assignments being completed before high-priority, lower-status ones? You may be working on the wrong priorities because of your law firm culture, and technology may not be able to help you to remedy that problem.

There is almost always a way to improve a process. Let's stick with prioritization. Perhaps you shift to a shared task list (or implement a task list at all, a simple technology that you may not be using yet), so the assigners can see what you are working on and re-prioritize for you or shift deadlines or merely have a more transparent view of what you are already working on. Perhaps you have a daily email that outlines the two or three things you are working on each day. Some of these are not great productivity or management approaches—daily emails can particularly feel like micro-management—but depending on the tempo of your law practice, these small tweaks to a process may ensure that everyone understands what work is being undertaken.

Again, if you are planning to practice as a solo, some of these processes will be simpler. Even if you are dealing with a process that is just your own, though, you may want to write out, step-by-step, how you complete a process just for yourself. You may find that, by writing out your process, you can more clearly see where the improvement can be made and a change or adaptation attempted.

Let's take a universal example: an email sent to the wrong people. For a lawyer, this can be catastrophic. You only need to do a quick search online to find stories about lawyers who have mistakenly breached lawyer-client confidentiality by emailing sensitive information to a journalist or other third party instead of sending it to their client or someone in the law firm. How does that happen?

The simplest answer is that someone typed in the wrong email address. But that is often not the entire story. When we create an email, we often approach it with a process like this:

- Fill the TO: line with the recipient's email address. Many people will use the auto-fill option, so they will start to type a person's name and accept one of the offered addresses.
- Fill the CC: or BCC: lines depending on who else needs to receive the email. They will repeat the same address lookup steps.
- Fill in the Subject line.
- Type in the email.
- Attach the attachments, if there are any.
- Send the email, either by scheduling it for a specific time or sending it immediately.

This is such a simple process that we do not even think about it, we do it so often. The layout of email software follows the same template, and we progress, as humans are wont, from top to bottom. In fact, if an email system was set up differently, we might balk at it even though it might be designed for a better user experience and one less likely to result in mis-addressed emails.

One problem is that, when we use auto-completed email addresses, we may select the wrong one. This is particularly true when we are not sure about the spelling or we are feeling pressure—either because we know what we want to say or because we are in a hurry—to get to the message body. Given this likelihood of valuing the message drafting step over the email addressing step, how do we minimize the risk of not sending that email to the wrong recipient?

In this case, we have multiple options that might minimize the problem. The first might be to disable auto-completion of addresses, the feature where the email application suggests possible recipients as you type in part of a name. This would mean that you are making a more active, deliberate step when you select a recipient because each one is validated by you when you choose it. This is a good example of how your technology already supports an improvement, without needing to add any technology. You just need to know how it works so that you can make the adaptation.

Another would be to re-arrange the steps of the process. One approach is to write the message *first* and address it afterwards. In that way, you move directly to the most complicated part of the process and take care of it first. You can draft your email and ensure it has all of the necessary files attached. As you write the email, you may find that your list of potential recipients changes. Once you have written the email, you can now go to the Subject line and provide a clear description of the message body. Then, at the end, you can select—with deliberation—the recipients of the email. This is a simple process change that you can turn into a habit over time. It does not require any new technology.

Practice Pointer

Efficiency and speed are not the same thing. As the saying goes, *haste makes waste*. The need to accomplish something quickly can cause you to rush and to make mistakes. The benefit of having a process that minimizes the risk of errors is that you can move more quickly and efficiently through it because you know you are following a set of steps, like a checklist. The more you use your process, the more efficient you will become and the faster you will be able to complete the process without creating unnecessary risk.

In the case of that misdirected email, while there may be repercussions for that error, it is a process that can probably be solved without new technology. Unless you are using an email application, particularly a web-based email app like Outlook.com or Gmail.com, your email client (Microsoft Outlook, Mozilla Thunderbird, etc.) should provide the ability to manage and disable auto-completion options. If not, you can always adopt a new email application or make your email drafting process more methodical.

Another reason to understand the process you are impacting is that, if you decide that you do need to acquire software, you will need to be able to map that process to the technology. If you do not know how a process works, you may miss critical gaps in what the technology can provide.

Let's say that someone has missed a court event that should have been placed on the shared calendar. An error of this magnitude can cause decision-makers to panic and skip the process analysis and definition of requirements stage. Your law firm may decide that, in order to avoid this, it needs to select a practice management system or docketing calendar solution to improve management of court events. These applications are far more complex and will impact many more processes than just the issue of fixing a missed calendared item. These technology platforms can bring many additional benefits as well, but this course of action may fix one thing and break others. Additionally, if there has not been an assessment of what the process is and how it failed, laying any type of technology on top may not reduce the likelihood of failure in the future. The application of technology will not fix a broken process. The process will need to be fixed; technology will provide the opportunity to make the process better.

Is New Technology Necessary?

This may seem somewhat counter-intuitive in a book about law practice technology, but technology is not always the solution. Many process problems can be overcome without the acquisition of new technology. Make this assessment first, before you expend resources on a new acquisition. You may find that all that is needed is a change in the process: an additional step or a better explanation for an existing step.

Perhaps the process is not the problem, but the people implementing it are. Law firms have consistently lagged in providing training for their technology. It is really only at the largest law firms that close to or 100% of lawyers have access to training of any kind for the technology they use. This drops to about one-third of solos and fewer than half of lawyers in firms with fewer than 10 lawyers.[15] If these numbers reflect the value lawyers place on training, then they may also reflect the level of training that support staff in law firms are able to receive.

This training deficit extends not only to existing technology but emerging technology as well. Despite the blanket impact of artificial intelligence on the legal profession, training remains something of an afterthought. In a Thomson Reuters survey of a variety of professions, lawyers were ahead of the curve on training in comparison to other professions but still only made it available in about 40% of law firms.[16] One would think, given the criticality of the technology's impact on practice and the already widespread misuse of it by lawyers in court filings, that training would be close to 100% on a risky technology.

The lack of training is something to remedy before adopting new technology. It may not be the solution to a process problem, but it may shine light

15. Am. Bar Ass'n, 2023 Legal Technology Survey Report: Technology Basics 30 (2024).

16. Thomson Reuters Inst., 2024 Generative AI in Professional Services Report: Perceptions, Usage & Impact on the Future of Work 27 (2024). The law firm respondents were split almost evenly across three organizational sizes: 1–10% (34%), 11–179 (35%), and 180+ (31%). This is not a normal distribution for the North American legal market. The survey participants were from eight countries.

on alternative solutions that can be accomplished with existing resources. When you consider the variety of costs in time and money that technology acquisition brings, training is probably a smaller investment and will improve productivity even if it does not entirely solve the problem you have identified.

Avoid Scope Creep

Once you decide to acquire new technology—that it provides the best road to solving the problem identified—the next step will be to focus as narrowly as possible on that solution. A common outcome in technology acquisition is scope creep: a technology project started with one goal and ends up with a much broader, often more complicated focus. This not only consumes more resources—time to acquire and implement, greater learning curve and impact on staff and lawyers, more money—but can end up providing solutions to problems that do not exist, and it can run the risk of not solving the initial problem at all.

This can be particularly tricky when you are considering acquiring a technology that has a great deal of integration. An email application is relatively simple. Its primary function is to send and receive email. Some email applications will include a calendar and perhaps a contact manager. But, for the most part, you can use an email application with a separate contact manager and even a separate calendar.

This is less true with some law practice-specific and business-oriented technologies. Many of these applications will have tight integrations of functionality that go beyond the narrowly defined problem you are trying to solve. To adopt one of them, you need to be open to making far greater change than the initial problem you may have identified.

In some cases, an integrated system will be the best option even if your initial problem is narrowly scoped. It may be that the integrated system provides X, Y, and Z functionality and you are only seeking to improve the X function. But if your law practice does not yet have something to fill the Y and Z gaps, then this may be an overall improvement even if it is more complex than you had initially intended. In many cases, though, more functionality—more bells and whistles, as the phrase goes—will result in a higher cost, and so you should have a high degree of confidence that you will have a future need for currently unused or unneeded functionality before you expend time and money on acquiring it.

A simple example of this is building in some resilience around your law practice documents. There should always be at least two copies. The most common approach is to store one copy on the computer you use (in your Documents folder or somewhere similar) and the other on a backup medium. One common solution is to buy an external storage device and to make a copy of your computer files and store them on the external drive on a regular basis.

A more complicated process would be to use the cloud to keep a replica of your computer files (perhaps in addition to the external hard drive). An added benefit to using a cloud service like Microsoft OneDrive or Box is that they often offer version control. This means that, if you find you have overwritten an important template or client document, you may be able to recover the earlier file. A backup system will not necessarily enable a simple way to do that. Adopting a cloud backup may provide you with more than just a backup copy of your current files.

It is likely that you may find that a discrete technology application does not exist for the problem you are trying to solve, and your only option, if you seek a technology solution, is a product that is far larger and more complex than you had initially intended. In that case, if you have not already considered it, you may want to look at training and see if you are just missing out on how to use existing functionality. Or—and it bears repeating—make the choice to not add any technology. The lack of a well-matched technology solution can sometimes suggest that most people have solved the problem with a process change. Sometimes this may be the wisest move.

This is a decision point. It may be that you want to do what you can with the systems and training and people that you have. That, if there is a risk, it is now more manageable than it was once you have reviewed and improved your process. Or, if the goal was to become more efficient, that training and deliberate action can move you closer to your goal. The alternative is to continue towards the acquisition and to prepare properly to ensure its successful implementation.

Identify Technology

Once you have identified the problem and know how you are going to pay for it—perhaps you even know how you will implement and ensure training—it is time to start looking for possible technologies. You may already have a technology in mind, but if you do not, there are a variety of ways to find possible matches. If you have nowhere else to start, a bit of technology research can help.

> **Practice Pointer**
>
> Yes, you are the customer. But keep in mind that, especially in the very small legal technology world, you are dealing with people on the other side of each product interaction. Be considerate of their time and efforts as you make your inquiries. If you do not have specific plans to acquire their product or one like it—you have not budgeted for it yet or you are not planning to adopt the technology for a year—be clear about that. It will let them know to follow up with you but not to waste your time or theirs on turning you into a customer until you are ready.

An internet search can be a good starting point, if you know the keywords to describe the technology you are looking for. Even better, if you have heard about a product or come across one in your search, you can start to use that as a keyword. As you search, you can narrow your funnel as you learn more keywords or product names.

I tend to find the product name approach the fastest. If you have found a product in an advertisement in an American Bar Association publication like the *ABA Journal* or *Law Practice Management* magazine, you can start with that. You can research that product by going to the product website. But it may be just as useful to search for the entire range of products. The search I use is "alternatives to [product name]," where the product name is the one I have identified, preliminarily, as a good match for what I'm trying to solve.[17] Try "alternatives to Microsoft Word," and you will see a variety of other word processors that are available. This list will include free and open-source office suites as well as freemium office suites like Microsoft Office.[18] Once you have a list of a handful of applications, you can start to do some comparison shopping.

17. If this sounds like a legal research approach you learned in law school, you are correct. You start with the known resource and work your way out from there.

18. Freemium is a portmanteau of "free" and "premium." Software is frequently only one or the other—commercial or free—with the smaller category of shareware. But shareware assumed that, after you tried it, you would pay. Freemium emerged with the move to cloud computing. Premium, fee-based products were made available to internet visitors for free. The free tier of the product might be free forever (like Google's Gmail or Microsoft's Outlook web app), but the goal was to encourage those free adopters to become paid adopters (of Google Workspace and Microsoft 365). There are lawyers who choose to remain on the free versions of the freemium applications they use.

This approach works whether you are looking for general business software or law practice-specific software. If your primary goal is to find alternative applications, search engines will help you reach it. If you are looking for product reviews and even customer feedback, this will be harder to find as you move away from common, commercial business software and into the more niche legal vertical products. There will just be more people talking on the internet about their experience with products like Microsoft's Exchange email server or SharePoint document platform than there will be for the practice management and time and billing software that is designed for lawyers.

When you are looking at law practice technology specifically, you may find the research a bit circuitous. In some cases, one or two service providers or platforms will have blanketed publications with advertisements or created great search engine optimization so their product is found online. It may feel as though there is not much choice. If you are worried you are missing out on products, make sure you are talking to your colleagues. Some bar associations will also have practice management advisors (PMAs), either on staff or on retainer, who are available to help guide your planning or technology choices.

Create a Short List

Now may be a good time to get comfortable with spreadsheets, if you are not already. Or you can create a simple table in Microsoft Word or your word processor of choice. Either way, make a list of the requirements you are looking for in a tabular row. In the rows below that, list the applications you look at and check off which products have functionality or features that match your requirements.

This is useful for a number of reasons. First, you may find that none of the products are matching your requirements. In this case, you need to start your research over, keeping in mind that the keywords you were using were not leading you to the resources you were hoping to find. This may be a good time to ask a colleague if they have any ideas. Another source of information may be a technology consultant, either one you have worked with before or one who has worked with lawyers.[19]

19. There is a school of thought that products developed by lawyers for lawyers, and technology consultants who have prior law practice experience, are better capable of supporting the technology needs of lawyers. I do not follow that school of thought. Technology products can be adapted to the practice of law without any lawyer being involved in their

You may find that the terms that one technology solution uses are different, if only slightly, from those used by another. Is there a fundamental difference between "bank-level encryption" and "military-grade encryption" or are they just marketing terms?[20] If you have a matrix of your criteria, you can start to see how different responses to your questions ("what sort of encryption does the platform use to secure my information?") vary.

Alternatively, you may find that every product you find solves your problem. Wouldn't that be great! That may be an embarrassment of riches, but having more than one possible solution is better than having none. It may also reflect that your criteria are too generic and that you may want to be more specific or detailed. If you end up with multiple products that meet your needs, start to look at what distinguishes them. This might include their pricing or their license. It may include what countries they host their servers in or other nuances that your law practice may value.

You may also find that, especially with consumer or business technology, you have multiple solutions that are largely indistinguishable. In this case, all you have to do is choose. There is rarely a wrong answer if you have defined your scope well and stuck to your selection criteria.[21]

There is unlikely to be an exact match for your needs at this point. You will probably have identified products based on the most positive information possible, which will be that provided by the product developer or service provider themselves. Now is the time to start to dig in a bit more. You should rank the products you have found and choose the highest ranked one for the next step. This is still not your final selection phase. But you will want to learn more about whether what it purports to do is *actually* what it does do.

---

development. Similarly, a lawyer can explain their ethical requirements to any technology consultant: ethics and the use of technology are not unique to the practice of law.

20. The answer in this case is "yes" to both. While there are some distinguishing features to different encryption levels, they would not be meaningful for most lawyers. You are trying to act reasonably, and so this sort of detail may have more to do with marketing than risk you are contemplating.

21. Buyer's remorse is a common cognitive dissonance when selecting and acquiring technology. If you wait three months or pay 50% more, you will be contemplating entirely different technology. The difficulty this puts you in is that, in three months or at 150% of your current planned expenditure, you could still wait three more months or spend an additional 50%. There will always be something new and improved. If you struggle with buyer's remorse, be aware that it should be expected and is not an indicator that you are making poor technology choices.

Cloud Computing and Other Emerging Technology

It is worth touching on the challenge that emerging technology or technology laws present. When a new technology appears that might serve a law practice, there is a heightened need to understand what impact it can have before you adopt it, due to your professional responsibilities. This is particularly true when the technology creates an unknown or as-yet untested risk around client data and lawyer confidentiality or other parts of law practice, as opposed to the *business of law* applications that you will use to run your law office.

The latest technology to raise this issue is generative artificial intelligence. Similarly, in the early part of this century, cloud computing caused widespread concerns among lawyers, particularly lawyer regulators, about the risks it raised for the profession.[22] It is not always obvious how to square a lawyer's professional obligations with an emerging technology.

In the case of cloud computing, this professional ethics concern was superimposed on the creation of the USA PATRIOT Act, which allowed for electronic surveillance and collection of electronic communications like email.[23] When lawyers primarily kept their communications on their own devices, there was a sense—perhaps not entirely defensible—that it was harder for a government to access those files. The move to cloud computing changed some of that calculation, causing law firms to be wary of storing client data in the cloud. It is true now as it was then, but anything that you can access via the internet may be accessible to others on the internet.

It seems quaint now, given how much the legal profession relies on cloud-based services for all aspects of their business operations. This is particularly true in solo and small firms where the blend of consumer and law practice-specific technologies is likely to be greater than it is in larger law firms. Common applications like Microsoft 365 and Google Workspace, Outlook.com

---

22. Cloud computing comprises a wide variety of services that are provided on servers that are outside the law firm and that may be shared with others. The most common of these services to impact lawyers—Software as a Service or SAAS—shifted law practices from having software installed on every PC to accessing it through the internet. For more on law practice and the cloud from an earlier perspective, see my book *Practice Law in the Cloud.* DAVID P. WHELAN, PRACTICE LAW IN THE CLOUD (2013), https://archive.org/details/practicelawinclo0000whel.

23. CHARLES DOYLE, CONG. RSCH. SERV., RL31377, USA PATRIOT ACT: A LEGAL ANALYSIS (2002), https://www.congress.gov/crs_external_products/RL/PDF/RL31377/RL31377.2.pdf.

and Gmail.com, accounting software like Intuit and Sage, document storage on OneDrive or Box, and many other tools are cloud-based. In some cases, the locally installed applications have disappeared or the product was designed from the start as a cloud computing application.

Lawyers are sometimes characterized as being luddites or slow to adopt technology, but I do not believe that is the case. They need to be able to assess the risks they are taking when they adopt technology, to understand how it will impact their professional ethical obligations. In fact, there were plenty of lawyers who were using the cloud perhaps without realizing it—most notably with web-based email—but I'd argue that even legal research sites like Thomson Reuters Westlaw or RELX Lexis were cloud-based, especially from the perspective of those who remember having to install local software for each service—and who continued to use it despite the intervening methodical assessments of cloud computing's risks by lawyer regulators. While lawyers seem to always be cognizant of their professional obligations, it seems that the adoption of technology is far more likely to be based on whether lawyers see that a technology fits into their law practice or not: whether it saves time, allows the generation of more fees, and so on. Not all emerging technology does that, and so a failure to adopt a new technology reflects less on the lawyer—or even the perception held by the lawyer regulator—and more on the product's role within a law practice.

In many ways, that is where the legal profession finds itself following the widespread availability of generative AI. There is a certain degree of caution but also significant adoption, although perhaps indirectly. Like many technologies, generative AI is being embedded in other tools and services that lawyers already use (like legal research platforms, office suites and productivity tools, and so on). Unlike cloud computing, where the failures and missteps of lawyers seem, in hindsight, to have been relatively rare, the negative impact of AI on the legal profession seems more pronounced. The remarkable number of documents filed by lawyers that have resulted in court responses highlighting the fake cases and entirely made-up confabulations feels unprecedented.[24] It

24. A European researcher has created a database with links to court decisions (numbering over 120 at the time of writing) calling out the artificial intelligence-generated filings of lawyers. Damien Charlotin, AI Hallucination Cases, Damien Charlotin (last visited May 27, 2025), https:/www.damiencharlotin.com/hallucinations/ [http://web.archive.org/web/20250527122309/https://www.damiencharlotin.com/hallucinations/]. The term *hallucination* is a term of art for these representations, but they are increasingly characterized as *confabulations* given that the latter term describes actual false creations, while the former refers to *perceptions*. There is no question that the fake cases, and the fake ci-

is becoming routine to hear of lawyers being disciplined for these misuses of technology, and one wonders at what point the regulators will be dealing with more severe outcomes than mis-cited cases.

If your search for technology solutions for a problem in your law practice leads you to an emerging technology, be aware of your heightened risks. There is no reason to avoid emerging technology, but you may find that you will need to do more research to understand the challenges it poses. For example, a lot of lawyers had to understand what secure web browser connections (http v. https) were once they were using information in the cloud.

They may also never have considered what happens when a cloud provider suddenly disappears and, unlike a local server failure where you may have a backup, all of your practice data is entirely unrecoverable.[25] Time moves on, and the shift caused by cloud and web encryption has led to most web browsers and all reputable online providers that store data using encrypted connections. You will even find that some law practice technology and business technology providers will anticipate your concerns about data loss.[26]

The moral of the story is that newer technology may give you an advantage over other lawyers or provide you with new ways to practice. It may also bring unknown risks that you will need to plan for as part of your technology adoption. There is no reason to push yourself or your law practice to adopt emerging technology unless it solves problems you have identified.

---

tations and language, are creations. See, for example, Andrew L. Smith, Felix Greaves, & Trishan Panch, *Hallucination or Confabulation? Neuroanatomy as Metaphor in Large Language Models,* PLOS DIGIT. HEALTH , Nov. 2023, https://pmc.ncbi.nlm.nih.gov/articles/PMC10619792/ [http://web.archive.org/web/20250318010456/https://pmc.ncbi.nlm.nih.gov/articles/PMC10619792/].

25. Before generative AI and even before cloud computing, there was an emerging pre-cloud variant called application server provider (ASP). It is very much what developed into Software as a Service (SAAS) cloud computing. When Red Gorilla, an ASP that provided online time and expense management, collapsed in 2000, it took a number of law firms' data with it. This early failure led to a more thoughtful consideration by law firms and those supplying them online services about how to provide data escrow or portability in the event of a dissolution. Stefanie Olsen, *Red Gorilla Can't Survive Capital-Market Jungle*, CNET (Jan. 2, 2002, 4:43 PM), https://www.cnet.com/tech/tech-industry/red-gorilla-cant-survive-capital-market-jungle/ [http://web.archive.org/web/20231204210605/https://www.cnet.com/tech/tech-industry/red-gorilla-cant-survive-capital-market-jungle/].

26. For example, a practice management cloud provider, Clio, offers a data escrow service for their law firm clients. Clio, *How to Switch Legal Software: A Guide for Law Firms*, CLIO (last visited Feb. 14, 2025), https://www.clio.com/playbooks/switching-software/ [http://web.archive.org/web/20250214085844/https://www.clio.com/playbooks/switching-software/].

Test Your Findings

This can be an expensive use of a lawyer's time. If you have staff to whom you can delegate the work, that may save you time and resources, although they may not have the insights needed to see the product from your perspective. Alternatively, this is another good place to bring in a consultant. They should bring not only the time but experience in testing out products for lawyers. Or they may be able to configure the product with your requirements in mind so that, when you do start testing on your own, you can maximize the impact of your participation in the testing.

If this is a relatively discrete app, one whose adoption does not impact other systems or require integrations to be created, it is probably something that you or a staff person can quickly test on your own. You may use it for a week and see how it fits into your workflow. After that week, you may determine that it is or is not a good fit, that the requirements are met or they are not. At that point, you may move on to your second-ranked solution or you may decide that you are ready to make a selection.

Your ability to do testing and product trials will depend on your resources available. For example, I wanted to move my email server. My current server lacked sufficient spam control and my inbox was increasingly being overwhelmed by spam and potential malware as exploiters and spammers adapted their communications. I identified two solutions, one of which was easier to migrate to, the other harder. I decided to migrate my email to the easier of the two solutions and found that, while it was better than what I currently was using, it was still far from minimizing the spam as much as I had wanted. I used it for 10 days and decided it was time to rethink my choice.

My original email server was still available as a fallback so I decided to move from the first-choice solution to the second one and test it out for a week or two. Worst case, I could still revert to my old server and keep looking if this did not solve my problem. In fact, what I found was that the second-choice option, while a bit more complicated to configure, had two additional spam control tools that it had not advertised in its marketing and that I had not known to ask about. This product solved my problem, and I was able to migrate my systems entirely over to this new server. It is sometimes impossible to know how well suited a product is until you are actually using it.

If it is a more complicated app, this becomes a more complicated process, because each product will require more effort to prepare for testing. Testing a practice management system or an accounting system, for example, will take more time and may not be something that you can easily pivot from. A trial or demonstration period can help by letting you see how the application functions. Even if you get a sense of the product, it may not provide you with enough information to move forward. Once you start putting client information into the system, you may find that it is difficult to retrieve it and return to your existing system. You may attempt to run parallel systems for a period of time, which creates an enormous amount of overhead impact for you and your staff to maintain client information in both systems and do it accurately. At some point, you will need to make your best guess at whether it is a good solution for your problem or not and then commit to moving forward if it is.

I think of these more complicated systems as a bit like buying a car. It is a multi-year investment and a significant one in terms of time and money. A test drive will help you get a feel for its abilities, but it will not unearth all the great features or the ones that you will eventually find irritating. You also do not have to keep that car forever. Give yourself a reasonable amount of time that you will commit to the product and keep that timeframe in mind. While you may have to commit to a complicated system without a full understanding of its abilities, you can adapt to that system just as you would to a car.

There are those who will argue that this reflects a flawed due diligence process. It may be true that you can perform a more extensive, deeper dive into a product, just as you can with legal research. At some point, though, you will start to experience diminishing returns, and the additional knowledge will not make your decision easier or clearer. Technology acquisitions can sometimes suffer from analysis paralysis, where the need to acquire just a bit more information or a bit more certainty inhibits a decision. This delay can have a financial cost as the problem you are experiencing goes unresolved, but you are spending time (and therefore losing revenue) in this fact-finding.

There remains the strong likelihood that a lawyer will tend to want systems that will adapt to how that specific lawyer practices law. This desire for close compatibility is understandable. At the same time, it can create risks in the acquisition process. One common outcome is when a law firm finds off-the-shelf software and decides to customize it to match the law firm's processes. This type of realignment may undo some of the software's benefits if the law firm's processes are not well devised. There can be substantial hidden costs in trying to make a technology adapt to a law practice rather than the other way around. It is often easier in time and money to adapt a law firm's processes to the technology, which will usually have been developed in a way that ensures that the product performs the way it is supposed to. System customization can start small and become more complex and costly over time, as new versions of the original software are released and potentially introduce incompatibilities with the law firm's unique choices.

Law students in particular may want to work with the technology as it is designed rather than trying to recompile it to fit their expectations. The technology may reflect the experience of its customer base, either lawyers or other professionals, experience that you do not yet have as a law student and will not gain even in the first year or two of your law practice. A new lawyer who is able to adapt to the technology will not only find less friction in adopting the new technology but should hopefully gain from the wisdom that has been baked into the product's development. As you gain expertise as a lawyer, you can start to see where your practice approach deviates from the software and start the process of finding ways to fill those gaps.

Practice Pointer

It cannot be overstated how disastrous customizing software can be for an organization. It should only be done when the organization has a very clearly documented process it needs to emulate. One organization I worked for adopted Microsoft SharePoint without considering how different it was from the network-stored files and folders that all staff used. They attempted to force this folder-centric system onto SharePoint, without realizing that SharePoint had constraints on file and folder naming. Teams started creating folder-in-folder storage without heeding Microsoft's recommendation, at the time, that folders not go more than three levels deep. This clash of process (deep foldering) versus how the software was designed (to rely on metadata, not folders) derailed the adoption of SharePoint. It added years to the project, which was to transition off networked file storage servers and on to SharePoint sites. Be flexible in achieving your goals and know the difference between what the technology has to do and what you would like it to do.

Beyond internet searches and talking to the sales or account representatives, you can ask the technology providers for references. Once you are over a few thousand dollars in an investment, I would ask for references. You may find that you know other lawyers who are using the same software or technology consultant or hardware.

If you do not, though, and particularly as a recent law school graduate, the simplest way will be to ask for references. These will be people you should be able to call and ask questions of. You should generate a short list of questions—both to be respectful of the other lawyers' time but also to ensure you are focused on the features most important to you—that can be sent to those customers and that touch on your greatest concerns. Focus less on whether the customer reference likes the product or service and more on how they experience the functionality or expertise you hope to get out of it: does it do X or are you able to do Y? Have you experienced any problems doing Z?

Product and Vendor Complexity

The old adage was that "no one gets fired for buying IBM." This conservative approach to buying technology has evolved over time ("no one gets fired for buying Microsoft"), but there is a kernel of truth to it. You may find that you want to take a cautious approach to your technology acquisitions. This is particularly true as someone starting out in the practice of law, who has little experience with law practice technology and may not have the resources—in time or money—to make risky technology choices. When you select widely used products from large corporations who are making regular investments in the technology, you are eliminating one area of concern around technology acquisition. As you become more expert with your law practice and your technology, you may start to diverge from that perspective.

There can be substantial benefits from using technology from a single vendor, whether it is hardware or software. A lawyer on a Windows computer who also uses Microsoft 365 and the Microsoft Office Suite, who uses the Microsoft Edge web browser and the Microsoft Defender security tools, will have a highly integrated system. If nothing else, Microsoft is likely to ensure that all of its products work together.

Given its primacy among the technology used by lawyers, you could do worse than a Microsoft-centric approach. It should give you wide compatibility with other lawyers and their systems. If you were to start working at a law firm or even lateral out of one later, this would be a portable approach across law firms. At the same time, you may find that other applications, made by competing vendors, provide features you would rather use.

Practice Pointer

Where possible, make these choices yourself. For example, Google Chrome remains the most popular web browser in North America. You may find that court and other websites encourage you to use it because they believe that their websites are designed for Chrome. This is usually not true, and the website owner or their staff may not realize that, unlike the older web browser Microsoft Internet Explorer, Microsoft Edge and Google Chrome use largely the same underlying software, the Chromium web browser. Web browser extensions found in the Google Chrome web store will work on Microsoft Edge. Websites "designed for Chrome" should render the same in Microsoft Edge, and the distinction is mostly aimed at Apple Safari and other web browser users. Another common place this arises is when websites recommend that you download the Adobe Acrobat PDF Reader. In most cases, the PDFs can be read within any modern web browser or a PDF reader of your choice. Before you download additional software and create new complexity for yourself, see if your current software handles the problem, even if the website suggests that it will not.

One benefit of using multiple vendors is that you can create your own array of applications or tools that are best suited to your needs. For example, you might use a Google Gmail account but still prefer to use Microsoft Word as your word processor and even Microsoft Outlook as your email client. This works best in a situation where you have multiple discrete applications that do not require integration. Where you need integration across applications, or the application itself is heavily integrated, as is the case with law practice management systems (where the component parts are not divisible), this use of multiple vendors may not make sense or not be possible. There are pros and cons to either approach. There is also nothing that prohibits you from changing your mind and your approach later in your career. Just keep in mind that technology change comes with costs, no matter which direction you are going.

In general, using multiple vendors for software makes more sense than using multiple vendors for hardware. At first, as a new lawyer, you will not need to worry about standardization for yourself. If you start your career at a law firm or government agency or court, you will almost certainly experience it there, and the decision to standardize will have been made for you. Computers, whether desktops or laptops, as well as peripherals like printers and monitors, can often be purchased at a discount if they're bought in bulk or through a business equipment plan.

These discounts and business accounts are usually through a single provider, someone like Lenovo or Dell. While you may be able to purchase anything you want from these vendors through the relationship, most organizations will buy multiples of the same device all at once: the same laptops, the same desktops, and so on. This provides a number of benefits to the organization. For one thing, it simplifies supporting those devices. They should all operate the same way, especially if they are all running the same software. They should all have the same internal components, which should reduce the diagnostic work for technology staff or consultants. If one fails, it can be replaced with an equivalent device and that should reduce the impact on the person using it, since it is familiar.

The purchase of multiple devices that share a standardized configuration means that, as law firms get larger, they can create a local stockpile of parts for these computers. Instead of a different type of processor or type of memory or hardware cable for each device, they can have parts that can be swapped into any purchased device. This reduces the likelihood that staff and lawyers, who are turning their time into revenue, will lose time or productivity.

This standardization usually extends to the software on machines as well, although I expect standardization mostly happens within law firms where there are dedicated IT staff. Otherwise, there may be no effective way to identify, configure, and then enforce software standardization. This standardization is exactly what it sounds like: every computer will run the same version of Windows, of Microsoft 365's apps like Word, Excel, and PowerPoint, and the same version of Microsoft Edge. If there is a license for Adobe Acrobat, everyone will have the same version and the license will be properly registered.

Standardization can be constraining in some instances, because, if implemented well, it should block the installation of unapproved or non-standard software. At the same time, it can help alleviate licensing issues by ensuring that staff and lawyers are not installing more copies of a product or products than are authorized. Standardization can reduce risk around license violations within the law firm.

There can be a large degree of technical complexity as a law firm or organization grows in size. Perhaps more importantly, it is not uncommon in legal organizations for people with more status to try to avoid standardization in ways that people with lower status cannot. This results in senior lawyers or law professors or judges having technology that is different, perhaps unique to that particular individual, that other people within the organization cannot have. Not only does this increase the workload for the technology staff, who now may have to learn to manage a much wider variety of tools, it can create hostility between the have-nots and the haves, and cause time and financial waste as more parts are required or more complexity is managed.

Larger Technology Purchases

This book will not cover large law firm technology purchases. They are not fundamentally different, except that the lawyer often will play a smaller or no role in the selection and implementation of them, relying instead on career technology experts and the law firm's business executives or managing lawyers. As a law student, it may be many years until you will have that sort of decision-making responsibility. However, let's talk about some of the elements involved in more expensive or complex purchases here just so that you are familiar with the terms and why, perhaps, you do not need to use them.

When you are dealing with more complex purchases or more expensive ones, you may be licensing technology rather than buying it to own. This can result in ongoing expenses as well as contractual obligations. In some cases, you will need to create a more defensible selection process—particularly if you are working in a government environment, although it can be a necessary or advantageous approach even if you are not—than the selection process that a solo or small law firm lawyer might do on their own. When I talk about large technology projects, these would be in the hundreds of thousands or millions of dollars, far beyond the entire technology expense for a solo or small law firm.[27] Most lawyers will never experience that sort of acquisition, and you will almost certainly not need to contemplate one in your first years of practice.[28]

---

27. This is different from the large law firm technology acquisitions exemplified by Cleary Gottlieb's purchase of SpringBok AI. Large U.S. law firms have created their own portfolio of technology products that may be as much for the benefit of clients to use as they are for the lawyers themselves, such as Cleary's ClearyX technology subsidiary. Sara Merken, *Law Firm Cleary Buys Legal Tech Company in AI Bid*, Reuters (Mar. 18, 2025, 1:02), https://www.reuters.com/legal/legalindustry/law-firm-cleary-buys-legal-tech-company-ai-bid-2025-03-17/.

28. This is not to say that many law firms are managing some very large license costs in law practice, like Microsoft Windows or 365 licenses, or even legal research platforms. A small law firm can quickly face five-figure or six-figure license or project costs. But in many

Large technology projects may use a request process to generate possible candidates who are interested in bidding for the work or who have compatible technology.[29] These processes can include requests for information (RFI) or request for proposals (RFP). Unless you have the purchasing expertise to develop these documents, you can hire a consultant who can help you to create them and manage the process. The documents themselves are common enough, but you will need to be very specific in describing your requirements. Just as you would do as a solo or small law firm lawyer when you are making an individual technology decision, you need to know what problem you are going to solve.

You will also want to investigate or elicit information about ancillary costs. How many staff will the project require from the vendor or from the consultant? What is their hourly cost? What is the ongoing maintenance cost for the technology? What is the maintenance contract like, and what does it cover? These are topics that exist even in the smallest technology purchase, where hardware will probably come with a consumer warranty, and software may have specific terms and conditions that you assent to when you make your monthly payment. The difference is that these clauses and obligations can be negotiable on larger contracts, and they also create substantially more grey area around a selection, a fog that you will want to disperse before you commit to any given technology.

A process complex enough to warrant an RFP may also result in a more complicated relationship with consultants and the vendors involved, and you may need to invest more time in understanding your partners and their business longevity. You will often see the term *due diligence* in relation to selection of these larger technology products or in the retention of consultants to complete a technology task.

Due diligence is one reason that more conventional, stable vendors are often selected over newcomers or those with less experience, just as they are

---

cases, there will be a single source provider so an RFP will not result in a different choice than merely picking the actual platform directly. This can sometimes be seen in government RFPs where the request for proposal document requires a feature or publication that is only available on a single product or platform. The outcome is pre-determined, and there is no need to go through this process unless you are required to do so.

29. At the solo practitioner and small firm end of the spectrum, there are gig sites like Fiverr and Upwork that allow you to post your technology need and freelancers can respond to your request. This can be a simple way to solve a unique technology problem—have something coded for a website or a logo designed or an Outlook email form created—without having to have technology staff available to handle it.

in more consumer-oriented purchases. There is risk management balancing in selecting known quantities. In these cases, though, due diligence does not mean the same thing as the term of art *due diligence*, which envisions far greater research into a company. You should do enough investigation to assuage any concerns you have, but you should not misunderstand the goal here to be to engage in the kind of deep research that an actual due diligence review would require. You are not buying the company: you are just working with it.

It is not uncommon to find products that offer a lifetime license. Keep in mind that this is not your earthly lifetime nor is it even the lifetime of your law practice. It is the lifetime of the product, and that lifetime may be curtailed at any point by the technology provider or its successors.[30]

The converse is true as well. Just because you can use a technology without updating or upgrading it does not mean you should. I have worked with lawyers who stayed multiple versions behind on Microsoft Windows, putting their law practice and their clients at risk for the sake of $100 and a bit of change management. While you should not take a lifetime license at face value, even a perpetual license will need you to maintain the integrity of your technology with updates and upgrades.

If you require a technology for a specific length of time, then you should speak to that vendor about how to ensure that it will be around for that period of time or whether they can guarantee that you will get support for the duration of that period. It is not uncommon for companies to close or to be bought out and for customers or products to be left behind. The best case is not to be

30. A good example of this is a virtual private network provider who bought out a competitor—not completing their own *due diligence*—and being surprised to find a large number of lifetime license holders. It cancelled all of the lifetime licenses. Scharon Harding, *VPN Owner Shows Buyer's Remorse; Claims Was Unaware of Lifetime Subscription*, ARS TECHNICA (May 14, 2025, 2:55 PM) https://arstechnica.com/gadgets/2025/05/vpnsecure-owner-says-it-had-to-cancel-unsustainable-lifetime-subscriptions/ [http://web.archive.org/web/20250515021903/https://arstechnica.com/gadgets/2025/05/vpnsecure-owner-says-it-had-to-cancel-unsustainable-lifetime-subscriptions/]. This is not an issue with small companies alone. When Broadcom purchased a server virtualization company called VMWare, it inherited a client base that had perpetual licenses. It has created an uproar in its handling of these license holders when it refused to extend their service contracts unless they bought new licenses. Scharon Harding, *VMWare Perpetual License Holder Receives Audit Letter from Broadcom*, ARS TECHNICA (June 26, 2025, 3:17 PM) https://arstechnica.com/information-technology/2025/06/vmware-perpetual-license-holder-receives-audit-letter-from-broadcom/ [http://web.archive.org/web/20250705115024/https://arstechnica.com/information-technology/2025/06/vmware-perpetual-license-holder-receives-audit-letter-from-broadcom/].

lured into lifetime licenses but to consider the intended "life" that the amount you are paying will reasonably guarantee. Additionally, if you are setting and following a budget and a technology renewal period for each component of your law practice's software and hardware, you should not be impacted by a false lifetime claim.

Similarly, look behind the meaning of marketing puffery. Cloud computing providers, in particular, seem to tout their security level of encryption. They may use terms like "bank-grade" or "military-grade," which may or may not reflect a common understanding of how secure it is. Instead, ask those vendors (if the information is not provided in their materials) what level of encryption they have implemented *specifically*: AES128, AES256, etc. Then take that keyword and look it up yourself.

When it comes to security, there is not necessarily a right answer: a higher level of security is not always required because a lower level may be *enough*. As a lawyer, you will have to act competently so the level you are most concerned about is the level that is widely understood to protect your clients' information. This level will likely change over the lifespan of your law practice. In the past 20 years, we have seen the standard of encryption, specifically the encryption standards (as shown by their names: 128bit, 256bit, 1024bit, and so on) increase. While AES128 has not yet been cracked with brute force, RSA1024 has, and implementations like web browsers and Microsoft Windows servers that used it have replaced it with later versions, and so the number is not enough information.[31] If you are unsure about whether a marketing term is a technical term, you can either research the term or speak to an expert, like a technology consultant. The more important question for a cloud computing provider may be whether they have suffered a breach before or not, and if they did, how they responded to it.

31. A brute-force attack means that an encrypted or secured resource is hit with repeated attacks often meant to guess a username and password. This is why you are locked out of an account after too many login attempts; it is a limitation on brute-force attacks. *Brute-force Attack*, WIKIPEDIA (last visited Aug. 26, 2025), https://en.wikipedia.org/wiki/Brute-force_attack.

Keep an Inventory

As you start law practice, this may be the easiest aspect of your technology to manage: keep a list. Keep an inventory of the equipment you purchase for your practice: it may be everything you can see on your desk, but it may be more extensive. As your law practice grows, keep expanding that inventory so you know what you are currently using. The inventory can help you to flag how long you have had a piece of equipment and prompt you to start planning for a replacement. There may also be an accounting benefit if you are depreciating your computer technology, so knowing when you bought something and how long you have been using it can be helpful.[32]

Similarly, keep track of any warranties you pay for or register for, so that you actively use the help or support provided by the warranty before you incur lost time or additional costs to solve your issue. I think it is common for people to have warrantied technology and still resort to an internet web search or informal help without taking advantage of their warranty coverage. If you have technical support or a warranty that is still active, the cost of those things has been included in your payment for the product or service. You would be remiss not to use them.

At the consumer end, unfortunately, the only recourse sometimes is to send the technology back to the vendor. This can mean having to work without your device for an extended period or having to consider who might get access to your client files if you ship a device to a third party. This is not a minor imposition. Not only are you without the actual device, but all of the productivity configurations you may have made will be lost while you are without that device. In larger organizations, there is often a spare device available so that you can continue to use a laptop or a printer or what have you. As you renew your own technology, it can be useful to retain the technology you replace, keeping one older generation at a time. That can give you a backup device should your new technology fail to work.

32. Your accountant may want to know what hardware you are purchasing so that it can be depreciated and result in a positive tax consequence for your law firm. If you go into solo practice, you might want to talk to an accountant early on, so you can determine how to ensure your technology acquisitions are treated as business expenses and not personal ones, in cases where they may be dual-use.

Your Law Practice Hardware

Your budget will determine the hardware you can afford. You may have preferences that will shift your costs, but there really is rarely a right or wrong piece of hardware to buy for your law practice. Prefer a laptop? Great. Want a wireless mouse and keyboard and headset? Fine. Gamer headphones with RGB color enhancements? Why not. Apple or Microsoft? It does not really matter. Microsoft products will work on desktops and laptops, phones and tablets, Android, Windows, Macintosh, and Linux systems. Additionally, applications that run on those devices can be used successfully in a law practice even if you decide not to go with Microsoft products. In very rare circumstances, like trial presentation software, you may find that it will only run on one kind of device, like an Apple iPad. Otherwise, your choice of hardware—particularly if you are leveraging cloud computing which will usually operate in any web browser—is unlikely to impact your success as a lawyer so long as you keep it up to date and in good order.

There are some areas where a lawyer might use hardware differently from how you are accustomed to using it as a law student. One suggestion that comes up frequently in law practice is to use multiple monitors. This is a common practice across any industry that works with spreadsheets or documents, so you may not feel this is novel (especially if you are a gamer and already have a multi-monitor rig at home). There is a 50/50 chance you will work in a law firm where the lawyers are using dual monitors, either two distinct monitors or one to supplement a laptop screen.[33] Some of these monitors can be rotated so they are taller than they are wide, accommodating a digital document so that it resembles the way you would hold a paper document.

In most ways, your law practice technology only matters to the extent that it is affordable to you, that it is current, and that it can be maintained (see below on *Patching and Updating*). Your selection of hardware should be based on your needs. A computer and phone are the key pieces of hardware you will want at the beginning, just as they are key to your law school experience. As you start to practice law, you may want to acquire peripherals if you find that you need them: printers, copiers, scanners, fax machines for those working

33. Am. Bar Ass'n, 2023 Legal Technology Survey Report: Law Office Technology 14, question 13 (2024). 51% of lawyers reported having dual monitors, while 6% used 3 and about 1% reported using 4 or more monitors. Solos are the least likely to report that they used dual monitors (30%) while lawyers in firms with 10 or more lawyers range from the mid-50% to nearly 70% using dual monitors.

with doctors or insurance companies, and so on. The practice areas and locales in which you practice (for example, if you are working most of the time out of the courthouse) will drive some of these choices.

Chapter 2 Exercises

A. Create a technology budget. Identify your current technology investment (primary computer, tablets, phones, Bluetooth headphones, uninterruptible power supply, keyboard, mouse, monitors, etc.). Determine how much longer each will last and devise a plan to pay for those future costs. You should also consider whether you want to make a new technology investment—move from a gaming PC to a laptop, for example, or add a second monitor—and how you would add that to your budget. Extend your budget out for three years to ensure you incorporate a renewal of most of your technology.

B. Identify a current technology problem you have in your life and what your ideal solution would be. For example, perhaps you like to watch online videos or play games, but they are extremely laggy. Video lag could be caused by your computer, or it could be your internet connection. With your solution in mind, list the steps you would take to first diagnose the problem and then identify two or three solutions (money is no cost for this exercise) that would result in your ideal solution. Use a specific technology problem, and identify specific solutions.

C. When you decide to buy new technology, where do you start? Do you have a trusted friend who is deep into technology? Or do you set yourself a budget and then start to do research? Write out your current process, in law school, and describe your current approach. Then consider what elements of your current process you will need to adapt when you reach law practice. For example, you may need to be more concerned about security and confidentiality and specifically address the issue in a way that you do not right now.

Chapter 3

Practice Management

Let's turn now to the foundations of law practice technology. It all starts with a legal issue. A client—there will always be a client—has a legal issue and has decided that they need professional legal advice. They find you and make contact. Your professional responsibility is now in play, whether you eventually take them on as a client or not.

This is an incredibly important part of your law practice and, while neither the activity nor the technology involved at this step is very challenging, it still needs to be done with deliberation. A client's initial contact triggers a number of professionalism questions that can only be answered or managed by getting information from the client. This client intake process is how you will gather the initial information you need to determine whether this is a client you will take on. It is where you gather enough to understand whether the client's legal issue is one you feel able to handle and whether it is one you want to work on. That determination will lead to the next steps, whether to agree to represent the client or to communicate that you are not representing them.

There are a number of professionalism rules to keep in mind. We'll cover them in more detail, but here is a summary of some rules, using the American Bar Association's Model Rules of Professional Conduct, that come into play as soon as you are contacted by a prospective client:

- Rule 1.1. This is where it all starts. You will need to act competently, and that requires the legal knowledge and other skills to represent the client. If you do not have the knowledge, this is where you may decide to make a referral if you are not confident you can learn enough to competently assist this client.

- Rule 1.0. This rule provides clear guidance that you will need to keep the potential client informed and what their informed consent looks like. As you are starting to think about your communications technology, this rule will be important.
- Rule 1.4. You will need to communicate with this potential client, either to confirm your representation of them or your decision not to represent them. This is one of the most important rules. A significant number of lawyers who are disciplined are found at fault because of poor communication with clients, and confusion over whether or not a client is represented is a common point of contention.
- Rules 1.16 and 1.17. The professional rules describe with specificity the duties owed to a prospective client (1.17) as well as the steps to take when declining to represent a client (1.16).[1]

There are other rules that might come into play—and more rules will apply once you consider the subject matter of the legal issue—but, for now, we can focus on the most basic of information: who is your client and how do we manage that information.

The Foundation of Practice Management

There are several technologies that can manage this information for you. Most of them are common in both the business world and within the legal profession specifically. These are the personal information managers (PIMs), although they will be known by their commercial product names. Microsoft Outlook or Google Workspace are two of the most common. In addition, lawyers have been able to purchase software or, increasingly, license cloud-based applications designed specifically for the legal profession to manage their client matters. These practice management systems have existed for decades, and

1. The American Bar Association's Model Rules of Professional Conduct are not binding in any jurisdiction. However, I will refer to them in most situations because most U.S. jurisdictions adopt the Model Rules in some form or another, and so they are largely the same or very close as official professional rules. Similarly, readers from Canada will find many rules of the Law Society rules of professional conduct to be the same or close to the ABA rules. When you are called to the bar in a jurisdiction, be sure to confirm the rules that apply to your new law practice.

it is worth taking a moment to mention them, although we will deal with them more extensively later on.[2]

Practice management software can be a nebulous concept, but it almost always involves one specific attribute: a high degree of integration between the multiple functions that it offers. This is different from how most lawyers will experience a Microsoft Office environment or how most law students will use either Microsoft Office or Google Workspace. For example, I might receive an email in Microsoft Outlook asking me about a topic that will result in a calendared event. Ideally, I would be able to add that email to my calendar and schedule time to work on it. Outlook does have a *reply all by email* function, but that assumes I want to meet with other people. What if I just want to add it to my calendar to ensure I have time to review, do a bit of research, and ask for input? In this case, I have to manually create a calendar item based on the email, cutting and pasting information from one to the other. This is an example of a lack of integration, although once I have created the event, Microsoft Outlook may then prompt me with relevant documents from my email inbox. The integration between component parts of practice management software is likely to allow for more automated functionality.

This text will touch on practice management applications in more detail later, but the distinction between integrated systems and multiple standalone systems is worth highlighting up front. As we discuss some of the components you will find within a practice management system, it will be useful to be thinking about whether the integration makes sense for how you want to practice law or whether you want some separation between applications and why. Many lawyers use a cluster of individual applications, so integration, while it can create efficiencies, is not for everyone.

2. I am going to refer to these applications as *practice management* systems rather than the common alternative term, *case management*, for two reasons. First, that is what their function is: they manage the practice, not just cases. They frequently contain hooks into accounting and financials, provide document connectivity and data integration, and extend to both clients represented and declined representation. Second, case management is a term that is used in courts for their systems. When we get to talking about electronic court filing (e-filing) and systems like Public Access to Court Electronic Records (PACER), we will be touching on CM/ECF: case management, electronic court filing. The court systems are, from a lawyer's perspective, a different set of functions and features than the practice management systems that lawyer's use day-to-day to manage their law practices. Calling them all "case management" is unnecessarily confusing and we might as well develop the habit of distinguishing between the types of systems from the start.

The integration is central to the key technology output of a law practice: the document. Whether it is a real estate contract or a divorce submission or a motion for summary judgment, the legal profession primarily captures its work in documents. This book will dig more deeply into these document management issues, but practice management applications tend to provide integration between the management of information about individuals—clients and others—and your documents and other systems.

Let's use Microsoft Word as an example again, this time in conjunction with a Microsoft Excel spreadsheet. We want to send out a single letter—perhaps for marketing or some other business development purpose—to a list of recipients. We might create a letter and type in each address. But that is a slow process, and we have technology that will help us. If we have enough addresses, we could use Microsoft's mail merge function to import that list to a letter template. We start with a blank letter and then save it as a template. We add to the template data fields that are drawn from the Excel spreadsheet, things like first name, title, street address, and postal code. When we select the mail merge option on the Microsoft Word toolbar or "Ribbon," the data from Excel will be used to populate the fields in the form, generating a new copy of the letter for each new row in the spreadsheet.

This use of document automation is a time-saver but is also mostly only used in extensive mailings because your contact data probably does not live in an Excel spreadsheet but is rather in your Microsoft Outlook contact manager. But Microsoft Word has limited ability to look at your Outlook contacts and the data within other contact managers.[3] You may work at an organization or use a shared address book and, despite Microsoft Word being able to look at Outlook contacts, Word will not see all of the address books that *you* have access to. So, despite having the data available in your systems, it will probably be more efficient to manually type a letter when you only have a few recipients, adding their names and addresses by hand.

While a technology solution is possible, it is not practical. The lack of integration between your contact manager and your Microsoft Word application means that the work to implement it is more complicated than the more simple, manual option. The one reason to consider using Microsoft's mail merge

3. *Use Outlook Contacts as a Data Source for a Mail Merge*, Microsoft (last visited Sept. 10, 2024), https://support.microsoft.com/en-us/office/use-outlook-contacts-as-a-data-source-for-a-mail-merge-4cfcf038-1bc4-4a73-b5e3-a3303302db13, [http://web.archive.org/web/20240910184733/https://support.microsoft.com/en-us/office/use-outlook-contacts-as-a-data-source-for-a-mail-merge-4cfcf038-1bc4-4a73-b5e3-a3303302db13].

with your Outlook contacts is that you can save the letter as a new template, connected to those contacts, for re-use. But you may also need to rethink how you use Outlook's contacts lists, to ensure that the addresses are where you need them to be for the merge to work. Given the way lawyers communicate, either re-using a document template going to new people or re-using addresses on a new template, this is probably not something you will do regularly. It means that the lack of integration between these related applications, although they can be automated, is not of much concern on a day-to-day basis.

Integrations and Inflexibility

In a practice management system, however, these sorts of functions may be highly integrated. A letter to a new client can be a template in the system that is already pre-configured to pull client data from the contact management area of the practice management application. This means that, once the prospective client has been added into the system—a necessary prerequisite to performing a conflicts check and bringing them on as a client—it is relatively easy to create a personalized letter to that person. Whether it is an engagement letter or a non-engagement letter, the integration gives you access to ready automation. You do not need to engage in preparing the data for a merged file.

It may feel like a small benefit, but time is what lawyers use to generate revenue, so even a small time saving has value. The integration means that learning how to build templates and embed form fields in them or to accurately pull information from data sources like spreadsheets or contact managers is no longer necessary for the lawyer or their staff. It can be a quicker road to some of the automation techniques discussed below.

At the same time, there is a cost to this path. In the early days of practice management software, a lawyer would tend to buy an application and install it. They would link it to their internal systems—their document management system, their contacts manager or customer relationship management (CRM) application, their billing system—where possible. All of the technology lived within their office walls, and they might pay for maintenance or support, but it was not uncommon to find lawyers who paid for software once and used it for years.

The advent of the cloud in the early part of the 2000s brought about a tremendous shift in software delivery and access. This impacted lawyers and practice management software as well. Instead of buying a product once, practice management applications became something you pay for on a monthly or annual basis. It was licensed as a subscription and would only keep working so long as the subscription was maintained.

The relatively small size of the legal technology market, the so-called legal vertical market, means that vendor lock-in has been and continues to be a real risk for lawyers.[4] When I worked on an early practice management system in the 1990s, it was wholly uncustomized when it was bought by a new lawyer customer. There were some modules that could be dropped into place, but the entire application was tailored to the practice of the lawyer making the purchase. While this high degree of customization was desirable when the product was acquired, it also made it very difficult for that lawyer to leave the product and migrate to a new one. It also ended up making supporting and improving the software difficult because each client's installation was so distinct from every other client. Lawyers might find themselves constrained by the slow improvements and, while wanting to move to a newer, more feature-rich product, simultaneously constrained by their existing product customization.

Practice Pointer

See what your local colleagues are using. It is not the only selection criteria, but if you know other people using the same software—especially if it is law practice-specific, where there are fewer users or online support options—it should be a factor in your selection. There are some applications used by lawyers where even users will acknowledge it may not be the best, but the local adoption rate means that they can ask colleagues for help with functionality, or it becomes easy to find local technology consultants who have seen the software before.

We have seen a bit of relaxation in law practice technology vendor lock-in over the years. There are a variety of reasons for that. In some cases, especially with legal research, the impact of widespread web search that was easier to use than Westlaw or Lexis has meant that most legal research products have a

4. Vendor lock-in is when acquisition of a product and its ongoing maintenance limits the purchaser to a particular vendor. *Vendor Lock-in*, Wikipedia (last visited Aug. 26, 2025), https://en.wikipedia.org/wiki/Vendor_lock-in. To move away from that acquisition, there may be substantial friction or even a complete loss of data. This is an important function for lawyers to consider due to the long-term retention of client data and other work product.

similar search approach. A lawyer can switch between legal research products relatively seamlessly these days without having to learn and remember a new way of structuring a search. In most cases, it will be the interface that is the biggest challenge, since most research products continue to revolve around a search box and a body of searchable content.

The cloud also had an impact on this vendor lock-in, particularly for lawyers who were using many standalone, as opposed to integrated, tools. If you needed a document storage option, you could license Dropbox or Box or any number of free-standing cloud storage providers. You could use Microsoft's storage of the day (SkyDrive, OneDrive, SharePoint) or Google Drive or even Apple's iCloud.[5] If you changed your mind, moving to another storage vendor was as easy as downloading and uploading your files again.

As lawyers adopted cloud-based integrated systems, however, lock-in became as much of an issue as it had with previous offline or on-premises legal applications. Once a lawyer had populated a practice management system with client contact information, critical dates, and linked all of that to case documents and to billing information, the challenge of leaving that product became much greater. It can be done, but a quick glance at the existing practice management applications suggests that, even if you can extract everything from a system, you may not be able to re-use it easily in another, competing system.

It means that, as lawyers make their early selections of software, they need to consider this threshold question: is it better to have a high degree of integration or is it better to have, as David Weinberger put it, "small pieces, loosely joined."[6] It is not a new question, but lawyers who lean towards integration—which will bring immediate efficiency improvements and will be simpler to bring online for a solo or small firm lawyer who may not have extensive IT support or skill—may be doing so at the risk of greater vendor lock-in.

---

5. This is not to say that vendor lock-in does not happen with simple or single-faceted applications like online storage. Once an organization starts to rely on that system, creating links from websites to files in storage, or creating shared files or even creating online forms that store data in the storage system, lock-in becomes an issue.

6. I highly recommend reading "Small Pieces, Loosely Joined: A Unified Theory of the Web" in its entirety. It is a helpful guide and, despite being published in 2002, continues to be relevant as we see the internet grow into closed gardens (Meta's Facebook, Instagram, Twitter, and others) where vendor lock-in is the platform's goal. DAVID WEINBERGER, SMALL PIECES LOOSELY JOINED: A UNIFIED THEORY OF THE WEB (2002).

Business Software or Legal Software

There is a second threshold technology question for any lawyer: do I need technology specifically designed for lawyers or can I acquire off-the-shelf business software?[7] Like other professionals—engineers, accountants, doctors—there is a blurred line between what is needed to run the *business of law* and what is needed to run the *practice of law*. The business involves communications (email and phones), scheduling (tasks and calendared events), financial management (accounting, billing, payables, banking) and more. A law practice will need all of these things.

At the same time, lawyers have specific needs. They need a trust account to manage their client funds ethically as required by Rule 1.15, something that may not be available from every accounting application. They need to maintain those emails and documents in a way to ensure they can preserve the client file until the client's matter is complete as well as to comply with any professional or statute of limitation obligations. Lawyers must secure their files and systems against unauthorized or inappropriate access. This may involve additional backup and disaster recovery options or records retention and workflow features. They will want to use the shared calendars with other staff and lawyers but may need to implement an ethical wall to avoid internal conflicts.

Technology selection often comes down to an individual preference. The practice of law is essentially an individual endeavor. You may work with a law firm or other professional entity, but, at the end of the day, the documents you sign, the counsel you give, the undertakings you commit to are your responsibility.[8] You will be able to make many individual technology choices to match your approach to law practice, even when you are working in a law firm.

---

7. For the purposes of this text, I am not distinguishing between open-source and commercial products. Open-source products tend to have a lower acquisition cost but have costs in maintenance as well as other risks, like whether the maintainers will keep maintaining it. Commercial software may have a high acquisition cost but yield greater certainty in long-term support. But there is not a good reason to prefer one or the other entirely. Almost everyone uses open source-based web browsers to navigate the web. Billions of people use the open-source Android operating system on their phones and tablets and in their cars. The choice to use open source or commercial products will be based on far more than whether it has an open or closed license.

8. This is not an abstract exhortation. The Federal Rules of Civil Procedure provide for sanctions if the documents you submit as "representations to the court" fail to comply with Rule 11. States have similar rules about the signing of pleadings. See, for example, Ill. Sup. Ct. R. 137 and Wash. State Super. Ct. Civ. R. 11.

The size of your law firm or the practice areas in which it is involved may provide some constraints on those choices. For example, if you practice primarily in tax or intellectual property law, both areas where there is extensive choice in types of specialty legal software applications, you may find that it is necessary to use a specific commercial product licensed by your law firm. These products can be uneven in their interface and their functionality. The lack of choice may require you to adapt to the application even if you would rather it worked differently, particularly if you had been using a competing product while in law school.

In the largest legal organizations, those choices may be constrained or application selections will be made for you by the organization. In part this is because, as law firms scale up in size, there is a need for them to hire on a consulting or permanent basis the technology expertise that is necessary to support this additional complexity: to manage information, to keep systems operating and updated, to secure them against intrusion. In these organizations, however, there remains a disconnect between the *availability* of a technology and *the use of it*. In other words, a law firm can lead a lawyer to water, but it cannot make them drink. Our natural inclination to do what feels most efficient may, in fact, cause us to avoid some of the specific features our technology offers because they are unfamiliar.

This is most clearly demonstrated in the relatively low uptake, year over year, of law-specific practice management applications. Despite all the obvious benefits to adopting practice management software, lawyers have never adopted these applications as broadly as general business software like email or calendars. Practice management software adoption has hovered in recent years in the 50 to 60% range in law firms.[9] Given the centrality of the types of information practice management software can manage to the success of a law practice, this relatively low adoption may seem surprising. The adoption rate drops as the law firm size decreases, with solos reporting in 2023 that practice management software was available in only 43% of their offices. The largest law firms (500+ lawyers) reported it was available in nearly 64% of their offices.[10]

9. The 2023 American Bar Association Legal Technology Survey: Law Office Technology report volume indicates overall case or practice management software adoption as being 52% of respondents in 2020, 51% in 2021, 63% in 2022, and 59% in 2023. AM. BAR ASS'N, 2023 LEGAL TECHNOLOGY SURVEY REPORT: LAW OFFICE TECHNOLOGY xxix (2024).

10. AM. BAR ASS'N, 2023 LEGAL TECHNOLOGY SURVEY REPORT: LAW OFFICE TECHNOLOGY 33, question 23a-u.

The availability of software in a law firm does not mean that it is used by lawyers. This is particularly true in large law firms, but it is an impact across the profession. Only about 39% of lawyers indicated they *personally use* practice management software. Those numbers are inverted compared to availability. Solos may have it available in 43% of offices, but 38% use it themselves. In the largest law firms, where it is available in about 64% of firms, only just over 11% personally use the software.[11]

The distinction as to who personally uses the software tells us a lot about how these law firms are structured. The smaller the law firm, the more likely that the lawyer will be interacting with these sorts of systems, merely because there are no other staff to do that work. A solo law firm is not necessarily a one-person shop—they may hire in-person staff or use virtual staff for both business functions like bookkeeping or reception or for legal functions like research or document preparation—but the lawyer is much more likely to select and utilize the practice technology.[12]

The solo lawyer's proximity to the decisions around technology selection can lead lawyers towards commonly available business software over law practice-specific software. If a lawyer buys a new computer and it comes with the Microsoft 365 applications (Microsoft Outlook, Word, PowerPoint, Excel), they may not search out additional software. A law student who has spent years through university and law school using Google products may have committed to Google Workspace (Google Mail, Drive, Docs). There is broad overlap between personal information management tools like Microsoft 365 and Google Workspace and practice management software. It would be unsurprising to learn that many lawyers end up practicing with a specific software by way of default, using what they first picked up or had access to rather than being more deliberate in their selection as their practice grows and evolves.

---

11. *Id.* at 38, question 23b-d.

12. The lawyer-to-staff ratio in a law firm may not be wildly different between a solo law practice and a large law firm. Large law firm lawyer-to-staff ratios have plummeted from more than 1 staff person per lawyer to under .9 staff per lawyer. A solo may have a similar ratio, but the aggregate in the law firm—to create IT departments and marketing and business development teams—will provide specialized support in those roles. "Professional and administrative staff to lawyer ratio of law firms worldwide between 2005 and 2016," showing a drop from 1.08 (2006) to .87 (2016). Raphael Bohne, *Professional and Administrative Staff to Lawyers Ratio at Global Law Firms 2005–2016*, Statista (July 6, 2022), https://www.statista.com/statistics/829790/professional-administrative-staff-to-lawyer-ratio-legal-services/.

Choices

It cannot be said too many times: it does not really matter what you choose. The component parts of these systems are sufficiently similar that, as a starting point, you will have enough to manage your practice whether you select a dedicated practice management system or you cobble together other applications more loosely. You will need a way to communicate, which can be managed with an email client and a virtual meeting application. You will want to capture information about each person involved in a legal issue: your potential client, other people who may be parties, who have knowledge about the issue as witnesses or experts, and so on. You will need a calendar to keep track of not only your interactions with your clients but other deadlines: court filings, tax filings, statutes of limitation, and so on.

If you have any familiarity with either Microsoft 365 or Google Workspace or a similar application suite, you can probably already see the basic technology elements for your law practice. Neither platform is sufficient to manage your entire law practice. You will need to find accounting and trust account management software, in particular, in order to comply with your business and professional obligations. There are also automation tools that can improve your workflow. There are productivity tools that will help you manage your time better.

Perhaps the most important thing to know with any tools you use to manage your practice is that the tool will not manage your practice *for you*. It is just a tool, no matter how expensive or familiar or comprehensive it purports to be. You will still need to decide how you will practice and what processes you will use to leverage the power of your technology choices.

Let's return to that prospective client and their initial contact. Whatever software platforms or technology you choose, the first information you will start to gather will be prospective client data. One day, someone will contact you and ask you for help with their legal issue. At that point, you will need to have a way to collect it, to store it, and to re-use it. Whether that ends up being a practice management application or Microsoft Outlook, the data will provide a basis for you to start to apply the necessary processes for your law practice. But how do you collect the data to populate your client systems?

Practice by Checklist

A good place to start is with the data you need to make your decisions. That requires you to determine—just like you would for trial advocacy or moot court—the questions you need to ask in order to elicit the information for your determination of accepting or declining to represent a client. Once you have your questions, you can use checklists to build the processes to ensure you are capturing the information you need. It can then be placed into the information technology tools you have selected.

Checklists do not sound like particularly advanced technology because they are not. But they have been shown to improve outcomes if they are used in a consistent way. Researchers have looked particularly at the medical field—where an error can be life-threatening—and how checklists can improve patient outcomes. As one researcher put it:

> Their implementation ensures consistent adherence to established protocols, minimizing deviations in clinical practice.... For example, surgical safety checklists have significantly reduced surgical errors, such as wrong-site surgeries and instrument mishaps.... Checklists serve as cognitive aids for healthcare professionals, ensuring the consistent following of critical steps.[13]

These are exactly the goals a law practice should have when dealing with a prospective client: avoidance of errors, aids for consistently following critical steps. It may be daunting to imagine that you need to develop these checklists on your own. After all, you are about to open your own practice or start practicing. What happens if you omit something from your checklist?

Fortunately, there are plenty of checklists designed for law practice. You will find them on bar association websites as well as those of lawyer regulators. After all, they want you to avoid discipline, and so many have developed free tools to help you negotiate each step of your practice. These checklists can give you a starting point that you can adapt to the way you practice.[14]

---

13. Emmanuel Aoudi Chance, Dia Florence & Innocent Sardi Abdoul, *The Effectiveness of Checklists and Error Reporting Systems in Enhancing Patient Safety and Reducing Medical Errors in Hospital Settings: A Narrative Review*, 11 INT'L J. OF NURSING SCI. 390 (2024), https://doi.org/10.1016/j.ijnss.2024.06.003.

14. As a rule, you should not limit your search for checklists to your own jurisdiction. Many practice management checklists are generic to the practice of law. However, as you get further into your representation of a client, you should keep in mind that your jurisdiction will matter more as you start to deal with substantive legal issues. At the same time, you can

Another reason to start using checklists when you practice is that you can build habits that you will use as your client's legal issue progresses. One part of your prospective client intake is to assess whether the client has a viable claim or one that you can assist with. Checklists can help you walk through causes of action and other legal issues in a consistent way to ensure that you have the information you need to take on a client's legal issue.

Checklists can also give you an idea about the type of technology you might want or need in order to fulfill a law practice management function. Checklists lay out processes that run law firms, and technology is a layer that you place on top of well-functioning processes that you want to improve. If you are not sure whether you need a given technology, you may be able to get some clarity by looking at a checklist that deals with the function you are investigating.

A checklist can be re-used on new matters and with new clients, and it improves the likelihood that important steps or tasks—filing timelines for court, communications with clients—are not overlooked when your case load gets heavy or your calendar is full. They provide a kind of muscle memory, ensuring that you do not skip important steps. Perhaps just as importantly, a checklist can be used to train others and ensure consistency as you add staff or work with other lawyers.

The checklist is a simple technology, and there are endless ways to implement a checklist. It can literally be as simple as a document with checkboxes on it with matching tasks listed next to it. It could even be paper based if your law firm retains a paper file, although it is likely to start as a digital document.

You may already use a task-based app on your phone, whether for a shopping list or for other routine activities. As you are considering your options at the start of practice, think about the re-usability of the information. While an app can be useful, it may be hard to share with others or to present in an alternate format. To that end, the ability to share and reuse a checklist should dominate your selection process. Criteria like mobile use and apps can become a plus factor for your initial choice.

The selection process is something that you should also start to become accustomed to as you identify and select technology for your practice. How do you choose? What are the criteria that matter most to your law firm's use of technology? This is not a one-size-fits-all question. Earlier, I mentioned some

---

look at statutes or other legal guidance to blend in the specific requirements for the jurisdiction in which you are going to practice if you find an out-of-state checklist that may be really helpful; just bring the correct law to the checklist.

selection criteria that might apply, but you will find that some become more or less critical depending on your goal.

At the start of your practice, when income flow may be low or slow, your budget may be the most important selection criteria: what can you afford to acquire and what can you afford to maintain? As your practice matures and your technology use becomes more expert and perhaps has to be used by others in your law firm, other criteria may push to the fore.

Practice Pointer

Each client and each of their matters will need to be treated as distinct. The earlier you think about how to keep each client's documents and communications organized to keep them distinct, the better. You might keep them physically separate or you might use technology like virtual folders or tagging to do so. This ability to keep information separated will help if something like a legal hold occurs. Also, unless you get involved in a case like Charles Dicken's *Jarndyce v. Jarndyce* that continues past the lives of the lawyers involved, a client file will eventually close. You may also need to—or want to—return the client's file to them. This means that, when you create checklists or other documents or communications that are tied to a client matter, you will want to be able to quickly aggregate all of those items. As you start to select the technology you use, consider how you will maintain the technology as well as the things you create with it.

It may be easiest to look at two simple, easy-to-access and affordable technologies as checklist examples. The first is to use a word processor like Microsoft Word. The second is to use a cloud-based app like Microsoft Planner. Both are available in business licenses of Microsoft 365, although Word is available both as a free web app and in all home and business licenses of Microsoft 365.

This may appear as favoritism for a particular vendor, but, within the legal profession, Microsoft is the most widely used office software suite. Even where lawyers have selected to use an Apple operating system for their primary computer, they may face having to use Microsoft software applications like Word.[15]

15. About 10% of lawyers responding to the 2023 ABA Legal Technology Survey report used a Macintosh OS-based system. Nearly 16% of solos reported using a Mac, while the

This book will often prefer a Microsoft approach because of that law practice reality, but you may find that your own selection criteria will also start with Microsoft because of compatibility concerns.

Do Not Reinvent the Wheel

As mentioned above, one of the benefits of the checklist is that it can be re-used. This does not mean that the first iteration has to be built from scratch, though. These are business processes, and they are not all unique to the practice of law. The first place you should start in a Microsoft-centric law practice is by looking at Microsoft's online templates. These will generally not be law-specific templates, but they may still provide a starting point, a comparable document that has already been properly formatted or formatted in a way that is visually appealing. You will find memoranda forms, checklists, and many other types of productivity documents.

When you are in your Microsoft Office or 365 desktop application, when you create a new document, it will suggest possible templates. You can also select to see *more templates* to look at the entire range of matching templates.[16] Find one that appeals to your approach, and you can then start to customize it.

It is even better when you can find law-specific templates as your starting point. Confusingly, these templates are often referred to as forms, but they are not always the same as a simple form that someone fills out. These templates are designed to be downloaded and edited for re-use. Start with your law school library's catalog and search for lawyer form books. In particular, look for continuing legal education publications, where lawyers often share their own checklists with seminar attendees.[17]

---

number of large firm lawyers dropped to about 5%. These numbers may be off because 7% of lawyers *do not know* what operating system they are using. Notably, that number is lowest (1.6%) among solos and highest in mid-size firms of 100 to 499 lawyers (18%). Am. Bar Ass'n, 2023 Legal Technology Survey Report: Law Office Technology 13 (2024).

16. At the time of writing, Microsoft Office 365 templates are freely accessible at Microsoft Create. https://create.microsoft.com/en-us. They are separated out by product type, but you can also keyword search across all types.

17. Another source to consider is your local public library or, if it exists, your local public *law* library. They will often license legal forms databases because they are such a vital practical tool. Look for forms from Gale, EBSCO, or NOLO Press. These products are geared towards self-represented litigants but provide additional samples that you can re-purpose for your law practice. Some law school libraries will also subscribe to these databases, both for educational purposes or because they serve the public.

Microsoft used to have a dedicated team focused on what is called the legal vertical market. Law firms, in other words. In the early part of the 2000s, Microsoft had an advisory panel made up of lawyers and technology consultants who serve law firms. They even created some law-specific templates like a Microsoft OneNote trial notebook. Most of this effort seems to have waned or been refocused on helping migrate larger law firms into Microsoft 365. The law-specific templates Microsoft provided have disappeared from the internet.

Westlaw and Lexis both have checklist resources, but you may find they are more finely tailored to specific types of issues than you need when you are first starting to practice law. For example, both Westlaw's Practical Law and Lexis' Practice Guidance have checklists for immigration visas, but each visa gets its own checklist. This may be helpful when you are dealing with a legal issue you have not dealt with before.

Practice Pointer

The drawback to creating a large number of intake forms on narrowly tailored topics is that they will need to be maintained over time as the law changes. We will touch on document management below where there may be some automation or re-usable elements that could help with this. Also, a substantial amount of information—name, address, jurisdiction, and so on—will be the same on each intake form. A simple desire to improve your own checklist may become more arduous if you are maintaining a checklist for each narrow issue you may come across.

They may also resemble less of a checklist and more of an outline. This provides an alternate approach, which is to take a process list from somewhere else and apply the formatting that you want to use for your checklist. Whatever approach you take, you want to end up with a list of the information you need and a way to record that you have received it. This information should stay with the client file, in whatever format that takes.

An application-based checklist can work as well. Microsoft Planner is a good example of an app that provides a web-based task list.[18] It offers some of

18. These can be found under a variety of names, not all very exact. Look for task schedulers or task managers. Some applications will bill themselves as project management applications, but true project management tools (including Microsoft Project) are far more

the functionality you should look for in any online task scheduler or manager. The tasks are shareable, so you can include your staff, other lawyers, or consultants in your workflow. The project plans can be copied, so that you can create a template and then re-use it for each client. There are integrations with your Microsoft Outlook calendar and a reminder system.

The most significant drawback to this app-based approach, whether Microsoft Planner or some other online app, is how to manage the information at the time you close your matter file. A Microsoft Planner plan can be exported to Microsoft Excel, which provides a snapshot of the project elements: who did what and when. This Excel file can then be stored with other electronic artifacts in a digital case file or printed off to go into a paper file.

Practice Pointer

This issue of ease of use versus long-term accessibility is a real one. The cloud has brought a variety of very strong business-oriented as well as law-specific applications. The downside can be exporting and downloading that data when a client's matter is complete. This can be especially true about a mobile app, particularly one that is tied to a phone and not cloud-accessible. While you can leave that data on the application, if the provider goes out of business or alters or eliminates the application, you will need to have an export path. If you identify that path before you start, you can build the export step into your law practice processes.

First Contact

Intake is a key part of your law office processes. It is where everyone comes into your practice, even those people who do not remain as clients. This means that you need to consider what information you want to gather from people you may never see again. It also means you need to be deliberate about how you treat everyone at this stage. One of the most consistent sources of clients is

---

complicated than most lawyers will need. Products available at the time of writing include Trello and Notion.

referrals from friends and family.[19] Your intake checklist and overall approach can ensure that, whether you are retained or not, you make a positive impact.

One area that will be covered later in this book is law firm marketing. But it is in your intake process where your marketing goals need to have a presence. This is where you can find out how someone found you and your law practice. Advertising? Website? Their best friend (and who that is)? Your intake process can help you to identify which clients are finding you using which source. This *conversion* information can help you make informed decisions about how to invest in those sources going forward. But you will want the prospective client to be asked at their intake, just in case you decide you are unable to help them with their legal matter.

The intake checklist does not have to live solely within the law firm, used only when someone physically walks through the door. It can provide a basis for online intake of clients if that is something you want to pursue. This requires you to have a website, which may not be a given, or a way to host an online form for your intake questions.[20]

An online intake form may require a level of technical expertise that goes beyond a simple contact form. For example, you may be asking someone for information, and they may need to choose from among different types of issues: different types of personal injury, different types of family law issues. This may require branching logic to ensure you ask the right questions based on their legal issue. Some online practice management applications will offer this intake feature. The benefit, again, of using a practice management system with intake form support is that not only do you not need to worry about the technical challenge it creates, you may have the ability to insert that data directly into your system for managing contacts and new clients. This elimination of double-entry by you or your staff can be a time-saver.

It is worth mentioning here that, no matter what path you take to create an intake process, you want to be careful how much you learn. If you have created a checklist for the process, you can better manage gathering enough—but

19. See, for example, the 2019 and 2017 Clio Legal Trends Reports, which found 62% and 59%, respectively, found legal representation through a family or friend. 2019 LEGAL TRENDS REPORT 20 and 2017 LEGAL TRENDS REPORT 16.

20. It may be surprising, but not all law firms have websites. In the 2023 American Bar Association Legal Technology Survey report, in the Marketing and Communications volume, 87% of law firms reported having a website. That number was lower among solo practitioners— about 65%—and nearly 100% in the largest law firms. AM. BAR ASS'N, 2023 LEGAL TECHNOLOGY SURVEY REPORT: MARKETING & COMMUNICATIONS TECHNOLOGY 12 (2024).

not too much—information. This can be useful because that first contact may create ethical challenges and potential conflicts of interest. As the American Bar Association puts it:

> Under Rule 1.18 of the Model Rules of Professional Conduct, a lawyer who was consulted about a matter by a prospective client, but not retained, is disqualified from representing another client who is adverse to the prospective client in the same or a substantially related matter if the lawyer received from the prospective client "disqualifying information"—i.e., information that could be significantly harmful to the prospective client in the matter. But, if the lawyer "took reasonable measures to avoid exposure to more disqualifying information than was reasonably necessary to determine whether to represent the prospective client," and the firm takes specified procedural precautions, then the lawyer's conflict of interest is not imputed to others in the lawyer's firm.[21]

One way to avoid learning disqualifying information is to follow a process using a checklist that limits what information is sought. This can mean providing specific warnings for a prospective client not to overshare during your initial inquiry—so your checklist should include the provision of these warnings—as well as delineating when you have gathered *enough* information to be able to proceed to the next stage of the client process: the conflicts check. It may even mean assigning the checklist to someone other than you (or another lawyer) to ensure that you do not receive any disqualifying information.

The Last Checklist Item

Your next-to-last checklist item on your intake list should be your engagement letter (or your non-engagement letter). Once you have decided whether to take on a client or to decline to represent them, you should let them know, clearly, what your intention is. If you are willing to take up their matter, there are specific things—like how much you anticipate it will cost them—that you need to communicate.

21. ABA Standing Comm. on Ethics & Pro. Resp., Formal Op. 510 (2024).

Model Rule 1.5 sets out that:

> The scope of the representation and the basis or rate of the fee and expenses for which the client will be responsible shall be communicated to the client, preferably in writing, before or within a reasonable time after commencing the representation.[22]

We will touch on fees and pricing your services later on. At this point, though, you will want to make sure that you and your prospective client know what happens next: they will work with you or they will need to find another lawyer. If you embed this step in your intake checklist, you can improve the likelihood that a prospective client does not mistakenly think they've become an actual client.

Your final checklist item will be to open a case file or to close the file if you are not taking on the prospective client's matter. A new client's case file will expand over time as you create documents, save your research and work product, and engage in the business processes of law: invoices, payments, and so on. Even for the cases you do not take, though, you will want to store the information you received during intake as well as your letter showing that you are not taking the case. While the rest of this text is focused on client matters you take on, much of the information relates to managing the information for the declined representation as well.

Chapter 3 Exercises

A. Create an intake form for a specific area of law. Be sure to include:
   a. Basic identifying information about the client;
   b. Information about parties, jurisdiction, and timing;
   c. Information about the area of law and the specific requirements for the legal issue the intake form covers.

   You may create your intake form based on templates you find online. Be sure to consider the jurisdiction, sources, and recency of any template you use.

---

22. A.B.A. Model Rules of Professional Conduct, r. 1.5(b) (Am. Bar Ass'n 2025).

B. Create a simple non-engagement letter in Microsoft Word. Start with a traditional letter and the content in the body of the letter. Convert it into a template by adding form fields for the name and address block and for other information that can be drawn from a data source like your Microsoft Outlook contacts, an Excel spreadsheet, or a practice management system.

C. You are the lawyer responsible for choosing the technology for your law firm (you can choose the size and resources—budget, staff, etc.—that are available to you). Given your law firm's needs, *under what circumstances* would you choose, and why, the following types of software:

   a. General business software like Microsoft 365?

   b. Legal-specific software, like a practice management application?

   c. Open-source software?

D. You have decided to select a technology from a startup company, one without any prior history of its performance. You do not yet know how long it will be around. What questions would you want to ask about the portability of your client information and files so that, should that vendor go out of business or change its products, you can ensure the viability of your law practice?

E. Microsoft and Apple are not the only operating system providers. There is a very small but dedicated group of lawyers who rely entirely on open-source applications and variants of the Linux operating system. Identify three challenges of using an open-source operating system and explain how you would overcome those challenges.

Chapter 4

The Calendar

The calendar is the beating heart of the law practice. It cannot be over emphasized the key position a calendar takes in a law firm. It is where client meetings are booked. It records filing dates and calculations on statutes of limitations. It shows when a lawyer is available and, when they are not, who else may be available to provide backup coverage.

When you are in a meeting or at court and an additional hearing or event has to be calendared, you will need to have up-to-the-minute information about your own and others' availability. You may need to provide access to your calendar to others, so they can help to manage your events and any ensuing conflicts. Whether you select to use an off-the-shelf calendar like Microsoft Outlook or an integrated one within a practice management system, it will soon be a vital part of the success of your law practice.

Not surprisingly, there is a professional responsibility related to your calendar. Rule 1.3 says that a lawyer will act with *reasonable diligence and promptness in representing a client.*[1] It is a short rule, but it touches on two important points: diligence and promptness. Your calendar will help you with both. A calendar is not just managing your responsiveness. So much of the practice of law revolves around critical dates that a failure to manage those dates can lead to accusations of malpractice and, sometimes, lawsuits for mistakes that end up hurting your clients.

1. *Id.* r. 1.3.

Deadlines and Malpractice

One sign of how important it is to have and maintain a calendar for a law practice is how it is perceived by your malpractice insurer. One of the expenses you will have when you start practice is legal malpractice insurance. Your legal malpractice provider may provide you with a discount on your insurance premiums if you maintain an electronic calendar.[2] This is very similar to how you might get a discount from your automobile insurance provider for being a safe driver or, more commonly these days, allowing them to install a device within your vehicle to ensure you are driving within safe parameters. The discount reflects an acknowledgement by the insurer that you are using technology to try to lessen the likelihood of needing to use your insurance benefits.

This is because missed deadlines, like court filings and statutes of limitations, can lead to legal malpractice claims.[3] You are more likely to be sued for malpractice than to be disciplined by your lawyer regulator for missing a deadline. As you start to practice and add more and more clients to your list of open matters, you will have more and more deadlines to juggle. This can probably be done using paper methods if you are a solo practitioner and are the only person who needs to see or access your calendar. As soon as you have staff or other lawyers to coordinate with, this level of additional complexity will necessitate the move to shared electronic calendars. Whether in print or on a device, you will need to be highly conscientious about recording your events and obligations.

In some cases, you will know a specific date and can put it on your calendar. For example, you have received a complaint on behalf of a client, and you

2. It is not just the calendar. An insurer is going to look at whether you have a plan for risk management, and this will include a number of topics covered in this book: engagement or non-engagement letters, calendars, conflicts checks and conflicts management using client consent, financial and accounting controls, and so on. As you think about your technology purchases, remember that they can contribute to savings in other areas of your practice.

3. Very few lawyers are disciplined in any given year, with the American Bar Association describing the number as remaining consistently between 0.2% and 0.38% of lawyers. AM. BAR ASS'N, 2023 PROFILE OF THE LEGAL PROFESSION 103 (2024), https://www.americanbar.org/content/dam/aba/administrative/news/2023/potlp-2023.pdf#page=103.19. On the other hand, lawyer malpractice insurance claims can be ten times that number, and most lawyers—the ABA estimates about 80%—will be sued at least twice in their legal career for malpractice. NEW LAW. PROGRAM, KENT. BAR ASS'N, LAWYERS MUTUAL OF KENTUCKY: PREPARING FOR LEGAL MALPRACTICE CLAIMS (2025), [http://web.archive.org/web/20250716150002/https://cdn.ymaws.com/www.kybar.org/resource/resmgr/nlp/2025/january/Preparing_for_Legal_Malpract.pdf].

can calculate the date that a response is due in court by looking at the local rules of procedure. Perhaps it is a business filing and so you know that it is due before or after a financial quarter. In others, there is more flexibility and, sometimes, uncertainty.

This is a good time to start to create habits and set expectations around your scheduling. For example, how fast will you respond to a client request for information?[4] A common customer service approach is to respond within 24 hours, but that will depend on your client's expectations. What about a prospective client intake form? You may need to do additional research or rework the information, perhaps creating a timeline of events or to calculate critical dates. You will need to perform a conflicts check. Each of these steps will require resources, primarily someone's time. You will want to create a timeline to determine the sequence and resources required for each step—like a project plan—so that you can estimate what to tell your prospective client about your response or decision to accept their case or not.

At first, you may not be sure how much time all of these tasks will take. If you have been able to take experiential classes during law school, you may be able to estimate the time or resources involved for some or all of the steps involved in client intake.[5] You can also speak to other lawyers, whether in your law firm or perhaps a lawyer who acts as a mentor, to find out the time they think it is reasonable for a new lawyer to take to complete this process. As you become more experienced, you will be able to assess your resource requirements more capably. Either way, you can schedule a response to a client within a given number of days after receiving the intake form. Whatever that number of days is, you will communicate to the prospective client by what date they can expect to hear back from you, and you can use your calendar as a prompt to ensure that your engagement or non-engagement letter goes out on time.

4. These are commonly called service level agreements or "SLAs" in the technology or service market. They do not need to be provided to the client, but it can be useful for you to document—for yourself and your staff—what the responsiveness level is that your law firm will provide.

5. In some instances, your law school experience may have exposed you to only a portion of the intake process. For example, you may have triaged cases for a legal services event to help move the person with a legal issue on to a legal services provider, whether a lawyer or Legal Aid or some other source of assistance. Since you would not perhaps have been providing legal services as a student, you would not have had to worry about conflicts checks and other steps in this process.

Practice Pointer

It is beyond the scope of this book, but your choice of practice area brings with it a variable risk of being sued for malpractice, as does the size of your law firm. When you are thinking about your first job in private practice after law school, you may want to consider whether the small firm you are joining or the practice area in which they want to hire you are a good match for your personal comfort level with risk. Since you are almost certain to receive disciplinary complaints or be a defendant in a malpractice lawsuit—never mind that the complaints may be unfounded and the lawsuit may be dismissed—you may want to have some awareness about how much being on the receiving end of those complaints or accusations will impact your enjoyment of the practice of law.

Your calendar will also act as a record of the work that you have performed. This sort of time tracking can be a challenge when you are busy. How much time was spent on client A before you pivoted to a call from client B and then returned to client A's matter? The billable hour remains a common way for lawyers to earn money, and it relies on accurate time-keeping. It is easy to find cases of lawyers being disciplined for billing more hours than there are in a day.

Even if you decide to use a flat-fee billing system, it is worth keeping track of your time. The flat fee that you charge your clients will be based on the work you anticipate doing for that client, often itself based on an average number of hours that it will take you to complete a set of tasks. If those tasks are taking you longer than you estimated, then the flat fee will fail to match the calculations you made when creating the fee. In that case, the flat fee may need to be raised—or the tasks reconsidered, by delegating them or becoming more efficient or eliminating them—to take into account the actual cost to your law practice.

When items are being added to a law firm's calendar or scheduling system, the process is sometimes referred to as docketing. This term seems to be used whether or not the calendared items are part of a court docket, and you will sometimes see calendaring software designed for lawyers referred to as docketing software.[6] This is not to confuse it with actual docket-related software that provides you with access to documents in a court docket. When the discussion turns to law practice calendaring, there can be an emphasis on trial or litigation-related events, which may not be relevant to your practice area or calendaring goals. This may be due in part to the fact that a significant number of law practice-specific software applications deal with litigation and trial-related processes, as opposed to transactional work. But it would be a mistake to think that careful calendar management is the work of a litigation firm. Any client event can be a critical one for you to manage.

Organizing Calendar Access and Retrieval

A calendar for a lawyer or law firm with tens or hundreds of clients can quickly become overwhelming to use. As you start to think about how you will use calendars in your law practice, consider how you will organize its contents. There are tools within many calendar applications that allow you to create different views of the events that are within the organization and to organize and make less cluttered the events that are your responsibility. Your ability to filter and manage the scheduling information will improve your likelihood of seeing key dates and events that are most relevant to you.

The most obvious is to distinguish between your personal calendar view and your ability to view the calendars of others, whether in your organization or elsewhere. In Microsoft Outlook, the ability to view multiple calendars must be configured, but you can overlay your personal calendar with that of others or with a shared group calendar. A shared group calendar has an owner but is not personal to that owner, allowing multiple people to add events to it separately from their own calendar. You can also integrate external calendars from other systems or people, such as a calendar provided to you for a class by your professor using Blackboard or Canvas or some other learning management system. You may want to practice with your course calendars so you can

6. While docket is something of a term of art in the legal profession, it also has a broader sense of being an agenda or a list of items to be dealt with. *Docket*, MERRIAM WEBSTER (last visited May 19, 2025), https://www.merriam-webster.com/dictionary/docket [http://web.archive.org/web/20250419101158/https://www.merriam-webster.com/dictionary/docket]. This may explain why it may be used generically for calendaring items and generating an agenda. I will tend to use *docket* only in relation to court-related items, but it is worth knowing that it can be broader than that.

get a feel for what it is like to juggle multiple calendar views. In practice, you might use shared calendars with external governance boards that you serve on or for shared projects with consultants supporting your law practice. They can also be used in law practice to segment different types of critical dates. For example, you might have a shared calendar for people's vacation so you know who is in or out of the office on any given day, and another for court dates, so that everyone has a shared view of the law practice's critical dates.

As you set up your Microsoft Outlook or other calendar for the first time, be sure to think about how you can share your availability with others and what you are comfortable sharing. A shared calendar can allow you to offload some of the email interactions that occur around trying to schedule meetings and other events. If you have made your availability accessible, people can use it to book time with or for you.

In some law firms, you will delegate your calendar access to a member of the law firm's staff. That staff person will then be able to manage your calendar, adding or moving events for you as they field calls or emails on your behalf related to your critical deadlines. You can also choose levels of information to share: do you show just that you have availability or not, with areas of your calendar blocked off? Or can people with access to your calendar see the general topic (which might describe a doctor's appointment or might refer to a client by name and the purpose of a call or visit with them)? You may want to share less information to begin with, rather than over-sharing and having to reduce access later.

This calendar delegation approach can seem a bit old-fashioned and assumes you have staff to support you. You are unlikely to have experienced, as a law student, the need or had the resources for other people to access and manage your personal calendar. As lawyer-to-staff ratios drop at law firms, you may find that no matter how large a firm you are in, you will need to continue to manage your own calendar. Some solo and small law firm lawyers will use virtual assistants to help them. These third-party service providers give the lawyer access to a part-time staffing resource to help triage calls and events, among other things. Although they are referred to as virtual assistants, they are actual people and are virtual only in the sense that they do not share your office space with you.[7] They are not artificial intelligence, although those sorts of virtual assistants are certain to appear as agentic AI expands.

7. Services like Ruby describe themselves as virtual receptionists, and you may want to try similar alternative terms to "assistant" if you end up wanting to explore virtual staff support based on the need you have identified.

Modern calendars and cloud- or server-based calendaring, whether through tools like Microsoft Outlook or practice management systems, tend to allow you to shift some of that process burden whether or not you have an actual person to whom to delegate calendar control. For example, you can set up your calendar with your work hours—say, 9am to 5pm—to constrain when people can place events on your calendar. You can also share your calendar with others in your organization. This will allow them to see your availability (whether you provide them with the details of your events or not) and, in the most efficient circumstances, allow them to add things to your calendar without engaging in a back and forth about availability.

Practice Pointer

If someone shares their calendar availability with you, use it to show you respect their trust. Once you can see someone's calendar, if they ask you to make an appointment with them, create a meeting invitation based on their availability. You do not need to email them first to ask them if the time—that you can clearly see on their calendar is available—is convenient. If it is inconvenient, they can counter your appointment request and move it to a time that is more convenient. When you are in Microsoft Outlook, use the Scheduling Assistant to line up the calendars of all of the people who may need to participate in a meeting or event and use it to find the best time. This will save countless emails backwards and forwards and show that you understand the purpose of shared calendars.

If you need to schedule a meeting with multiple people, some of whom do not have access to a shared calendar or for whom you cannot see their availability, you can still avoid a lot of emails by using a group calendar app or a simple online form. For example, from within Microsoft Outlook, you can insert a simple poll into an email message or, if you have a business license to Microsoft 365, go to Microsoft Forms to create a simple calendar poll that you can send out to your event participants. There are also dedicated apps for that, like Doodle, where you customize a form and each person can respond with their availability. The benefit of sticking with a Microsoft option is that you can keep the information within your law practice. Like many Microsoft applications, there are some simple templates you can start with for finding a meeting time or scheduling an event and, once you have made one, it is easy to copy to re-use the template for a new event or purpose.[8]

When you provide that level of visibility into your calendar, it allows other people to schedule meetings and events with you whether or not they have been delegated rights to work on your calendar as if they were you. This is helpful when you are asked to schedule a meeting with someone. If you license the business version of Microsoft 365, you also get access to their Bookings tool. This allows you to create pre-defined meeting templates (say, "client meeting for 30 minutes") that you can share with other people, even those outside your organization, for them to initiate a meeting. This shifts the burden of having you or even a staff person with delegated access having to create each appointment. It allows the person who wants to schedule the meeting to go ahead and do so, knowing their calendar and yours.[9]

A day- or week-at-a-glance, or even an agenda list of upcoming events, is not the only way to organize a calendar. This may still provide you with far more information than you can manage or sort through. As you start to think about your law practice and your calendar, you will want to think about how you will be able to look at just the items related to a particular client or a particular matter or involving a specific person or group of people. This is something you can accomplish in Microsoft Outlook, but it can require a number of manual steps or connected systems.

For example, you might use Outlook's category system. This is a system of labels that you can apply to your events or emails. Each calendar item or email can have a category attached. There are only 25 colors for Outlook category labels, but it appears to allow unlimited labels. You might assign a client name to a category label and then apply it to events and emails for that client. Or you might always put the client name at the start of a calendar item so that you can filter on their name. You could also create hashtags inside the description of each calendared item—#SmithConnie #JonesBakery #Employment—to provide other keywords that you can filter on or retrieve in a search.[10]

8. Microsoft Forms https://forms.office.com.

9. There are other tools that do this, including systems like Calendly or even the Google Workspace calendar, which can be made public. It is critical that, if your calendar is made visible to anyone outside your law practice—or anyone within your law practice who may be subject to an ethical wall—they not be able to see the details about your clients and the matters on which you are working. In general, showing what is blocked and what is not should be enough for others to send you meeting requests that you are likely to be able to accept.

10. Email can be organized into client folders and so may not be as difficult to manage as calendared items.

Microsoft Outlook can be very uneven in how it exposes its support for these filters. If you access the calendar in Outlook on the web, the filter option is limited. You can really only show types of events and limit them by category. The Microsoft Outlook app on your computer will have more functionality. If you access the Change View option in your Outlook calendar, you can create and save views based on your most common filters, and you can filter on more facets of your calendar. For example, if you have a hot case at the moment and need to regularly see what is going on in just that matter, you could develop a filter just for the events relating to that client.

The difficulty with these approaches is that you need to develop a stable, shareable way to do these things, which becomes harder as you add staff or lawyers to your practice. And then, even if you have a common, agreed upon way to do this, you still have to be consistent in always following the process you develop. Any misstep—failure to calendar an item, failure to tag it properly, failure to assign it to the right person—can lead to missed deadlines or worse outcomes for your clients and your law practice.

One of the benefits of practice management or database-driven systems can be that they make these linkages for you. If you want to see all of the calendared items for a client, you can access the list by using the client-centric views within the practice management system. The filtering system will be built into the application's integrated design by default. Similarly, in systems like accounting or other business operations, the data-driven approach means that it is usually very simple to pull together all of the items that relate to a given person or entity.

Simple Automation in Outlook

Most products that lawyers use to practice law offer some opportunities to automate what would otherwise be manual steps, like labeling an email or an event or moving it to a folder. They may not be terribly sophisticated, but they can close the gap between a set of manual steps and full automation. Microsoft Outlook Quick Steps are a good example of this.

Imagine that a prospective client has reached out and submitted an online form, perhaps received by you and your staff as an email, or they may have sent in an email directly without using your online intake form. You or your staff will need to respond and determine whether to set up an initial intake meeting. As described above, you may need to categorize information or, if they emailed

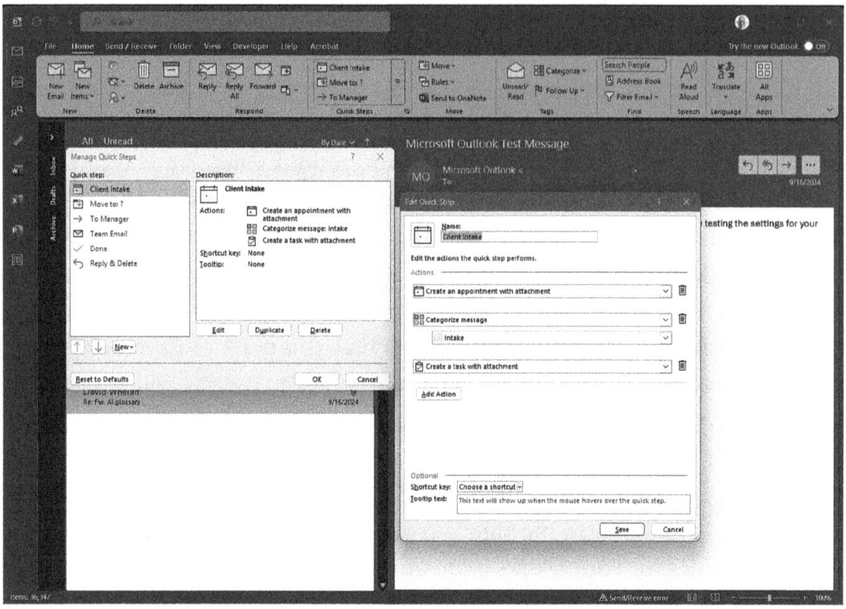

Figure 1: Edit Quick Step, Client Intake

you directly, you may want to direct them to an online form that gathers some of the intake data in advance, to manage your potential conflicts. While there is probably no way to create a workflow that moves from Task A to Task B to Task C in that order, you can create a Quick Step to initiate multiple tasks at once.

Quick Steps are available for all types of documents or items in Microsoft Outlook. We will look at them in relation to email later on. Quick Steps can allow you to tie together the different parts of Microsoft Outlook so that you do not have to click around the app to get your work done. In the example above, I have created a Quick Step called Client Intake. I have saved it, and I can now invoke it whenever I have a new email that requires me to initiate the client intake process. When I click on the Quick Step on Outlook's Ribbon, it will execute the three steps:

- It will categorize the email with the *Intake* label, applying my yellow label to it
- It will create a new appointment, with the email as an attachment
- It will create a new task, with the email as an attachment

The label function is obvious and saves just a few mouse clicks. The creation of the appointment and task would normally take someone a bit more time, and so these can create some efficiencies by way of automation. The ideal situation would be that the appointment and task were pre-populated with some of the information from the email. Instead, Outlook will just open a new calendar item and a new task item, and they will need to be completed manually.[11]

This sort of automation can reduce the likelihood that someone will forget either step to create the calendar or task item or forget to label the email. But it is a modest example of the sort of automation you might be able to apply if you are working with a system where these processes have tighter integration. In particular, one area where calendaring almost demands automation is in rules-based calendaring, where you are trying to implement a daisy-chain of events based on a court-determined starting point.

Rules-Based Calendars

The concept of templates in relation to documents has been mentioned previously. The use of templates extends to almost every area of your law practice, though, so look for ways to use them in everything you do. Wherever there is a repeatable process or activity, you may benefit from a template. There is a good chance that some other lawyer or business has already created one, but, in the worst case, you can always develop your own.

In the case of calendaring and docketing, the law is replete with template-ready events. For example, let's say your client is selling a property. Once the offer is made and accepted, it kicks off a number of activities that need to occur before the closing on the property. These are often "x days after y" sorts of events, which means that you can create a template of linked calendar events to capture them.

Similarly, many courts use a standard set of events that occur in a daisy chain, with the first leading to the second and so on. This is particularly clear in the United States federal courts when a *fast track* order is used, and the dates in the daisy chain are spelled out.[12] In the law practice technology world, this

11. There are more programmatic ways to have Microsoft Outlook create and populate events or emails, but they are beyond the scope of this book and would require more development knowledge than the average lawyer will have. However, there are ways to create templates within Microsoft Outlook that carry their own scripting and can perform specific tasks that the default application will not.

12. See, for example, this Microsoft Word template for a fast-track scheduling order from the United States Middle District Court for Florida. The draft order includes the time-

is referred to as *rules-based calendaring*. Not surprisingly, practice management software will frequently offer this as a feature. But there are standalone products aimed at the litigation-specific law practice that provide rules-based templates for you based on your jurisdiction needs. These templates can be designed both for your practice management software or for your Microsoft Outlook or Google Calendar.[13]

> **Practice Pointer**
>
> Check the court rules for your jurisdiction. If you are unsure about how to calculate the rules-based or fast-track dates, it will be spelled out in court or other rules. For example, in the Federal Rules of Civil Procedure, Rule 6 talks about how to calculate due dates when there is a holiday or a weekend or when the filing is required in a period that amounts to hours. You should never guess on a filing date. Be certain and, if nothing else, call the court to confirm the date once you have done your calculation.[14]

When you apply a template, it will set the future dates for you based on built-in logic, calculating the "x days after y" rules for your jurisdiction. The template should be able to adapt if, for example, the scheduled event lands on a Saturday (often this means moving it to the following Monday) and perform calculations of the interval of days between events for you. It is clearly a set of tasks you could do without technology by entering each event manually, doing the calculations yourself by hand. But manual entry introduces the possibility of error as well as involves additional time and work for you or your staff. Rules-based calendaring will not work for every client matter, but it is a great

---

line—90 days after the date of the order, 150 days after the date of the order—that will be used for every fast-track order. http://web.archive.org/web/20250528143204/https://view.officeapps.live.com/op/view.aspx?src=https%3A%2F%2Fwww.flmd.uscourts.gov%2Fsites%2Fflmd%2Ffiles%2Fjudges%2Fforms%2Fflmd-barber-fcra-fast-track-scheduling-order.docx&wdOrigin=BROWSELINK.

13. Two examples of these applications are LawToolBox and CalendarRules. They create the templates based on court rules (in the case of LawToolBox, both US and many international courts, including Canada) and you license the rule templates for your calendaring application.

14. FED. R. CIV. P. 6.

example of a relatively simple automation that can reduce your law practice risk and make you more productive.

Add-ins, Macros, and Scripts

There is a broad area of add-ons for online office suites, including Microsoft 365 and Google Workspace. Microsoft Outlook users will see some of these called add-ins. These are generally narrowly defined applications that sit within the Microsoft or Google app and extend the app's functionality. They are often not developed by Microsoft or Google but have been created by someone who had a very specific idea and wrote a program to perform that function. Lawyers will find these add-ons for legal research, for document management, and rules-based calendaring, among many others. There are far too many to discuss in this book, and many will be niche in their scope, mostly of value to lawyers with a particular approach to practice in a particular substantive area. These add-ons will vary in cost, complexity, and compatibility with your law practice technology.

In addition to add-ons, you can create (or perhaps have created for you) macros and scripts that can automate common functions in your office suite.[15] In Microsoft Office products, you can customize the Ribbon to add a Developer tab. The Developer tab is where Microsoft Office's macro capabilities are accessible. This tab will allow you to create, by recording each step as you do it, a macro. When you find that you are doing something—or asking your staff to do something for you—over and over again, you may want to consider saving it as a macro. In that way, you can reduce the multiple steps you are taking to an automated process.

Macros and scripts are something you can create on your own, but they may require more technical knowledge than you have or want to acquire, given that they tend to be based on a scripting language created by Microsoft. Despite this, there are still some very simple automation tools you can use within the Microsoft Office suite to save time and without any technical know-how. Sometimes this involves using them in a way they were perhaps

15. My first stop when I am looking how to solve something to do with Microsoft Outlook, whether it has to do with the calendar or email or other components, is this somewhat dated looking site called Slipstick. https://slipstick.com. It has a lot of information about the nuances of supporting Microsoft Outlook and has been a regular source of pointers on how to do something or fix something.

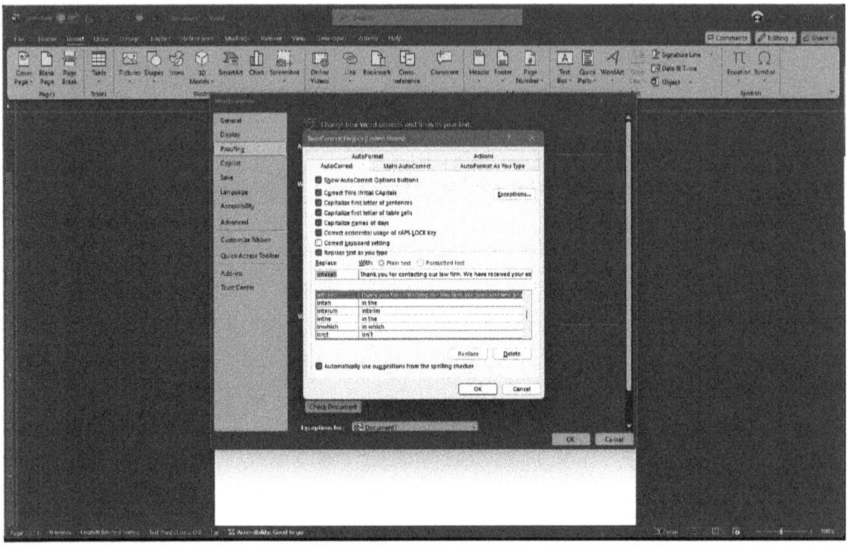

Figure 2: Auto-correct client intake

not intended. We are starting to see artificial intelligence embedding some of these—in particular, auto-correct or suggested next words—in office suites. But even that is leaving untapped potential. An auto-correct is designed to replace one thing with another, as simple as that. You can create small text snippets—like contract clauses or basic statements of law like the standard for summary judgment—and invoke them with easy-to-remember commands.

In the example above, I created an auto-correct that would be invoked if I typed "intake!!" I used double exclamation points because it is unlikely that I would type those normally (unless I was really excited) and I would not want the rule to be invoked whenever I typed the word *intake* alone. You can come up with a similar regular pattern for your own auto-corrects. The next step was to create the new text I want inserted by the auto-correct function. I have a long text snippet that I can insert—"Thank you for contacting our law firm ..."—even though it is not actually *correcting* anything. It is just leveraging the basic replacement functionality that auto-correct uses. Auto-correct can be used as a template alternative, where you may have a custom phrase or piece of information that does not need to live in a template but might still provide personalization to your email or meeting invitation. It is common to see people add some default text to their signature block, for example. You might include "with warmest regards" or "have a nice day" and have that inserted in your email whenever you add your signature block. This is limited in its utility because it can only be inserted where the signature goes, which is usually the end of the email. An auto-correct could allow you to insert custom text blocks anywhere in your email or other documents.

As you continue through this book and consider your ongoing selection and use of technology tools, keep in mind that you may not always be looking for a new application to replace something you are comfortable using. You may only need an add-on or script or some small piece of technology, one that you may be able to create yourself, to fill a gap.

Chapter 4 Exercises

A. Create a calendaring template that pre-populates dates based on practice rules in a local jurisdiction. You may create it using any tool you like. For example, it may be as simple as creating a Microsoft Word table or Excel-based checklist with the formulas to calculate future dates.

B. Shakespeare closes "Henry V" with a quote about how Henry's son "lost" France—the country Henry had just successfully conquered—due to the mismanagement of the people in whose care he was left.[16] Make a list of some of the risks that your law practice might experience by having multiple people able to access a calendar and the impact that might have on your law practice. What if someone leaves the firm? How do you know when a change is made (especially when it is an error)? Can you determine if a calendar has been shared and with whom, especially if it is shared externally? How would you mitigate these risks?

16. "Whose state so many had the managing / That they lost France and made his England bleed" WILLIAM SHAKESPEARE, HENRY V (1599).

Chapter 5

Time and Billing

Before you know it, whether it is the first prospective client or a later one, you will have an actual client. You have completed intake and done a bit of research to understand their case. You will send them an engagement letter using a template and secure their signature. Before you send that letter, it is time to think about a key business component of law practice: money.

Law practices have failed because lawyers fail to ask their clients to pay them. This may sound absurd, but getting paid is not something that is widely discussed in law school. If you have not experienced the need to bill and secure payment before you got to law school, you may not be familiar with this aspect of running a business. It is a fundamental element of the *business* of law practice.

At the same time, there are limits to what a lawyer can do to recover their costs. When a client pays them money, how the lawyer will handle it will differ depending on the purpose. An area that law students and many new lawyers are unfamiliar with is trust accounting, which is where client money that you have not *yet* earned has to be banked separately from money you have already earned, from this and other clients. We will discuss accounting further on, but it is enough for now to say that the money you collect from your legal work may not immediately be able to go directly into your personal or law firm operating bank account.

But back to money. It is important to know what you are going to charge your client and how. Your engagement letter will need to spell this information out. ABA Model Rule 1.5(b) sets out that

> The scope of the representation and the basis or rate of the fee and expenses for which the client will be responsible shall be communi-

> cated to the client, preferably in writing, before or within a reasonable time after commencing the representation....

If you have not yet had a discussion with your prospective client about what your representation of them will cost, you should do so at the earliest possible moment. Ideally, you will cover it in the engagement letter and have them sign to acknowledge they understand. But even well before you start the intake process for your first client, you will want to have thought about how you will price your legal work and how you will get paid.

What Are You Worth?

One of the first decisions you may want to make as a law student about to graduate into law practice is how you want to be paid. Lawyers are famous for billing based on the time they spend—often in 6-minute increments or one-tenth of an hour—on a client's matter. You may have thought about this already and calculated what you'd like to earn based on this incremental hourly system although, as we will touch on below, this is just the income side of your equation. This 6-minute approach seems easy until you start to have to track that time and ensure it is captured and assigned to the appropriate client. There are plenty of tools to help you, but it is a productivity challenge that you will need to manage.

An alternative to hourly billing is to charge your client a flat fee based on the type of matter it is. You determine the flat fee for the representation you are providing based on your prior experience so that it will approximate your previous costs to deliver a similar service in a similar matter. Even without getting into the unbundling of legal services—where you may provide representation on a discrete step within multiple steps needed to resolve a legal issue—it is possible to provide legal services for a flat fee. The benefit of a flat fee is that both you and the client know how much the client will be paying for the work you and your staff will be performing. Keep in mind that you do not need to only use one fee approach: you may create a tier of relatively simple work that is something of a commodity—easy to delegate portions to staff, easy to repeat, easy to complete using productivity tools like document assembly—for flat fees. Or you may offer highly expert services that have a regular set of tasks, like taking a case to an appellate court after another lawyer has lost at the trial court, for a flat fee. You can use hourly or other fee structures for more complex or less knowable work.

The big question is how to determine that fee, whether it is tied to a time increment or is flat based on prior work. This can create a chicken-and-egg challenge where, until you have done the work, you may not know what to charge them for it. There can be a lot of variation between two client matters that look the same on the surface—two divorces, two house sales, two misdemeanor traffic cases—that can make pricing difficult.

Practice Pointer

Look for practice management guides on pricing like the one written by Jessica Bednarz and Lauren Lester. These resources can provide both guidance on how to think about pricing but also templates to use as you start to communicate your fee approaches to your prospective clients. Bar associations and regulators know that pricing and billing are key parts of law practice and may be an unfamiliar subject area for lawyers who have not been responsible for them before. There are also consultants who work on law firm pricing, and, at large law firms, there may be legal project management teams that focus on costing and reproducibility of work. It can be a complicated process to ensure that their clients' costs are comparable to what other law firms are charging and are used to position the law firm to be competitive when a prospective client is seeking bids for work.

One place to start is to look at what other lawyers in your area are charging for similar services. In some cases, you can see from lawyer advertising that a lawyer is charging a certain amount for a will, for example. Transactional document creation can provide a lot of opportunities for flat rate billing. Not only is the output often knowable—a will, a tax filing, and so on—there are often productivity tools to help you automate the more routine portions of the output. Transactional practice areas are a good example of how you might approach a client matter by using not only your own skills, but also automation and delegation to less costly staff, to offer a repeatable fee for a relatively straight forward service. It may still take you some time to decide how much you *need* to charge, as well as what you may *want* to charge to earn a profit, as well as what your clients will be able to afford for your legal services.

This is not a technology issue but, like all law practice technology challenges, it involves a process or data input that will impact your use or acquisition of technology. You will need to know what it costs to run your law practice in order to know what you will need to charge to pay your bills and to earn an income. If you have not already thought about these costs, making some calculations while you are a law student can help you to know what may be required. One benefit of starting at someone else's law firm is that they have already done this math: costs for space, for staff, for legal malpractice insurance, for third party help like accountants or technology consultants, for bar admission and continuing education, and, among other things, for the technology you are going to use.

Near the start of this book, we looked at your technology budget. That amount, as well as all of your other costs, contribute to the cost known as your overhead. All of that needs to be paid for before you pay yourself. Once you have figured out what your cost-per-hour is for that overhead, then you can start to determine how much more beyond that amount you need to charge your clients to pay your own salary and the salary of your staff.

Once you have determined how much you need to charge and what method of fee structure—hourly, flat fee, contingent, etc.—you are going to charge your clients, it is time to start managing your time to ensure that the money you charge accurately represents the time and resources it takes to perform the work. Even if you are using a flat fee structure for some clients or some matters, it is worth monitoring and recording all of your time (and, when you have them, your staff's time) spent on every aspect of a client's matter. You may find that, as your expertise grows, you are taking less time to accomplish a particular matter and able to release that time to work on other client matters or to use the time in a different, possibly revenue-generating, way. Even if that does not cause you to change what you are billing clients, it may change your calculations on what you are earning yourself and what your law practice profit may be. Time is at the heart of how lawyers earn money and run their business.

Similarly, keeping track of time can show when, no matter what you do, it is costing you more in time and other resources than you are charging for a service. You may decide to increase what you charge for that service or you may decide to drop the service entirely, referring the prospective clients to another lawyer. Time-keeping and time management can be one of the best tools for gathering data about your law practice and using that data to make decisions. The earlier you develop a time-keeping habit, the better.

Client	Matter	Time	Task
Student bar association	Volunteering	1.5	Board meeting
Contracts	Studying	3	Review notes, update outline
Legal Research & Writing	Studying	2	Work on table of authorities

Table: A simple time sheet for a law student

Law school is a good a time as any. You do not need any special software to get started. A Microsoft Excel or Google Workspace spreadsheet will be enough. You will want to track the date and the amount of time you spend and then provide some categorization to help you use the information later. You might record your time in tenths-of-an-hour, but even if you default to 15- or 30-minute increments, it is good practice. Your categories might include "work," "school," "volunteering," and so on. They can be general labels or as specific as you want, but keep in mind that too much specificity can make it harder to aggregate your data. For example, "volunteering" is a high-level topic, where "Celtic law student board meeting" and "SBA board meeting" may give you more detail about what you were doing, but that detail may not help you manipulate the data at that higher level. Just as when you are in law practice, you do not need to measure the time you spend outside of work or, in your case, law school. Keep in mind that it may not always be clear: is attending a gathering of other lawyers for a birthday or a continuing legal education program after your normal work hours "work" or social? Or both? After you have developed the habit of updating your spreadsheet—perhaps at the end of a day, if you have large chunks of time involved, perhaps throughout the day as you are working on small projects or items—you can start to see how your time use breaks into your categories.

Practice Pointer

I think the better habit to develop is to update your data *throughout* the day, as you may miss or forget things that you worked on that are in the smallest increments. If you only do it at the day's end, your perspective is an eight or more hour day and you may forget some of the smaller increments of time you spent. If I am sure I was working on something but cannot remember what, I will use my calendar to see if I recorded it as an event. I will also often use my email sent folder as a prompt to remind me of things I was working on. I may have forgotten an email that took me 15 minutes to draft. To accurately record our time, it can require thinking differently about the work we did: "I sent email for 30 minutes" as opposed to "I sent an email to Professor A that took 10 minutes, and 3 emails to people involved in my law school club that took 20 minutes."

Automatic Time Recording

If you are charging based on the amount of time you spend on a task, you will need a tool to track your time. As mentioned above, even if you are not billing by the hour, gathering some ongoing data about how you are spending your time—on which client, and doing what tasks—can help your future planning for your law firm. It can also help you explain to your client how you used the time for which they are being billed if you are using an alternative fee strategy.[1]

The most certain method of recording your time is to do it yourself, manually, as soon as you complete the task. While this is extremely simple from a technology standpoint, it can be extraordinarily difficult once you try it in real life. You may still want to see if it is an option for you when you are first starting out. Once you develop the habit, you may find that it becomes routine to stay on top of your time reporting and recording.

You will come across lawyers and others who insist on paper calendars and paper notepads for their work. They may apologize for this very basic technol-

1. It is common for law firms to write off work that they either know or think that a client will not want to pay for (because the client has asked them to write it off). These write-offs can amount to substantial amounts, a value that needs to be considered when you are contemplating your fees. ABA Legal Technology Surveys have found that clients have requested from 7% to 10% over the years, ranging from about 5% for solo practitioners and as much as 14% for large law firms. AM. BAR ASS'N, 2023 LEGAL TECHNOLOGY SURVEY REPORT: TECHNOLOGY BASICS xi (2024). If you have calculated your fees without considering write-offs and you have set your overhead at $100 and your salary at $100, writing off 10% ($20) means that your salary is now $80 since your overhead costs will remain the same since you are doing the work even though you are not being paid for it.

ogy, but paper can be a highly reliable option if it becomes part of your habit and may be faster and more resilient than an app or other tool for capturing time spent. We tend to think of silicon-based applications when we think of technology, but paper retains its position as a key technology for supporting your law practice management.

Your typical day-in-the-life as a lawyer may provide you with the type of client work that is largely contiguous, with each task occurring one after another, with easy-to-manage start and end times. For example, you head into the office in the morning, and you need to do some research. You open a spreadsheet and create a new entry in your time sheet for the time period for which you are billing. You spend two hours engaging in research and then start to write a memo. You rough out a draft of the memo in an hour, you break for lunch, and, mercifully, your phone has not rung. Unless you have been peeking in at your email, these tasks and events are largely contiguous and large chunks of time, easy to document for your time management.

Practice Pointer

We will look at creating Microsoft Excel worksheets, below, that connected from one to the other. One sheet listed entities, and the other listed the people at those entities. You can create a similar arrangement with your time tracking. Your timesheet could be the first page of the workbook. It could link to a second worksheet that lists clients and matters, as well as common tasks that you perform.

You will want to capture who the work is for and the type of task you are performing. Not surprisingly, you will not be the first lawyer in history to perform that task. Over time, the legal profession has come up with standard sets of billing codes that can help to streamline how lawyers charge but, fundamentally, these are things we spend time on.[2] This is particularly beneficial

2. Two of the prominent code sets are from the American Bar Association's uniform task-based management system (UTBM) and the Standards Advancement for the Legal Industry (SALI). The ABA code lists are free to download. Some of the older code sets are available as PDF documents—here is the one for both litigation and non-litigation tasks (Am. Bar Ass'n, Uniform Task-Based Management System (1995), https://www.americanbar.org/content/dam/aba/administrative/litigation/leadership-portal/utbms.pdf [http://web.archive.org/web/20250425032717/https://www.americanbar.org/content/dam

if you end up licensing software for your time-keeping and billing in your law practice, as the software application may implement these uniform codes in their system. This will make moving between applications easier in the future as well as saving you from having to come up with your own task labels from scratch. You also may not be sure, the first time you try to bill something, how to characterize it. These lists are good reference points as you emerge from law school to being your law practice.

Let's look at our day-in-the-life again. Once you have completed your legal research task, you can return to the spreadsheet and enter the time at which you stopped. An easy spreadsheet formula can subtract the start time from the end time and give you a number. Alternatively, if you are working in large, clear blocks of time, you can just write the equivalent of "two hours" or "one hour." In practice, you would not use the words but would probably write "1" or "2"—or perhaps "2.1" if you had worked for 2 hours and one 6-minute increment—so that you can add the numbers up in the future. As you practice your initial time sheets, always think not only about what you are capturing now but how you will use it later. In reality, if you use an app, it will take care of this aspect for you.

You can then transfer this number to another system, if you are using your time recordings to bill your clients. If you have a column in your time-keeping spreadsheet that captures clients and a second column for their matters—as the table above shows—you can use your spreadsheet to filter each client to see the time spent on each matter or for the client overall. You can now turn to your next task and repeat the process for as many tasks or hours as you have available.

This is the simplest approach and one you can easily and immediately practice in law school. It fails to take into account the complexity that comes with a growing law practice, and it is almost certainly not going to scale up as you add staff, all of whom will need to contribute to a similar system. You will definitely outgrow a time-keeping method based on a spreadsheet, but it is an adequate place to start.

It will also be challenging if you end up in a law practice where there is a lot of uncertainty throughout your day. For example, you may be practicing criminal law, and, in the midst of working on an evidentiary motion for one

/aba/administrative/litigation/leadership-portal/utbms.pdf])—while more recent ones, like Criminal Law, Real Estate, and Workers Compensation code sets are already prepared in a spreadsheet format.

of your clients, the phone rings. A family member of a different client is calling because they are having difficulty reaching their family member—your client—who is in detention, perhaps due to a limitation on phone privileges or a lack of funds. You focus on the immediate, urgent need and forget to note the time you stopped the motion on client A and started the call about client B. When your law practice contains interruptions that you are not able to control or manage, time-keeping manually will become more difficult. You may already have experienced this if you have worked a summer in a law firm or are working at one during the school year. It is not uncommon to find yourself being asked to do multiple tasks where each person assigning work to you is unaware of the other work you have already been assigned. As you become accustomed to juggling multiple priorities, you will need to also keep track of how long you spend on each one in turn.

In this case, you may be able to use technology to help you (and you may have seen this in a law firm where it was available or mandated for your use). Your phone may record the time a phone call started, identifying the moment you were interrupted from the task you were performing for the first client. Your phone will likely also show how long the call was, as well as any subsequent calls you had to make to the detention center and to the client's family member. As you are managing your time, look for this sort of metadata about your activities to help you determine the amount of time spent. Your time-keeping app may not be connected to devices like your phone calls, and so you will need to manually move this information over to whatever tool you are using to record your time.

Practice Pointer

We forget how often we are interrupted during the day. Each interruption comes with a cost. Think of the last time you were studying and a friend stopped by for five minutes or you had a notification or text that required your attention for just a moment. Over an hour, you can easily accumulate five or ten minutes of interruptions that you may not remember to account for in your time. Interruptions come with their own cognitive cost as well. A single text message can cause your mind to reset, requiring you to spend time returning to the interrupted work at hand. Research has found that it can take more than 20 minutes to get back to the same point we were at before the interruption.[3] Think of the tools you use in law school—perhaps you listen to music on noise-cancelling headphones or you sit in a carrel where people may not find you—to minimize interruptions. You may need to identify similar approaches once you are in law practice, finding a quiet location in the law firm or closing your office door if you are able, to enable you to focus and be as productive as possible.

You do not want to guess on your time allocations for a client. Bill padding is a disciplinary issue, and so a guesstimate is an ethical risk.[4] If you are not sure that you can accurately track your time manually, you should look at time-keeping tools to help you. These will not be perfect either, but they may give you more detail. These applications are often able to manage multiple ongoing tasks by running timers for each activity. For example, you may run a stopwatch or timer on the first task and then start a second one when the phone call comes in. Starting the second timer will stop the first but retain the time spent to that point. Once you stop the second timer, you can return to the first timer. Since these timers will be integrated into the time-keeping application, the tracked time can be applied directly to the client and matter information in your system.

3. Research on work fragmentation by Gloria Mark and her colleagues has been cited for the past few decades for the observation that it takes time to return to interrupted work: "When people did resume work on the same day, it took an average length of time of 25 [minutes], 26 [seconds].... This was reported by informants as being very detrimental." Gloria Mark, Victor M. Gonzalez & Justin Harris, *No Task Left Behind?: Examining the Nature of Fragmented Work*, 23 Conf. Hum. Factors Computing Sys. 321 (2005), https://doi.org/10.1145/1054972.1055017. Additionally, in Mary Czerwinski, Eric Horvitz & Susan Wilhite, *A Diary Study of Task Switching and Interruptions*, 22 Conf. Hum. Factors Computing Sys. 175 (2004), https://doi.org/10.1145/985692.985715, it was found that multiple-document, longer-lasting activities were harder to return to. It is not hard to imagine that sort of task or situation in a law firm or law school environment. More recent research has suggested that it does not help if the interruption—say, a friend asking you about the topic you are currently studying—is related to the work being interrupted. The Cost of Interrupted Work: More Speed and Stress, Gloria Mark, Daniela Gudith & Ulrich Klocke, *The Cost of Interrupted Work: More Speed and Stress*, 26 Conf. Hum. Factors Computing Sys. 107 (2008), https://doi.org/10.1145/1357054.135707.

4. See A.B.A. Model Rules of Professional Conduct, r. 1.5 (Am. Bar Ass'n 2025) for details on billing clients.

Just the Time

If you do not need to use a time-keeper app that can be integrated with a billing application, there are a wide variety of productivity tools you can select from. These are applications that you install on your computer. They run in the background and keep track of what application you are in at any given moment.[5] At the end of the day, you can see all of the apps you ran and how much time you spent with each one, including each web browser tab you utilized. This will not always tell you what you were doing, but it can capture more minutely task-switching you are engaging in while you work.

This can be a fantastic productivity tool to determine how you are actually spending your day. Some of these applications will be designed or marketed for employee surveillance—to allow employers to monitor what their staff are doing when the manager cannot see them—and I would avoid using these tools for that purpose. If you want your staff to make the same productivity gains as you, then encourage them to use it in the same way as you will. The applications should not be used to remotely monitor or keep tabs on your staff. Focus on the information it provides you about your productivity, and then record the time that you spent engaged in the work or other categories of activities you are tracking. If you find obvious places where you are not using your time well—perhaps too many hours on YouTube—you can make those adjustments on your own.

At the end of the day or week or whatever time period you set for yourself, you can check to see how you are spending your time. You may want to review your time more often at the beginning so that you can discover anything unexpected and start to adapt. Also, keep in mind that these applications run on your computer, so they do not manage anything that does not happen on the computer (or, in certain cases, on your phone). One reason I like the simple method of a spreadsheet is that you will inevitably have time and tasks that are going to have to be captured manually; it may be easier to start with a system that can capture everything rather than having multiple places your time and tasks are recorded and then having to consolidate them.

5. Timely and Worktime are examples of this application. https://app.gettimely.com, https://worktime.com. Chrometa is another example, but it has integrations to lawyer practice management systems. https://www.chrometa.com.

Time Plus Billing

Time-keeping and billing functionality is often available together in an application. However, these programs are fundamentally different from the time tracker apps mentioned above and are unlikely to attempt to automatically capture your task time usage. Rather, they are more like a spreadsheet method in that you need to manually enter your time into the system. They may offer multiple timers or stopwatches so that you can keep track of multiple tasks at once and bill them to the appropriate client.

Another place where they shine is in the integration of the time recording with other systems and with the billing feature. If you have adopted a simple spreadsheet method of managing your time, you will still need to move that information over to a client bill. Once the bill has been created, it needs to be sent and tracked for payment. You may even want to find a way to send your bill electronically and have it paid online too. This process sounds simple, but it involves a bunch of systems working together. You are used to paying for things online, but that is just the last step in the process. There were many steps in generating data around the costs and getting it on to the invoice or payment prompt that reached you and that allowed you to complete the payment.

All of this is possible in a law practice. It requires us to return to the primary question you will be asking yourself: what problem am I trying to solve and what is the best way to solve it? Since time-keeping is such a widespread business need, the options that you have may be broader:

- Simple, manual spreadsheet
- Time-keeping app, no billing (export time to other systems manually)
- Time-keeping app with billing integration
- Time-keeping app with billing integration and ebilling
- Time-keeping app integrated with practice management system (which has billing functionality)
- Practice management system with internal time-keeping and billing functionality

Lawyers are not the only people who bill based on time spent on tasks or who base their flat fees on the time spent on projects. Freelancers, consultants, and many others will use time and billing systems to get paid in their line of work. You will need to sort through these permutations to decide which is most appropriate for you and how you work, as well as the sophistication of your clients, some of whom may prefer or only be able to work with paper invoices. If you prefer to have a collection of discrete applications in your time management and payment process, having a standalone time and billing application may be the best choice. If you are using a practice management app, though, you may not need to acquire anything additional, depending on the time and billing functionality in the system.

It cannot be overemphasized that your time-keeping needs to be accurate, but the time you record also needs to be able to be fed into a system to generate your bills. Unless you are tracking time solely for productivity analysis, you should be looking at time-keeping that either integrates with or is internally connected to a system with billing outputs. Otherwise, you will spend a lot of time creating and managing the billing processes, moving data backwards and forwards.[6]

Time in the Cloud

Some applications may make more sense as locally installed applications. Time-keeping is one that may be ideally suited for cloud computing, for all the same reasons as time-keeping on a paper planner or notebook. You never know where you will be when you need to handle a client matter. If your time-keeping application is located on a single device, and if that device is unavailable to you, you may be forced to make spur-of-the-moment notes and remember to add them later. You may decide that you want to limit your technology selections to time-keepers that have mobile apps in addition to a locally installed computer app. This will require you to plan to synchronize your time recording across devices or otherwise move the time data from your phone to your computer.

A cloud-based time-keeper can keep your single source of time management always available, by mobile device or while you are in the office or working remotely. If you are worried about cloud computing and the risks of confidentiality and inadvertent disclosure but want to try using the cloud, time-keeping data will be among the lowest risk data you could start with. You

6. I say "you" here loosely. It may not be you but instead a bookkeeper or office manager you hire. But whether you do it yourself or pay someone to do it, there is a cost that you can minimize by using automation where possible.

would still not want this information about your clients to be exposed, but an exposure of it—as compared to client documents or evidence or personally identifiable information—would likely be less damaging to your client than other data loss merely because you are not capturing a great deal of information in the time record.

Time-keeping is a good example of what is essentially a utility technology. It is relatively generic, and yet is a key tool for managing your law practice. It will need to be highly available and accurate, and yet it does not really need to have anything law-specific about it. Most any time-keeping or time and billing app, including those used by freelancers or other small business owners, will work in a law practice. The only things that may be unique to a law firm are the types of labels for your time (like drafting a motion) and the time segments that you use, if you bill by a portion of the hour. Law practice-specific time-keepers will be useful primarily if you can leverage their integrations with other law practice technology.

Chapter 5 Exercises

A. Spend one week during law school recording your time. You should capture at least work and school, and within the school category, capture a level of detail that includes time spent on each class or club or activity you spent time on. Use a spreadsheet to capture the data and then create a visualization—chart or some other output—that shows the breakdown of your week's worth of data. Did you find any surprises? Do you feel your time invested in school and work activities is balanced with the other parts of your life?

B. Imagine that you are about to start your own law firm, and you want to investigate practice areas that would allow you to engage in value-based billing, rather than hourly billing. Research three practice areas that are appealing to you, and write a summary of which ones involve pricing strategies that you find appealing and would feel comfortable asking clients to pay.

Chapter 6

Legal Research

Let's return to the client matter at hand. Your prospective client has contacted you. You have entered their details into your calendaring system to set up their initial intake, taking care not to disqualify yourself from your current cases. Once you or your staff have information from them about their legal issue, you are ready to assess whether you can take on their case or not. As you gain experience, you may know immediately that this is not a case you are prepared to work on.[1] But you are likely to find that you need to do some legal research in order to understand whether there is a viable claim or other legal advice you can provide to this client. This is where your legal research technology comes into play.

1. You should already be thinking about referrals in areas where you are not comfortable or do not want to practice. However, keep in mind that referrals between lawyers are a form of networking as much as a practical ethics issue. You should only refer prospective clients when you know they have a case that someone could represent them on, just that it's not you. This means that, if you perform your legal research and find they have no case or a low likelihood of success, break that news to them rather than refer them on.

Practice Pointer

The rules governing your professional conduct allow you to take on new client matters in areas in which you have not practiced before.[2] As you are going through the intake process, you can make an initial assessment but, especially when you start out, you are going to need to do some legal research. The research stage will give you a much better sense of what is familiar to you and what will be a stretch. If you decide to take on a client with a matter in an area of law with which you are unfamiliar, you may need to identify additional resources to enable "necessary study" or, as the comment to the Model Rule suggests, you may want to coordinate with a more experienced colleague. There may be technology tools available in that practice area that you may not have discovered on your own that can reduce your learning curve.

You will have been using legal research applications almost from the start of your law school journey. These applications, like Thomson Reuters' Westlaw and RELX's Lexis, will be so familiar to you that you may not think of them as legal technology. Legal research extends far beyond the web browser, however, and is a critical part of law practice. The majority of respondents to an ABA legal technology survey reported that they spent between 10% and 30% of their work time engaged in legal research.[3] In fact, if you are entering a larger legal organization—a firm or government agency or court—you may find that your initial work is overweighted towards performing legal research as compared to other types of tasks.

Unlike many other law practice technologies, because legal research is a foundational law practice skill, it will come as no surprise that the amount of time spent by lawyers engaged in legal research was consistent across all firm sizes: while 67% of solos fell into that 10% to 30% range, so did roughly 60%

---

2. A.B.A. Model Rules of Professional Conduct, r. 1.1, cmt. 2 (Am. Bar Ass'n 2025): "A lawyer need not necessarily have special training or prior experience to handle legal problems of a type with which the lawyer is unfamiliar. A newly admitted lawyer can be as competent as a practitioner with long experience.... A lawyer can provide adequate representation in a wholly novel field through necessary study."

3. Am. Bar Ass'n, 2023 Legal Technology Survey Report: Online Research 13, question 12 (2024). 22.7% reported using 10%–14% of their work time, 12.7% reported 15–19%, and 23.8% reported 20%–29% of work time was used for legal research.

of lawyers working at firms with more than 500 lawyers. While law librarians are not typically found at law firms with fewer than 50 lawyers, their presence at the larger law firms does not seem to have a substantial impact on whether a lawyer is performing legal research themselves.[4]

This is, in part, because lawyers cannot fully delegate nor retreat from legal research for professional reasons. It is part of their competent legal representation of clients. Legal research also comes into play when a client's matter appears in a court setting. Rule 3.3 of the ABA Model Rules requires candor towards the tribunal.[5] This is explicit when it comes to legal research. While the first section discusses facts and the third section discusses evidence, the second one looks directly at existing legal authority:

> (a) A lawyer shall not knowingly ...
>
> 2) fail to disclose to the tribunal legal authority in the controlling jurisdiction known to the lawyer to be directly adverse to the position of the client and not disclosed by opposing counsel....

This is not the entirety of the obligation that is impacted by legal research. As we are seeing in the court decisions and application of fines and discipline of lawyers in relation to the use of artificial intelligence, many jurisdictions require a lawyer to certify the accuracy of their court submissions. This undertaking includes the unsurprising baseline that the law *must exist*, whether it is being relied on or being attacked:

> (b) Representations to the Court. By presenting to the court a pleading, written motion, or other paper—whether by signing, filing, submitting, or later advocating it—an attorney or unrepresented party certifies that to the best of the person's knowledge, information, and belief, formed after an inquiry reasonable under the circumstances: ...

---

4. *Id.* at 14, question 13c (2024). 89.2% of solos responded that they never used a law librarian or that the question was not applicable. This number rose to 93% in law firms with 2 to 9 lawyers and 93.3% for law firms with 10 to 49 lawyers. The "not applicable" dropped precipitously for firms with 50 to 99 lawyers and those that were larger. To be clear, this is not a value issue. A law librarian is a staff person in a law firm and is part of overhead. There is a law firm size below which it is the aid of a professional law librarian is not affordable.

5. A.B.A. Model Rules of Professional Conduct, r. 3.3 (Am. Bar Ass'n 2025), https://www.americanbar.org/groups/professional_responsibility/publications/model_rules_of_professional_conduct/rule_3_3_candor_toward_the_tribunal/.

> (2) the claims, defenses, and other legal contentions are warranted by existing law or by a nonfrivolous argument for extending, modifying, or reversing existing law or for establishing new law[.][6]

Legal research enables you to understand what the existing law is and to explore how or whether it might be extended, modified, or used to reverse existing law. Lawyers who submit confabulations to the court in the form of non-existent cases and citations are failing to understand and use their legal research technology competently.

Legal Publishers

The selection of legal research technology may be among the simplest technologies for a lawyer to adopt. They are largely search and retrieval systems with a wide variety of content that you can license to improve your search results. They often require no additional software and are accessed entirely over the internet, although some legal publishers provide software add-ons or plugins to create integrations with local law practice software. Just as with Microsoft, there are dominant products like Thomson Reuters Westlaw and RELX Lexis, as well as a wide variety of other platforms.

Practice Pointer

During law school, you will have access to two or three large legal publisher databases, perhaps more. There is a good chance that your access will not be as extensive when you arrive at your first law role. You may have a favorite platform in law school, but you should already be considering how portable your research skills are. The better you are at performing research on any platform, the more adaptable you will be when you start to practice law. Additionally, it will help to remove some of the vendor lock-in you may feel about comfort with one legal research platform over another. While you are in law school, practice your research on as many platforms as you are able. This will not only expose you to new information collections but will give you greater confidence in your skill development.

6. FED. R. CIV. P. 11.

Perhaps surprisingly, despite starting with legal research as their core business, many of the legal publishers have pushed into other areas of legal technology, with varying degrees of success. You can license time and billing software from a RELX unit and practice management software from a Thomson Reuters one. Some of these applications are discrete, standalone applications that may be ideally suited to solving a very specific, narrowly tailored problem like litigation event chronologies.

Many of these applications were developed initially by standalone companies and were acquired later by the legal publishers to meet a perceived need in the legal professional market. Over time, the law practice technology portfolios of Thomson Reuters and RELX have fluctuated significantly as they acquired and then shed or shut particular products. Some of these have been attempts to integrate the most common tools—like Microsoft's Office products—with the legal research and other products licensed by the lawyer. For example, Lexis for Microsoft Office and Lexis Create+ are plugins that enable connections between Microsoft applications and the Lexis platform.[7] Keep in mind that these plugins may have very low adoption among lawyers, far lower than the actual subscribers to the legal research platform. You should approach adoption of these add-ons with some care and be aware that commercial provider priorities change and the tool you rely on may be discontinued. You may find a great deal of variation with the maintenance and updates of these plugins, depending on the publisher's interest in developing them out and the interest which the legal market shows in adopting them.

Most lawyers will adopt one or the other of the two primary legal research services, Thomson Reuters' Westlaw or RELX Lexis. However, many lawyers do not use any fee-based legal research service, especially in solo law practices, where they are most likely to do their own legal research.[8] Even in law practices where fee-based legal research services are licensed, many lawyers will start

7. Lexis for Microsoft Office. https://appsource.microsoft.com/en-us/product/office/WA104380757 Lexis Create+ https://appsource.microsoft.com/en-us/product/office/wa200004714.

8. Am. Bar Ass'n, 2023 Legal Technology Survey Report: Online Research 17, question 4e (2024). 27.7% of solos reported that they never used a fee-based legal research service. This answer may not include all legal research, since, unlike other questions asked by the survey, there is not a question about whether a fee-based legal research service is available (even if it is not used by the lawyer).

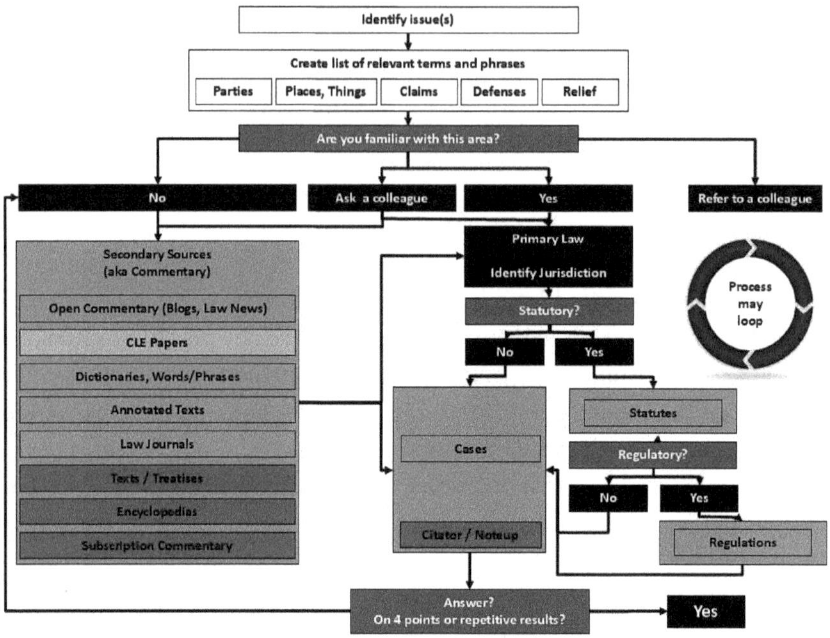

Figure 3: Example of search strategies that include asking colleagues

with a general internet search using Google or Microsoft Bing when they are starting their legal research.[9]

This is not surprising when you think about how lawyers acquire and use information. While this text is focused primarily on law practice technology, lawyers have a variety of information inputs in their practice that do not use technology. For one, they may just contact a colleague in the firm or in the same practice area and get some advice or a head start on a client matter, getting either an answer or a direct referral to a legal research resource that contains the answer they need, or the next link in the chain they can follow. Lawyers may have attended a continuing legal education (CLE or CPD) course and retained the materials, and they may consult those books or presentation

9. *Id.* at 26, question 16. Surprisingly, this number rises with the size of the law firm—although other data shows that larger law firms are more likely to license commercial legal research technology—with 39.6% of solos saying they start with a general search engine or directory and 63.9% of lawyers at firms with 500 or more lawyers.

slides.[10] A general web search using Google or Bing may remind them of a starting point or a term of art or a relevant case.

Commercial and Free-to-Use Information

A common question when lawyers are considering their legal research needs is whether they need to license anything at all. This may be surprising to you as a law student, where you have most likely had free access to both Thomson Reuters Westlaw and RELX Lexis throughout your degree program, where your law school has paid for your access. You have probably not experienced the need to manage how many hours of usage you spend on either product, how many pages you print or download from them, and so on. You may not even be aware that your usage can be tracked and so you will most likely tie each legal research activity to a client matter for accounting purposes, even if a client does not end up paying for it.

These are all considerations you may already have come across within a law firm or other environment, outside of law school, where there are more concrete costs to use these legal research platforms. In particular, it will be common to find that the law firm or legal organization you join—or start, if you decide to go solo—only licenses one of the products you used in law school. As you start to contemplate your law practice overhead costs, and the portion that will be paid to a legal publisher, you may need to consider that what you can afford is different from what you have had access to during law school.

Practice Pointer

It is not uncommon for lawyers to visit their local courthouse law library or even a public law school library to perform research without those limitations if they are concerned that their research time will be more extensive than their paid subscription will allow. When you start

10. You may find that, when you graduate and prepare for the bar exam, you suddenly have an instant library in your bar prep materials. It is not uncommon for lawyers to keep those materials in their first few years of law practice as a quick refresher on areas of law they may have forgotten after graduation.

to practice, you should ask your colleagues if they know of free-to-you alternatives—perhaps through your bar association membership—that can help you balance your need to have confidence in your research output with the costs of doing the research. Free legal research is a common option for lawyers, and you should include it in your assessment of the tools you will deploy for your clients. As you gain confidence, you may need these resources less often, but they can help—especially if your legal research skills are platform-agnostic—you to balance your need to research with the costs associated with doing so.

Legal research is an area that is ripe for consideration of using free or free-to-you legal information resources. This is particularly true because legal publishers are providing substantial amounts of freely accessible government information within their databases. That information is often available for free on government websites. While the editorial enhancements the legal publishers make to the content they incorporate into their platforms inform the license fees they charge you, you may find that the value of that editorial content diminishes as you become more knowledgeable about the areas in which you practice.

Some lawyers will make the decision to rely solely on publicly available information. This is relatively easy to do in North America, where you can find legislation, regulations, and case law for free from most jurisdictions. Both the United States and Canada have legal information institutes (LII), and Canada's has been funded by the legal profession through dues allocations paid to their provincial lawyer regulators. These LIIs are a great starting place for online legal research.[11]

There is also a wide variety of public commentary about the law. There are large, coordinated blog networks—in particular LexBlog—that host or encourage the writing of current, substantive articles about changes in the law.[12]

11. The United States LII is hosted by Cornell and was the first of its kind, created in 1992. Regional and national LIIs exist across the world and can be an excellent source for international legal research when your commercial license does not extend to foreign countries' legal information.

12. LexBlog (https://www.lexblog.com/channels/) is a commercial entity. It is different from loose affiliations of bloggers that may also exist on the internet. LexBlog is a mixture of hosted and syndicated content, with the latter coming from across the internet (my personal

There are law-firm powered expertise portals as well, including Mondaq and Lexology. They will publish timely articles by lawyers who specialize in the areas they write about. While, in your early career, you may want to license legal publisher treatise content, over time you may find that this need diminishes as you can find and follow experts who regularly publish about your practice areas and whose insights you trust. This information may exist on smaller or more niche publisher websites, both freely accessible and behind paywalls.

It is worth taking a slight detour into what may be a selection criterion when it comes to any information-based or current awareness technology. It is common for those platforms to provide two points of entry. One is direct, where you go to the platform and engage with a search box or browse the linked content.

The other is through platform alerts, where the platform sends you information based on criteria you have set for it. This is often distributed in the form of news alerts in your areas of practice, but it can be far more nuanced: if you are trying to secure a new client, you can follow their industry more closely or even follow news about them in particular. You might only follow court opinions or other primary documents, like a pending bill that you want to track through its iterations in a legislature, to see if it actually is likely to become law.[13] The most common way to receive this information is via email. As you become more expert in an area of law, you may rely more heavily on just seeing the latest changes in your practice area. Look for alerting options when you are considering how you will use your legal research subscription.

There is also a middle ground where there are legal research products that sit between the legacy legal publishers and the freely available internet research. As an alternative approach to the LII platform, American bar associations (whether they are lawyer regulators or voluntary membership organizations) have licensed legal information products for decades. The Ohio State Bar Association helped to develop CaseMaker, a legal research product that was adopted as a member benefit by bar associations across the

blog is syndicated by LexBlog). Some blogs that were incubated as part of the now-defunct Law Professors Blog Network may have moved to a standalone approach, like The Business Law Professor's blog (https://www.businesslawprofessors.com/).

13. This can be useful in more ways than you might imagine. First, you will want to know for your own ability to represent your clients and remain on top of the changing law. Second, you can share your analysis with current clients or prospective ones as marketing outreach, so that they are aware of possible changes that might require them to secure your services.

U.S. Over time, competition arose between Fastcase and Casemaker, resulting eventually in the two merging, and then Fastcase being purchased by a European-based legal publisher named vLex.[14] More recently, RELX Lexis has developed its own bar association-affinity platform called Decisis, which is available in about 14 states and at a number of regional bar associations.[15]

This means that, when you join a bar association, you should consider whether the member benefits it offers include free access to a commercial product like vLex Fastcase or RELX Decisis. This can be a cost-savings by reducing your overhead outlay for a commercial legal publisher as well as being an inexpensive—you are already paying the membership dues—supplement to using free legal information straight from the courts, agencies, legislatures, and municipalities who are publishing their law directly to the internet.

Practice Pointer

While you are in law school, investigate whether your state bar association has a student membership. Many do, and they are often free. This may provide you with a way to start to explore these free-to-you legal research tools while you are still in law school, platforms that you might not otherwise experience before you reach law practice.

While bar association-sponsored legal research benefits are common, they appear to be an underutilized resource. Most respondents to an ABA survey reported that they did not use a bar association-provided commercial legal

14. *Casemaker and Fastcase Merge to Become the Leader in Legal Research and Analytics*, FASTCASE (Jan. 5, 2021), https://www.fastcase.com/blog/fastcase-casemaker-merge/ [http://web.archive.org/web/20241212203800/https://www.fastcase.com/blog/fastcase-casemaker-merge/]; *Legal Tech Disruptors vLex and Fastcase Merge to Form World's Largest Global Law Library*, VLEX (Apr. 4, 2023), https://vlex.com/blog/vlex-fastcase [http://web.archive.org/web/20250322092114/https://vlex.com/blog/vlex-fastcase]. vLex has itself been acquired in late 2025 by Clio.

15. Bob Ambrogi, *Legal Research Service Decisis Makes Inroads Against Fastcase as It Expands to 20 Bar Associations*, LAWNEXT (May 9, 2025), https://www.lawnext.com/2025/05/legal-research-service-decisis-makes-inroads-against-fastcase-as-it-expands-to-20-bar-associations.html [http://web.archive.org/web/20250513211041/https://www.lawnext.com/2025/05/legal-research-service-decisis-makes-inroads-against-fastcase-as-it-expands-to-20-bar-associations.html]. Also, Bob Ambrogi is a long-time observer of the legal profession and technology world, definitely worth following on whatever platforms you can find his observations.

research resource.[16] Perhaps not surprisingly, of those who reported using the bar association affinity offering, the lawyers were predominantly solo practitioners.[17] However, considering that you are likely to join a bar association that has access to a free legal research service—many state and regional bar associations offer some legal research member benefit—it is worth keeping in mind that this is an option. Even if you end up determining that you need to license a larger or more complete commercial legal research platform, you may end up with cost-related reasons to work within a service that does not have a usage fee. For example, you may take on a pro bono case or work with a group where you are unable to bill them for their research time; a free-to-you service will give you the option to use something more focused than general internet searches.

Really Simple Syndication

Most legal research will involve you going to a resource and engaging with it, whether you initiate a search or browse through the platform's content. Since legal matters can pose very different fact scenarios from one to the next that require individual approaches to research, these will always be primary methods of researching. The advent of artificial intelligence-enabled search only impacts your search results; you retain the professional responsibility for knowing what the retrieved documents say.

You may also use news resources—search alerts, newsletters, and so on—to remain informed. Many of these can be defined within your legal research platform which you access with your web browser and will be sent to you as an email. In many cases, though, you may have the alternative of setting these news updates or alerts to rely on a technology known as really simple syndication or RSS.

RSS is sometimes called a newsfeed because it is a file that is generated by an information platform to provide the latest updated information available on that website. It is constantly updating, like a news ticker or 24-hour news streams, so it is an efficient way to stay current on changing information. RSS remains a bit of a niche research tool, used heavily by experts like law librari-

---

16. Am. Bar Ass'n, 2023 Legal Technology Survey Report: Online Research 44, question 31. 12.9% of respondents indicated that, yes, they accessed fee-based online legal research via a bar association. 87.1% said they did not.

17. *Id. at* 45, question 32.

ans and less so by practitioners, but it can be a feature to seek out when you are looking at licensing access to an information platform: does it support RSS?

Less than a quarter of lawyers ever use RSS feeds and only about 6% use RSS feeds once a week or more frequently.[18] In the last few years, as publishers have tried to find ways to engage with an increasingly fractured readership, there has been a search for alternative methods of delivering information. This has seen a resurgence in email newsletters, powered by blog-like sites like Medium, Substack, and Buttondown, but it has also led to some increasing chatter around RSS, since all of those platforms support it. RSS is available as an alert output when you create an alert on Westlaw.

While RSS will remain a niche information and research tool, there are dedicated RSS tools that you may want to investigate if you are one of those people who feel overwhelmed with email newsletters and alerts. An RSS feed can provide an alternate information delivery method, distinct from your email inbox, allowing you to manage your research and current awareness separately from what may be more critical court- or client-related emails.

Microsoft Outlook supports your ability to follow RSS feeds, but, while it is a relatively simple interface, it also is more clumsy than other standalone feed reader products.[19] RSS feed or newsfeed readers are common and provide a more feature-rich approach to digesting your research news. This can include creating filters to remove certain feed items based on keywords and the ability to highlight or save items for later retrieval. Some feed readers will offer the ability for you to share items, allowing you to create a curated list of resources that can be published to your law firm staff or to clients via the internet.

RSS newsfeed readers include mobile apps like Feedly or Reeder or online RSS readers like RSSOwl or OldReader.[20] Since RSS presents updates

---

18. *Id.* at 60, question 42l. 76% of lawyers never used RSS. Solos were less likely to use RSS than large law firm lawyers. However, there is little difference between the heaviest users: about 4% of solos and 5% of large law firm lawyers reported accessing an RSS feed once or more per week, and they were nearly identical—2.3% of solos and 2.4% of large firm lawyers—in reporting daily use.

19. *Subscribe to an RSS Feed*, MICROSOFT (last visited May 28, 2025), https://support.microsoft.com/en-us/office/subscribe-to-an-rss-feed-73c6e717-7815-4594-98e5-81fa369e951c [http://web.archive.org/web/20250528101932/https://support.microsoft.com/en-us/office/subscribe-to-an-rss-feed-73c6e717-7815-4594-98e5-81fa369e951c].

20. There are dozens and dozens of RSS readers, many of them freely available, and they are designed for web browser, PC, and as phone apps. Microsoft Outlook as an RSS reader is probably only worth a consideration if you (a) spend all of your work time in Outlook and (b) have no other alternative. The mobile apps probably offer the most flexibility for digesting this sort of current awareness information which will continuously appear,

and alerts that you can create without having to resort to sending an email, you can reduce the number of emails that flood into your inbox with current awareness. RSS newsfeeds can be merged so that, in applications like Microsoft Outlook, where a single feed appears almost like an individual email, you can further reduce the clutter to make it easier to monitor and manage your incoming information. Since RSS news updates are often current awareness and not necessarily time-sensitive, isolating them from your primary communication technology, your email inbox, can lead to a productivity gain.

Generative Artificial Intelligence

One of the areas where generative artificial intelligence is most visible to lawyers is in their legal research technology. The major publishers have been quick to apply generative AI and, almost as quickly, to reposition their AI implementations in light of the continual emergence of confabulations in court documents. You may be starting to see legal publishers refer to the AI implemented in their tools as *extractive* as opposed to *generative* AI. This is, in part, due to the concern that many lawyers and judges have that AI is creating things that do not exist (confabulation) and extractive AI should only be able to use information that already exists.

Similarly, legal research technology is increasingly relying on or marketing the use of retrieval augmented generative AI (RAG). This also makes sense because, in addition to lawyers not wanting what one lawyer described as "an eager assistant available 24/7 to handle all of your mundane or tedious tasks [that] also has both a pathological lying problem and an inability to keep a secret," RAG relies on curated information sources.[21] Even if the underlying large language model (LLM) was trained on generic, internet-accessible information, legal publishers have large information collections that they have curated. These collections can be used with RAG and should reduce the likelihood that confabulations occur.

There are many generative AI tools that are available for a lawyer to license directly or to use outside of legal research technology. They may or may not

around the clock. PC apps or web apps are often the most feature-rich and offer features that allow you to create an RSS feed on sites that do not already offer them.

21. Nicole Black, *How to Implement AI at Your Law Firm*, ABA Journal (May 23, 2025), https://www.abajournal.com/columns/article/how-to-implement-ai-at-your-law-firm [https://archive.is/AzRip].

use a form of RAG and may not restrict their results or outputs to legal information or even to reality. A lawyer may try using an OpenAI, Anthropic, or Mistral generative AI chat application, but the results may be substantially different from what they would experience using the same large language models—the legal publishers are frequently licensing the same name brand off-the-shelf LLMs that are available to lawyers directly—embedded within a legal research application that has included RAG.

This immersion of AI within traditional legal research technology makes selection and use more difficult than it once was. A lawyer who uses these AI-infused legal research tools will need to be vigilant about ensuring that a results set actually exists—the documents retrieved and cited are real documents—and that the things that it purports to say are actually being said by the court or legislature or creator of the underlying document.[22]

It may be worth noting that legal publishers have been using other types of artificial intelligence for years. In particular, they have used natural language processing for decades, as legal publishers shifted from requiring searches using Boolean connectors ("dog AND bite /p injury") to allowing researchers to search using phrases and sentences ("Who is liable if a dog bite causes an injury?").

As the large web search engines started to change how people searched the internet, legal publishers moved along with them, focusing their products around a search box. This use of what the legal publishers are now sometimes referring

22. As of writing, the AI interfaces in Thomson Reuters Westlaw and RELX Lexis are optional. You can perform legal research without using the AI functionality, a situation that may continue so long as courts and law firms limit the use of generative artificial intelligence (and other forms, if only because the concerns raised about generative AI are impacting other AI developments). See, for example, the United Kingdom's judiciary's guidance on using AI (recommended not to use it for legal research), COURTS AND TRIBUNALS JUDICIARY, ARTIFICIAL INTELLIGENCE (AI): GUIDANCE FOR JUDICIAL OFFICE HOLDERS (Apr. 14, 2025), https://www.judiciary.uk/wp-content/uploads/2025/04/Refreshed-AI-Guidance-published-version-website-version.pdf [http://web.archive.org/web/20250606171535/https://www.judiciary.uk/wp-content/uploads/2025/04/Refreshed-AI-Guidance-published-version-website-version.pdf], or a U.S. magistrate's standing order for AI use in matters before them. JEFFREY COLE, THE USE OF "ARTIFICIAL INTELLIGENCE" IN THE PREPARATION OF DOCUMENTS FILED BEFORE THIS COURT (last visited Apr. 30, 2025) https://www.ilnd.uscourts.gov/_assets/_documents/_forms/_judges/Cole/Artificial%20Intelligence%20standing%20order.pdf [http://web.archive.org/web/20250430153544/https://www.ilnd.uscourts.gov/_assets/_documents/_forms/_judges/Cole/Artificial%20Intelligence%20standing%20order.pdf].

to as *extractive* AI has been around longer than some of the other technologies that have caused concern for the legal profession, like cloud computing.

The natural language processing AI has been submerged for decades within the legal research platforms in the same way that we are now seeing generative AI become embedded. Similarly, it was trained on or was implemented by searching on and retrieving from a known body of information: primary law sourced from government publishers and secondary information licensed by or produced by the legal publisher.

In the long term, this is likely to be how lawyers primarily interact with generative AI when it comes to legal research: through the familiar search box on a legal research platform and not as a separate application.[23] They will also continue to have the imperative to validate their research—just as they would have done with any other legal research, on paper or on computers—and comply with any court orders about submissions involving AI before the court. By the time you are ready to enter the practice of law, this area may be more settled than it was when generative AI first came to widespread attention.

Knowledge Management

There is an entire field known as knowledge management and, while it is relevant to the practice of law, I am using the term in a more colloquial, narrow way.[24] A lawyer will gather a substantial amount of information during their law practice. Some of this is captured as documents or things that are provided to or created by the lawyer. Other information can be more ephemeral in nature, but it does not need to be. In particular, legal research may be a task that a lawyer repeats without taking advantage of the expertise they have gained from previous iterations. There are tools that can be used to capture this experience as it happens, allowing a lawyer to re-use the information for future cases.

23. The emergence of agentic AI is unlikely to change this dynamic. Since a good deal of legal research is done within proprietary commercial platforms, agentic AI may not be able to work within a legal research environment unless it is implemented by a legal publisher within the platform.

24. For more typical law firm knowledge management topics, look later on at document management and document automation. Both topics cover the management of templates and retention of precedent documents that capture firm knowledge for future use.

The first place to start is to look at your legal research platform and see what it allows you to retain. In many cases, you can store your searches so that the ones that are more productive can be re-used. Or, if you are approaching a trial date and want to make sure the law has not changed from your pleadings, you can save and re-run those searches. The legal research platforms supporting generative artificial intelligence allow you to save some of the "conversations" you create with the AI. As with every other aspect of your law practice, look for ways to re-use what has been successful in the past without starting from scratch every time.

Research Notebooks

You are not limited by the tools or functions within the legal research platform you are using, however. In addition to these features, you should consider using a research notebook. A research notebook can enhance your ability to repeat research and ensure, like the checklists mentioned above, that you are not skipping steps in your research. It can also be a place to jot down the information you gather—linking out to the cases or other citations you have found during your research—so that you can synthesize it prior to preparing whatever document (letter, brief, memorandum) you will be using the information in.

It is more than an outlining tool, which can be found within any word processor and which tends to provide only a linear hierarchy of information. Research notebooks provide you with ways to organize the information you are gathering. Microsoft's OneNote and Evernote are two examples of notebooks you may have access to or that have been commonly used by lawyers.[25]

Microsoft's OneNote is available for free although it will also come with any Microsoft Office or 365 account. It takes a folder-centric approach to keeping notes. You create what is called a Section, and within each Section you create pages. This allows you to mimic file and folder organization like the paper files you may inherit or create in your law office.

The benefit of a research notebook is that you can keep track of your research while it is occurring. If you get interrupted, you can return to where

25. Microsoft OneNote and Evernote used to represent two very different approaches—tagging v. foldering—to information organization. This distinction has lessened over time and Evernote in particular has moved towards more of a personal information management approach, incorporating to do task management and calendaring. Those features remain separate from OneNote, as they are encompassed by Microsoft Outlook.

you were in your research notebook and get a prompt or starting point. It is like a scratch pad with notes—search keywords that were or were not successful, tangential research topics or resources—about the steps you've taken in your research. Without something like it, you may find that you forget what you have found or what you have looked for. Once you have recorded the information in your notebook, you can return to it, like you would with a law school class outline, when you come into contact with the same situation or topic in the future.

Remember that legal research will be integral to your decision about whether to take on a client's legal issue or not. You will want to be certain that you have found the legal research resources that will help you make your decision. Similarly, if you have staff or lawyers who are also supporting this intake process, a research notebook can be shared with them. You can work on it simultaneously and gain the network effect of multiple people's contributions.

Once again, do not forget templates. Just as you can with email and calendars, it is easy to create a Microsoft OneNote template. Imagine that you have a specific set of folders you create for each new client: communications, pleadings, and so on. Your OneNote template can mimic that in a research notebook and, when you have a new client to process through intake, you can create their notebook with the template. It is a time saver but also a way to maintain consistency between clients.

Chronology and Other Mapping Tools

Legal research is a broad topic. It goes well beyond using legal publisher platforms and looking at the law. Sometimes you need a tool that helps you to sort through the information you have received from the client and sift out the most important pieces. This is the issue spotting that you will have been doing as a law student, identifying the facts and rules that are relevant while avoiding the distracting ones.

You will almost certainly have created a chronology at some point in law school, whether you thought of it that way or not. For example, you may have received an essay assignment with a fact pattern that needed to be organized by who did what first. Many legal issues have a time component. A chronology is a standard way of organizing information relevant to a legal issue that requires knowing in what order things happened. It can also be used to create a single view of stories or documents that come from many different sources, none of which are, individually, able to express the entirety of the events that encompass the legal issue.

There are tools that can help you to map out this information. Unlike research notebooks, which are general business applications, some of these mapping tools can be specific to law practice. There are both standalone timeline applications as well as ones built into practice management software.

Sometimes information management requires a non-linear approach. In that case, you can use something simple like Google Drawings or Microsoft PowerPoint to create a visual that connects different elements together. Think of the prototypical conspiracy theory wall, with dozens of pieces of information pinned to a board and connected with interlacing strings of red yarn. The more complicated this sort of presentation of information becomes, though, the more likely you are to want to move to a dedicated mapping tool, often termed a mind map. Mind maps provide more flexibility for creating information elements and then linking them together, supporting a higher degree of complexity than typical office suite applications and often without the default constraints of an 8.5" x 11" page size.[26]

Specialty Legal Research Tools

The largest legal publisher platforms will tout their comprehensiveness. In reality, no platform is comprehensive. This is particularly true as both of the major platforms license third-party legal publisher content, and those publishers sometimes withdraw behind their own paywalls.[27] Some publications stop being published and may be kept in their aging format on the platform or

26. This can be in the eye of the beholder. I use PowerPoint for a lot of my mind mapping because it is (a) a tool I already have a license for and (b) it is easy to use since it relies on the same knowledge I would use creating a slide deck. In PowerPoint, you can reset the slide size to as big as you want. I have in the past made a slide that was 3 feet by 5 feet, to enable me to place on it the information I wanted without having to shrink it down to a size that was hard to read. I would not be able to share the slide as a presentation on a projector because of that size, but the slide itself is a functional mind map.

27. A good example is American Lawyer Media, which first left Thomson Reuters Westlaw for RELX Lexis in 2011. *New Agreement Makes LexisNexis the Exclusive Third Party Distributor of Industry-Leading Legal Content from ALM*, LexisNexis (Apr. 4, 2011), http://www.lexisnexis.com/media/press-release.aspx?id=1301921219332215 [https://web.archive.org/web/20110611040727/http://www.lexisnexis.com/media/press-release.aspx?id=1301921219332215]. American Lawyer Media then announced it was leaving Lexis in

may be dropped as their currency declines and the risk to a lawyer in relying on them increases.

You have almost certainly been able to access HeinOnline during law school, a platform that re-publishes law journal articles and that has developed several niche information collections of legal information. It is with these other legal publishers that you will find a variety of online legal research tools geared towards specific practice areas. Some of these platforms are legal publishers who, like Thomson Reuters and RELX, have grown from legacy print publishers into online legal research platforms. Others will be new entrants and may be based on traditional linear legal information (like books, journal articles, and so on), or they may provide more narrowly tailored resources, like dockets or analytics.

Substantive Topical Tools

The first group will probably be the most familiar. Practice areas that have a large amount of public legal information or that rapidly change or that have very narrowly tailored expertise are likely to have specific legal research technology available. Tax law and intellectual property law are two of the common areas where you will find legal research tools that may contain within themselves all of the information tools for a lawyer who practices solely in that substantive area.[28]

These information providers may themselves be subsidiaries of the large legal publishers and contain overlapping information. Thomson Reuters' tax platform Checkpoint, for example, will overlap with Thomson Reuters Westlaw tax content. For a tax professional, though, it may provide a more concentrated set of materials, designed for both lawyers and other professionals who work within the tax substantive area. Similarly, while there are extensive online public resources for looking up patents and trademarks from the United States Patent and Trademark Office, or for Securities and Exchange

2025. *ALM to Remove Legal News from Lexis and Bloomberg Law by 2026*, AALL CRIV Connection (Nov. 4, 2024), https://crivblog.com/2024/11/04/alm-to-remove-legal-news-from-lexis-and-bloomberg-law-by-2026/ [http://web.archive.org/web/20241130234409/https://crivblog.com/2024/11/04/alm-to-remove-legal-news-from-lexis-and-bloomberg-law-by-2026/].

28. A lawyer or law firm that is this narrowly focused is often referred to as a "boutique" lawyer or firm. They are often more specialized than a larger law firm that practices in the same substantive area of law. *Boutique Law Firm*, Wikipedia (last visited Aug. 28, 2025), https://en.wikipedia.org/wiki/Boutique_law_firm.

Commission (SEC) filings from the Electronic Data Gathering, Analysis, and Retrieval (EDGAR) system, dedicated intellectual property or securities lawyers will want to consider legal research platforms that blend those sorts of search tools with the commentary and primary law that is commonly used in the practice area.

Dockets and PACER

A common legal research task is to retrieve documents from a court's docket. These may be the decisions of the court or other filings that have been made by parties. We will touch on electronic filing further on—where you will file your own pleadings and documents with a court—but there are many other instances when a court document will need to be retrieved.

The federal court system offers the Public Access to Court Electronic Records (PACER) system. This is the other end of the case management and electronic court filing system into which lawyers file their documents. Anyone can create a free account on PACER to search and retrieve court documents.[29]

Analytics

A relatively recent addition to the legal research technology world is the analytics platform. These systems provide information about the metadata on cases and other activities that you may want to use to inform your professional decisions. There is a wide variety of analytics tools, some with broad applications or applications beyond legal research while others are very narrow, focused on helping you make very specific decisions about a case and its likely outcomes.

Let's start with a free resource, the Interactive Data Analyzer from the United States Sentencing Commission.[30] The portal provides sentencing data for the past ten years, which can give you insights into what the sentencing outcomes were in particular federal courts. You can navigate the data using demographic data or information about the type of crime, criminal history, and other factors you might think will impact your client's possible outcomes.

---

29. A free account on PACER will prompt for a method of payment, like a credit card, but you can skip this step. Additionally, if you keep your PACER activity under $30 (about 300 pages) every financial quarter—three-month periods ending in April, June, September, and December—then you will not incur any charges for PACER use.

30. https://ida.ussc.gov/analytics/.

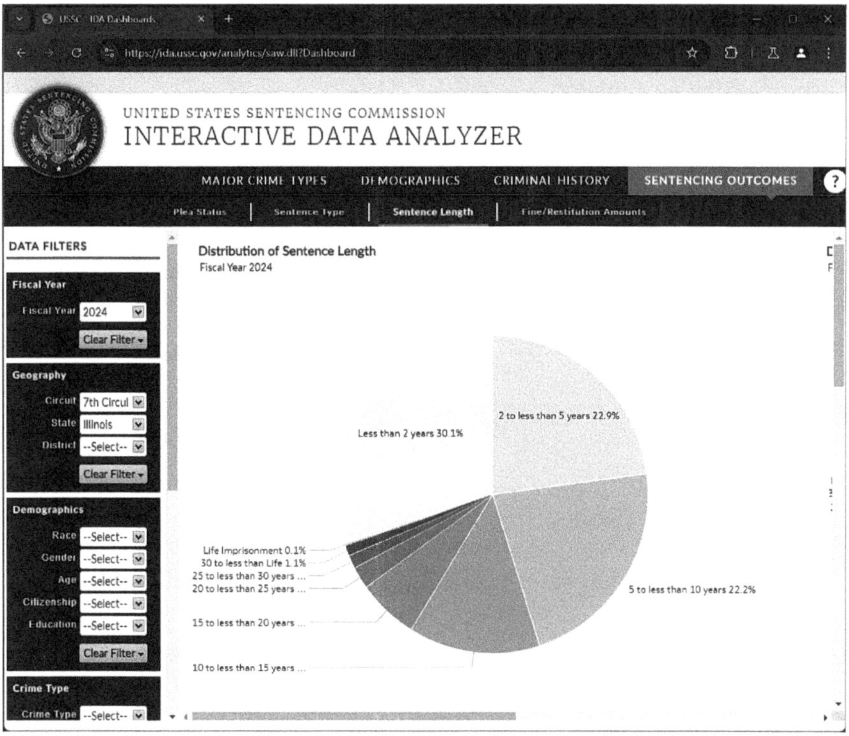

Figure 4: Interactive Data Analyzer screenshot

There is also information on how many cases go to trial and how many are plea agreements.

That should give you a sense of what a legal analytics platform will provide. They look at the information behind the legal matter, the case's metadata: who the judge was, what the settlement or jury award was, who the parties involved were. Law firms use this metadata to help them make decisions about where to file a case—also known as forum shopping—as well as what arguments or postures might be appropriate to take with a particular judge or in a particular jurisdiction.

A lot of this data will be available in legal research platforms where judicial opinions can be found, but it can take expertise and time to mine the information. It requires the legal publishing platform to have marked the documents so that those segments—counsel names, judge names, outcomes—are clearly identified and made searchable. A legal analytics platform can help you move more quickly to using the data and making decisions and skip the data-crunching steps. Analytics platforms frequently gather data far beyond case decisions and outcomes. Law firms will use these tools to identify new prospective clients, perform assessments of expert witnesses, and estimate the costs of taking on a matter.

Unsurprisingly, this sort of complex, niche research tool is more likely to be found and used in a large law firm than in a solo practice.[31] However, even in law firms with over 500 lawyers, only about 40% of respondents to an ABA survey reported using an analytics tool, compared to 27% of solos. The type of usage was largely the same across firm sizes, with all firm sizes using analytics tools primarily for legal research, then for developing case strategy (including outcomes as well as judicial decision-making history), and after that, for business development.

The Web Browser

In the end, choosing your legal research technologies will be among the simplest technology choices you make after you have selected your office suite (email client, word processor, and so on). For one thing, you will have as much experience using most legal research platforms as you have had with your office suite, unless you have joined a law firm and are having to transition to Microsoft Office from Google Workspace. For another, while there is a great deal of complexity within these platforms, they are largely isolated from other systems you will use. The selection of a legal research tool will, for the most part, not impact any other technologies you choose because they live on their own islands on the internet. Any integrations that are available will be optional, and you can assess whether particular add-ons provide a productivity boost or not before you decide to enable any integration.

It would be an oversight to leave legal research without discussing the one technology you will control when dealing with most of these platforms: the web browser. Except in very rare cases, your web browser will be the window through which you view every legal research technology you use. Since legal research was probably the first cloud-based system most lawyers used, it is not surprising that we may forget that it is used by way of a second piece of technology. The web browser is so fundamental it often disappears into the background as we focus on what it displays to us. Legal publishers, and other

31. Am. Bar Ass'n, 2023 Legal Technology Survey Report: Online Research 63, question 43.

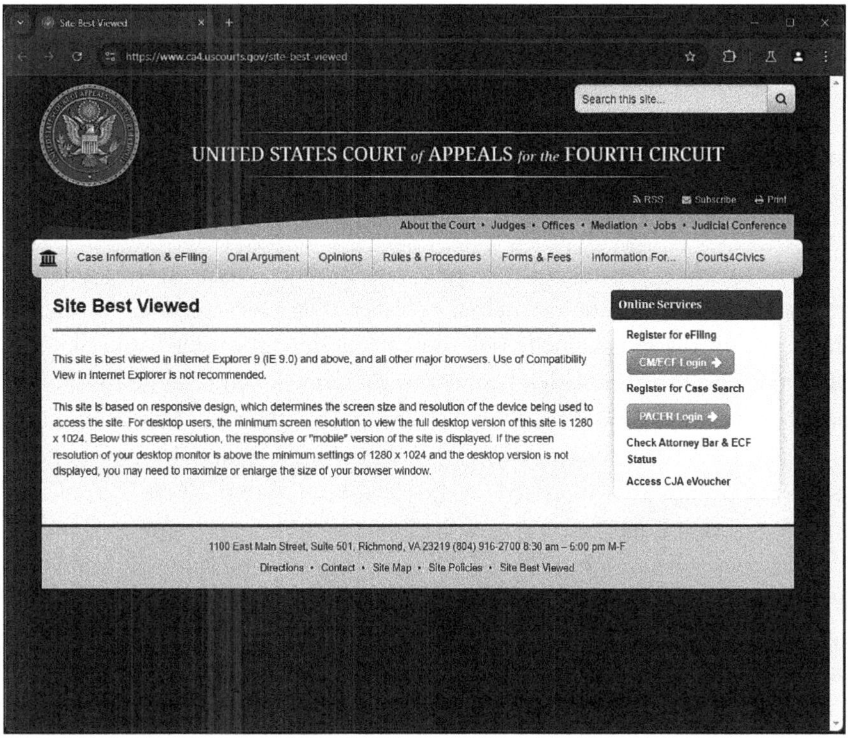

Figure 5: US COA Fourth screenshot for Internet Explorer 9

web-based or cloud-based providers, will design and develop their products with these browser choices in mind.

Not surprisingly, Microsoft Edge is highly visible in law firms that have a Microsoft-centric technology environment. It is hard to quantify its impact, though, as Microsoft Edge remains a standard, pre-installed component with Windows computers. As we have seen with other law practice technologies, just because it is available does not mean it is used. It is just as likely that a lawyer will use the Google Chrome web browser, even if Microsoft Edge is also installed on the same computer. Chrome remains the dominant web browser in the consumer world and is likely to be a web browser you have used or might choose for your own law practice. Some lawyers may use more than one browser, including Mozilla's Firefox, for privacy or other productivity gains enabled by segmenting usage between different vendors.

Historically, loyalty to a single provider's web browser made more sense when Microsoft was developing its own web browser (Internet Explorer). Web sites were faced with having to adapt their design and technology infrastructure to accommodate the nuances of each of the web browsers that might be commonly used. It was not uncommon for a legal research website—like the United States Court of Appeals for the Fourth Circuit, shown above—to indicate a specific brand and version of a web browser for compatibility purposes.[32] If you did not use that browser, you might find you had trouble accessing or using the information on that platform.

Unfortunately, this meant that your web browser might determine your access to information not just on that website but on every website. Nowadays, this sort of browser specificity will most likely impact people using the Apple Safari web browser, which is now the only major web browser that is not based on the Chromium (not Chrome) web browser. Lawyers who use Google Chrome or Microsoft Edge are largely using the same underlying application, as those web browsers are based on the Chromium web browser. This means that a Microsoft Edge user can visit the Google Chrome web store and install a web browser extension designed for the Chrome web browser.[33] Similarly, while it seems to be less common than it once was, if a website has been designed with a specific web browser in mind, the experience between Microsoft Edge and Google Chrome should not be significantly different, not enough to cause the website to be inaccessible or unusable.

Your web browser may not be a tool you are able to choose if you work in a law practice that standardizes on a single web browser. But even if that is the case, it should not make much difference. The most important aspect of web

32. Unwittingly, this browser specification by the court creates a sense that the court is, itself, not current with technology. Although this page was viewed in 2025, Microsoft Internet Explorer 9 came to the end of its life in 2016, almost 10 years earlier. *Internet Explorer 9*, WIKIPEDIA (last visited August 28, 2025), https://en.wikipedia.org/wiki/Internet_Explorer_9#End_of_life. While there may still be a very small number of people using Internet Explorer 9, and the court may just be establishing how far back its backwards compatibility goes, this should be an unnecessary detail. Website designers can see what web browsers are being used and can intercept and deliver web content.

33. *Add, Turn Off, or Remove Extensions in Microsoft Edge*, MICROSOFT (last visited June 3, 2025), https://support.microsoft.com/en-us/microsoft-edge/add-turn-off-or-remove-extensions-in-microsoft-edge-9c0ec68c-2fbc-2f2c-9ff0-bdc76f46b026 [https://web.archive.org/web/20250603161033/https://support.microsoft.com/en-us/microsoft-edge/add-turn-off-or-remove-extensions-in-microsoft-edge-9c0ec68c-2fbc-2f2c-9ff0-bdc76f46b026]. Microsoft has also created its own store for web browser extensions and many of the add-ons designed for Google Chrome can be found there too: https://microsoftedge.microsoft.com/addons/microsoft-edge-extensions

browser selection is that you stay on the most current version.[34] It will be your gateway not only to legal research but to your banking, accounting, documents, and more. You should not risk being on an older web browser version, like Microsoft Internet Explorer 9, for the sake of your practice as much as to ensure that you have a positive experience with your legal research tools and other web-based information and resources.

Chapter 6 Exercises

A. Create a free account on the PACER website, skipping past the optional payment method step. Using a case provided by your instructor or that you have identified by recent current events, locate the docket and download a single document (complaint or opinion/order). Compare your experience to using a legal publisher product, retrieving the same document from the publisher's docketing content.

B. Create a Microsoft OneNote research notebook. Customize it to mirror how you currently capture information about a new case or topic, if you have a method. For example, use the process you learned in first year legal research and writing or a similar class. If you do not have a process, your instructor can provide you with some guidance. Also, there is a simple template in OneNote to get you started at the URL in the footnote.[35]

C. Other than cost, what are the most important features of a legal research platform for your individual approach to research? List the features and describe why they are important to you. List at least five features and rank them in order of importance. Then identify which legal research platforms are most likely to match those feature preferences. You can use a different area of law practice technology but, in general, law students will have the broadest experience with law-specific technology through their use of legal research applications.

D. You know how to search the internet using web search engines like Google, Bing, or DuckDuckGo for restaurants, lodging and travel, and

34. See, for example, Thomson Reuter's web browser requirements for Westlaw focus on the current version. https://www.thomsonreuters.com/en-us/help/westlaw-classic/setup/system-requirements. The same for Lexis+. https://supportcenter.lexisnexis.com/app/answers/answer_view/a_id/1102039/~/system-requirements-for-lexis+.

35. https://perma.cc/AZ8A-3KHD.

current awareness. Thinking about your own research abilities, how confident would you be to start your legal research outside a commercial legal research platform, using one of those web search engines? What makes you more or less confident? How would you validate your research without access to a commercial legal research application? Where would the AI-enabled versions of the web search engines (Google Gemini, Microsoft CoPilot, and DuckDuckGo's DuckAssist) fit into your open web searching?

Chapter 7

Conflicts Check

Your prospective client intake has now progressed to perhaps the final step before you can make a decision, which is to ascertain whether being hired by this client would result in a conflict of interest.[1] Conflicts checking can be done with the same variety of standalone and integrated law practice technology tools that we have experienced in the steps up to this point. While you may find applications that promote themselves as designed for conflicts checking, there are many ways to accomplish the same activity. At the end of the day it is a process, and the most important thing is that you accomplish the check, not what technology you use to do it. Since you are looking at people and entities (like corporations or organizations), you may find that, to begin with, you can use your contacts manager to fulfill this professional obligation.

There are, unsurprisingly, a number of professional ethics rules that you need to consider when you take on a client and deal with conflicts of interest. They include:

- Rule 1.7 and Rule 1.9, which deal with conflicts of interest that your engagement with your prospective client would cause with clients who have already engaged you, whether their matters have concluded or not.
- Rule 1.18, which specifically spells out that the issues around a prospective client and a current client whose interests are materially in conflict with one another.

1. There is an entirely separate technology application related to conflicts of interest as it is defined more broadly, often in relation to government work. This may apply to your law practice, but this book is only looking at the lawyer-specific issue of professional ethics conflicts as they arise in relation to clients.

The rules are warnings for you to be sure you know what impact your prospective client's case may have on your current and former clients. It is not dispositive of whether you can take on a client. You may represent a person whose spouse subsequently seeks your advice on a matter that might impact your original client. A conflicts check will warn you about the existence of a risk. There remain methods, such as securing the informed consent of the impacted current and former clients, to acknowledge the conflict and allow you to be engaged by the prospective client.

A conflicts check is really a check for people or organizations and their relationships. A contact management tool will help you to manage this information although, just as you will find with other law practice processes, there are also a variety of standalone and integrated software options. Before we talk about those, let's talk about what you need to capture.

At a basic level, it is the name, address, and other basic information that allow you to identify your prospective client and their relationships. If they have changed their name—through marriage, gender transition, or adoption, for example—knowing previous names or even aliases will be important. If the client is a company, have they operated under other names or do they have or are they a subsidiary, where you might need to know their place within a business organization. You will also want to know who else is involved in the legal issue. Is it a company against whom the prospective client may have a claim? A spouse from whom they want to be divorced? Company information, the details about the spouse and any children, and about other people with a potential interest in the legal issue should be captured during your intake process.

Contact Managers

This entity and relationship information that you collect during the intake process should then be saved into your contact management system so that it can be used for conflicts checking. This is data you will maintain throughout the lifetime of your law practice. It is a cumulative asset, so describe and document each person or entity and their relationships as completely and precisely as you can for future you. The next time you perform a prospective client intake, you should be able to refer back to see who previous prospective clients were—whether or not they engaged you—and who else might have been involved in their legal issue. You will be able to compare your existing contact information with the new information you have gathered from a prospective client and see if there are any connections.

At a minimum, you will want to use something that allows you to track a lot of data. This is not something that can be managed efficiently on paper or on a paper analog, like a Microsoft Word document. The technology you use for conflicts checking relationships should itself be able to support creating relationships between pieces of data.

Microsoft Outlook or Google Contacts would be an adequate start. I say adequate because they are essentially flat data files. You create a contact record with name, address, phone number, and other information related to that person. But when you create a second contact record, even if those two records are related (spouses, siblings, business partners, and so on), many contact managers, including Outlook and Google Contacts, do not allow you to establish programmatic linkages between those contact records. This means that, while you can search for or sort by a last name, you will not know merely by looking at a record whether it is related to other people in your contact management application.

Both Outlook and Google Contacts provide a very basic way to create relationships between contact records. In Microsoft Outlook, you can apply categories. The contact or people categories appear to have the same limitation as they do for emails or calendar items: many categories but a limited number of colors.[2] The visual limitation of 25 colors that may impact the use of calendars is probably less significant when applied to contact management. Google Contacts allows you to provide labels to a contact record, just like you can with email and calendar items. You can create an unlimited number of labels and apply them to as many contact records as you like. For example, you might create a new label for each prospective client as part of the intake process. You would be able to see if you had an existing label with the same or similar name as you create the label. This categorization will allow you to establish relationships between contact records, but it can become haphazard.

---

2. The categories are not visible on Microsoft Outlook for the web. Open up the desktop Outlook client and select a contact to apply a category. *Organize Your Contacts with Color Categories*, MICROSOFT (last visited Aug. 28, 2025), https://support.microsoft.com/en-us/office/organize-your-contacts-with-color-categories-4d4e6521-aee8-4929-bea3-4a12e830fbfb. You can sort by shared color so this may be a secondary way to create relationships: green for lawyers, orange for courts, and so on. But this would require you to think in advance how you would use this second layer of organization.

These informal tagging or labeling schemes lack any obvious hierarchy, so you may not know if you are forgetting a tag because there is no relationship between the tags or labels themselves. It also lacks a central information organization function called a controlled vocabulary. If you are not careful, you might end up with a system that allows minor variations—Grace Smith, Gracie Smith, Grace P. Smith—for the same person. Libraries use a system called authority control to ensure that people are described as often as possible with just one name.[3] The authority control database will show variants so that someone who has a version of a name can use the authoritative one.

You will need a process for your law practice that creates a similar system, which may be as simple as "last name, first name [middle name] [married name]" for each client. Unlike a library, which may have to organize people whose names are written in a variety of languages, you are most likely going to be dealing with anglicized names that are ordered in a consistent way. This consistency will help you create a standard approach to your naming convention.

As you are thinking about how to organize your contacts and connect them to each other, you will want to think about how the labels themselves are created. One way is to decide to use a controlled vocabulary, like a library's authority control, so that every label is created in the same way and is consistent with existing labels: do you use uppercase and lower case? Just lower case? How do you determine when you need to create a new label and then how do you go back and apply it retroactively to existing contact records that are missing it? You may also find that you need to limit who can create labels to ensure consistency. When multiple people are involved with tagging or labeling information, you can start to see more variance if there are not specific guidelines or templates that help to enforce the labeling pattern.

Much of this can be managed with process: create a how-to document to help ensure each contact is created and managed in a consistent way. For example, you might have labels that describe the type of case (family, criminal, wills), the type of client (prospective, open, closed), or party position (plaintiff, defendant, appellant, appellee, expert, guardian). When a prospective client is going through intake, their client contact record would be created, and one of each of these labels would be applied to it. If they returned with additional matters, the contact record would be updated with additional labels.

---

3. *Authority Control*, Wikipedia (last visited Aug. 28, 2025), https://en.wikipedia.org/wiki/Authority_control.

Relational Data

Some lawyers recognize the limitations of these flat systems—where relationships can be wrangled but do not link together data records—and use a more data-centric application to manage their contacts for conflicts checking. One place to start is a spreadsheet. While it may not be a great contact manager, missing the features of Microsoft Outlook or Google Contacts, it can be a more powerful conflicts management tool.

The upside to using something like Microsoft Excel or Google Sheets and the power of a spreadsheet is you can start to create some relationships and build logic and formulas into your conflicts checking. Since a spreadsheet can capture all sorts of data, you are not proscribed by the limited fields that your contact manager in Outlook or Google Contacts offers. Additionally, most contact managers will allow you to export your contact lists as data files, so you can populate your spreadsheet without having to rekey the information. As you gain new contacts, you can export and import the incremental data changes.

Microsoft Excel is such a notable application for lawyers that multiple books have been written for lawyers on how to use it—including Microsoft Excel for Legal Professionals, published by the ABA—as a multi-purpose tool for law practices.[4] There is a great deal of repetition within a law practice, and tools like spreadsheets can create efficiencies once you have a good handle on how they work.

A significant benefit to using a spreadsheet is that you can use it to create relationships within your data that may not be possible within your contact manager. This may make your conflicts checking faster and more extensive, since you can both capture more information and quickly see connections between it. This relational data is possible in a spreadsheet (although you can easily use a spreadsheet without any relationships built into it), but it is deeply embedded in systems like practice management applications, which will be designed around fully relational databases.[5]

---

4. Affinity Consulting Group, *Microsoft Excel for Legal Professionals*, Am. Bar Ass'n (last visited Jan. 13, 2025), https://www.americanbar.org/products/ecd/ebk/410996728/ [http://web.archive.org/web/20250113080916/https://www.americanbar.org/products/ecd/ebk/410996728/], updated in 2024. See also: N.J. Inst. for Continuing Legal Educ., N.J. State Bar Ass'n, Microsoft Excel for Legal Users: 2023 Seminar Material (2023), https://njsbamaterials.com/MI135823.pdf. A Microsoft Excel class would be an excellent investment in time and money prior to starting to practice law.

5. For the truly hardcore law practice technologists, some practice management applications, like Clio, provide deep visibility into their database structure with tools like SQL for

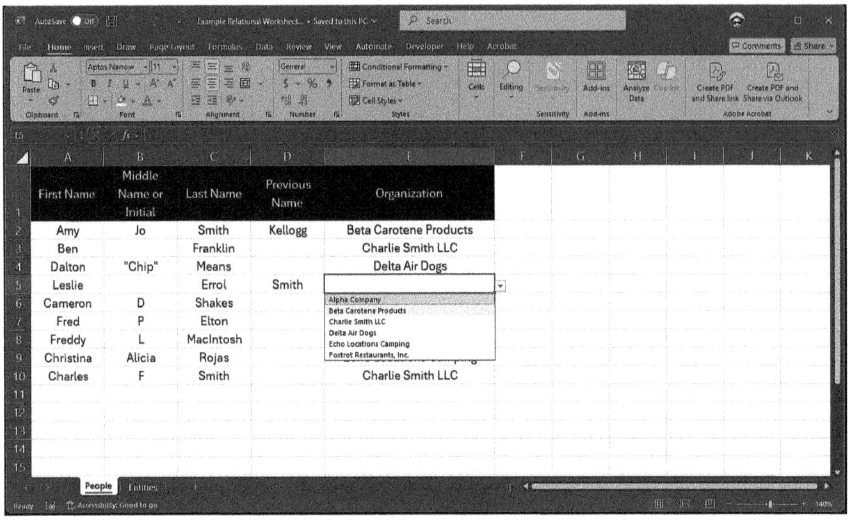

Figure 6: Microsoft Excel spreadsheet image of linked worksheets

For example, you may have multiple people using the same business name and address. You may need to enter that information for each person at that business and update each record separately if there is a business change of address or phone number. What happens if you type the business name incorrectly on one of those records? A tool like a spreadsheet or relational database can help you create the necessary controlled vocabularies, to ensure you use the same term each time, or allow you to link to an existing record rather than re-key the data multiple times, risking introducing errors.

In this example, then, you may have a list of people by first, middle, and last name, as well as some of their contact information. A spreadsheet is also called a workbook, and it is comprised of one or more worksheets. Each worksheet can contain different information organized in the most appropriate way for that data.

You would place your contacts list on the first worksheet in your spreadsheet workbook. This will be your "People" worksheet. On a second worksheet in the same workbook, you could create a list of Entities: companies, organiza-

---

Clio (SQL being a common database programming language used for creating, exploring, and manipulating relational databases). https://www.clio.com/app-directory/sql-for-clio/. I think it would be a relatively infrequent need for a lawyer to access data with that granularity—unless they were migrating their data to a new platform—but it may give some lawyers peace of mind to know they can engage with their data at that level.

tions, whatever information may be shared among the people on your contact list. You can then return to your list of people and create a drop down or "pick list" that pulls only the entries from your Entities worksheet. Here's what that might look like in Microsoft Excel. You can see the two worksheets at the bottom of the screenshot—People and Entities—and the drop-down list that is showing companies to choose from, drawn from the Entities worksheet.[6]

In the screenshot above, you can see that there are multiple people listed. If Amy Jo Smith belongs to the same organization as Leslie Errol (formerly known as Smith), there is no need to type the organizational information a second time here. Instead, you can choose from the pick list—created from the Entities worksheet—to indicate the organization. If the organization changes its address in the future, the only place this data would need to be updated would be on the Entities page, because each entry on the People worksheet is just a link, a relationship.[7] You can see how this might expand to allow you to have a worksheet that just includes lists (practice areas, types of matters, roles like judge or defendant or agent, and so on).

This sort of use of law practice data can take some time to plan out. Again, a relational database in an already-developed resource like a practice management application does that work for you, although it may not create relationships exactly the way you would have done had you created your own. Either way, once the relationships are developed within the data source, you should experience a boost in efficiency because you have fewer pieces of duplicate information to manage.

The real downside to using a spreadsheet and a contact manager that are separate is that duplication. Each copy of information that you have to manage will create new risk as you try to ensure the copies are exactly that: identical copies. A goal whenever you are dealing with data, whether in a law practice or any other environment, is to create a single source of truth.[8] If you do not have a single source, then you need to start to manage copies of information or delegate that management to someone accountable for it. Once these

---

6. This is a copy of the spreadsheet, created in Microsoft Excel, described in the text. https://1drv.ms/x/c/5e82142ae93b4352/Eak0bWvfQ3dNgPIoZPzmRIwBsQxMAXBppZ-PA9FAge83Ejw?e=PksCkH.

7. This is a dead simple example. However, you can see how it might be useful for things like doing mail merges as well. The ability to have your contact data in a relational resource can give you options far beyond just performing better conflicts checks.

8. This phrase is a term of art. *Single Source of Truth*, WIKIPEDIA (last visited Aug. 28, 2025), https://en.wikipedia.org/wiki/Single_source_of_truth.

copies become out of alignment, you risk all sorts of professional issues: you may send bills to the wrong address and go unpaid. You may not realize that someone has moved companies because you updated their address in one data set but not in a second one. You may have updated your contacts record with someone's new last name—and congratulated them on their marriage—but failed to make the update in your conflicts checking data, creating risk that, in the future, you will miss the name change and their new relationship. This might have a legal impact, if you submit a document with the wrong name to an agency or court, but also a reputational one, if you communicate with your client using the wrong name or communicate with someone like a represented party without communicating to their lawyer.

This is not to suggest you should not use Microsoft Excel or another spreadsheet. You should just be prepared that, the more collections of data you create, the more you will be required to manage the duplication of data. You will want to decide how to connect new records and modified records in your contact management tool with whatever data tool you use to manage your conflicts checking. You will also want to have a way to validate or verify, periodically, that the data is the same in both systems. It is one reason that law practice management software is a valuable tool for lawyers: it removes the overhead required to manage various datasets due to its integrated approach.

You can probably manage this sort of data duplication when you are just starting out as a lawyer or are a solo practitioner and your staff is small. A good law firm operations manual explaining the steps for each process can help to ensure that everyone knows where information needs to be updated and to use consistent, controlled vocabularies. But, if there was any area of your law practice that would benefit from a relational data tool, contacts management and conflicts checking would be the one.

Customer Relationship Management

Keep in mind that the data you are gathering is not just for the narrow purpose of completing the intake process. It is data that you will use to communicate with the prospective and possibly future client. It will add to your conflicts checking data for future prospective client intakes. You may also end up using it for marketing or other outreach that you do in order to generate new business. Friends and family tend to be significant sources of referrals of future work for lawyers. You will want to maintain that information not only for your professional obligations and for current communication. You will also want it for marketing and keeping in touch—things like birthday cards or important anniversaries, for example—with your clients throughout their lifetimes, even after you have successfully resolved their legal issue.

If contact managers are the first step and relational data tools like spreadsheets are the next, then the third level is customer relationship management (CRM). These applications are relational databases just like practice management applications. The difference is that they are focused primarily on the customer journey and business development and are thus business of law products, and they may not incorporate much in the way of tools to manage a client's legal matter on the practice of law side.

Not surprisingly, CRM applications tend to be more common in large law firms, where the complexity can be supported more easily.[9] In contrast, contact management applications—either standalone or integrated, for example, within a Microsoft Exchange email server or Microsoft 365 environment—are approaching full adoption no matter what the law firm size.[10] This is not to suggest solo lawyers or small law firms cannot use a dedicated CRM product. As with so many other business applications, cloud-based customer relationship management apps are easy to find and license for a single person.

Practice Pointer

If you get a CRM, do you still need a contact manager? Or a law practice management software platform? You will have noticed that there is a lot of overlap in capabilities, with a CRM and practice management app particularly providing wider sets of features as well as being relational databases. This is where your individual preference will most likely drive your technology selection. You may find a CRM that does most of what you need to do for managing your clients and supplement it with

9. Am. Bar Ass'n, 2023 Legal Technology Survey Report: Law Office Technology 26, question 23a-b (2024). About one-third of solo practitioners have a CRM in their law firm while about two-thirds of lawyers in firms with more than 500 lawyers indicate their firm has one. I think this latter number may be a bit soft, as many lawyers will not use the CRM themselves, and I would expect nearly 100% of large law firms to have a CRM function, if not a dedicated application.

10. *Id.* at 26, question 23a. 15% of solos say there is no contact management software at their firm while 2% of lawyers in the largest law firms say there is not one available in those firms.

document management or other tools that fill in the gaps. Or you may decide you want to go with something far more integrated, like practice management software, or the entirely other direction by only using discrete standalone applications, loosely connected. There is not a right answer so long as you are able to competently represent your clients. It is most important that you are aware that there is more available than merely contacts management and that you can run any sized law firm with sophisticated contacts, conflicts, and marketing relationship apps.

The widespread adoption of CRM, even if it is heavier in larger law firms, supports the notion that any sized law practice can get the benefit of its enhanced contact management capabilities. But it also may indicate that cloud-based CRM applications have lowered the technical bar and costs so that a solo lawyer or small law firm can take advantage of what might only have been an enterprise-level product in the past. Cloud-based applications give you an opportunity to try more complicated systems like CRM on a short-term subscription and without any hardware investment: you open up your web browser and you are at your CRM application. You only need time to test and trial it and money to license it; every lawyer can have those resources.

A CRM is not just a more complicated contact manager, though. It is a different type of software that also happens to manage contacts. It is designed to help you track your relationships with those contacts. Every contact with a client can be kept in it: emails, phone calls, meetings, unplanned interactions at community events, and other interactions can be recorded. It can give you a wider understanding of your interactions with a client, insights that you may miss if you are only looking at paper phone messages or voicemail or your sent emails individually.

Unlike more basic contact management apps or even relational data tools, a CRM will give you the ability to track your contacts as they move around over the course of your law practice. What if a lawyer changes firms or moves to a new company? What if a client gets divorced and remarried? Contact managers will enable you to manage the current information, and practice management apps will enable you to manage the current relationships. A CRM may offer you a greater ability to see where that person was in the past and what relationships they are a part of, both past and present.

We have not yet touched on client communications, but a CRM will help you with that aspect of your practice as well. What is your law firm's process when someone calls? How is that information recorded so that you not only know someone called but you can also ensure they get a call back or that their request has a follow up task connected to it? In a CRM, you can record every person who contacts your law firm and—as mentioned above as part of your intake—manage how they found you. But what if they call you a second time? Or you have other interactions with them: you see them at a professional event or out at a social gathering, or you meet a colleague of theirs. All of these direct and indirect contacts can be captured to give you a better understanding of this prospective or current client. You can get insights into how they interact with you if every contact—phone call, email, text—is recorded in this way. You will need to have a way to follow up on these contacts, and a CRM can help you to manage that workflow.

You may want to start to do this in law school, since a solo lawyer could manage some of these CRM tasks with their Microsoft Outlook or Google Contacts contact manager. There is a note field on most contact records. Perhaps you put information in there as you learn it about students or lawyers you meet during law school: birthdays and anniversaries, partner's or children's names, where they went to law school or what city they grew up in, the type of tea or coffee they drink (or avoid), and so on. I have even put notes about my contacts like "morning person" or the name of the mutual friend who introduced us or their kids' ages or where they are going to university, things that contact managers are not really designed to capture in an organized way.

These sorts of personal notes can be useful when you are following up with someone. They are small details that may be shared by your client with you and then forgotten if you do not store them somewhere. But imagine how surprised and connected your client will feel if you have refreshed your memory about them before you call or meet. Customer relationship management does not require a great memory when you record the information your clients share with you about themselves.

A CRM will not just help you manage the inflow of information. It can help you to see when you last contacted someone, so that you can follow up and maintain a relationship with them. It can help you keep track of key dates in their lives or their business, allowing you to proactively communicate with them about happy events or successes, so that they know that you are thinking of them outside of just the times when you are billing them for your expertise.

You may start to think this sounds an awful lot like the intake process. A CRM may, in fact, be an excellent way to start your interactions with prospective clients. Web-based CRM platforms can have online intake forms that allow you to capture much of the basic information you need and automate the scheduling of an initial interaction with your law firm. Since this data will be inserted immediately into the system, it can be used for both prospective and retained clients for future conflicts checks. The CRM, then, can provide you with new automated workflow options that go well beyond a more basic contact management app.

This management of the customer *relationship* is not something you will have likely learned about in law school. Instead, it is an application of the business of law practice, known as business development. Large law firms will have business development teams to help them maintain these relationships and look for ways to mine or expand existing ones. They will be monitoring business newspapers and platforms to see when existing and prospective clients are mentioned. They will be monitoring court dockets to see who is being sued. They may be proactively sending out messages connected to key events like birthdays or anniversaries, to keep the law firm on the client's radar. Since you will be meeting new people and will be contacted by prospective clients all the time, this aggregation of information will only grow over time. Your ability to start to make these connections—"it is nice to meet you, do you know Sally? I noticed that she works at the same company as you"—will help you to expand your business and client network.

A CRM is perhaps the most complicated approach to managing your contact information. This chapter is about conflicts checking, and so CRMs really provide you with far more information than you might need for that function. It is a good example of a relational database that is available for lawyers but that may be outside of the law practice management applications that a lawyer might ordinarily consider for their firm. CRMs are a business of law application that can be applied to law practice because the business of law and the practice of law are often intertwined.

Dedicated Conflicts Checking Applications

There are also dedicated, standalone conflicts checking applications designed for lawyers. They may provide additional functionality beyond that of a practice management application, and certainly more than you would get in a non-relational data system like Microsoft Outlook or Google Contacts. However, if they do not look directly at the contact management or other data sources you are creating, they will create the same challenges as any system that duplicates your contact management approach. You may need to refresh the data on a regular basis with exports or imports from other data systems or create an additional process to ensure that the conflicts data is kept current.

Just as with spreadsheets, that duplication is not a reason not to use them. Unlike spreadsheets, they may have an easy way for you to import your contacts or other methods of relying on your single source of truth, whatever it is, and still providing you with accurate analysis of potential conflicts. Whatever your solution, it should keep the re-keying of data to a minimum in order to reduce risk and ensure you are operating as efficiently as possible.

Chapter 7 Exercises

A. Construct a simple spreadsheet that presents client data in a relational format. Connect two sets of data to reduce re-keying or duplication of data. Your end result should be a list of clients sorted by name with other information related to them—organization connection, party type—being drawn from other parts of the spreadsheet. Use Microsoft Excel or some other tool that supports relationships between data.

B. Draft an engagement or non-engagement letter for a client. Feel free to use a template. Create a mail merge letter that pulls data from your spreadsheet: name (first, middle, last), address, and so on. Test it against your spreadsheet, and print off one of the letters to paper or PDF to show your output.

C. We have been primarily looking at conflicts checking, whether in an app or spreadsheet or CRM, from the perspective of a single system. What other information sources might you have, like evidence from a client matter or documents created for a client, that could also contain information about parties or entities that pose conflicts? How would you access those as part of your conflicts check, going beyond the contact management system?

Chapter 8

Document Automation

I do not think it is a controversial position to state that Microsoft Word is the cornerstone of law practice technology. That may not be the most aspirational viewpoint, but I think it is true of our current state and has been for decades. Once Microsoft Windows became dominant in law firms and their office suite overtook competitors like Corel WordPerfect, Word has maintained an outsized impact on the legal profession.

This chapter, then, focused as it is on document automation, really needs to start with Microsoft Word and the functionality it has built to support lawyers. There is a great deal of power in the word processor that you should understand before you start to consider how to extend it with add-ons and other automation tools.

There are no professional rules that have to do with document automation, which is a process. There are court rules that relate to word count, and rules that set out other formatting requirements. You should have these in mind when you start to draft a document for court, but the information they describe will involve common formatting for any Microsoft Word document.

Some of the rules are simple and obvious:

> (b) PARAGRAPHS; SEPARATE STATEMENTS. A party must state its claims or defenses in numbered paragraphs, each limited as far as practicable to a single set of circumstances.[1]

Some of them will be very specific, particularly when you get to appellate courts. You should be curious about, and ask your colleagues and the court about, local

1. Fed. R. Civ. P. 10.

rules that apply to formatting. For example, while the Illinois Supreme Court rules for documents filed in Illinois state courts are relatively lenient:

> Rule 10. Size and Specifications of Documents Filed in the Illinois Courts
>
> (a) Page Size. Except as otherwise provided in these rules, the page size of all documents filed in all courts of this State shall be 8½ inches by 11 inches. The court encourages use of recycled paper if the filing is in paper form.
>
> (b) Legibility. Documents filed shall be legibly written, typewritten, printed, or otherwise prepared.[2]

The guidance on documents filed in Illinois through electronic filing are more specific, in part to ensure that the file can be filtered through optical character recognition (OCR).[3]

> When possible, the following parameters apply to e-filed documents submitted through eFileIL:
>
> a. Optical Character Recognition (OCR) PDF.
>
> b. Minimum 300 dpi (dots per inch), Maximum 600 dpi—scanned in black / white mode.
>
> c. Page Size: 8½ x 11 inches.
>
> d. 12 pt. font
>
> e. First page, top margin of each e-filed document should be two inches.
>
> f. A one-inch page margin on all sides (top, bottom, right and left sides).
>
> g. The OCR PDF document should be created directly from the program creating that document, rather than from a scanned image of the document.[4]

What if you opened up your word processor and, through no fault of your own, the font had defaulted to 11-point instead of the 12-point preferred by the e-filing web site? You could select all of the text in your document after

2. ILL. SUP. CT. R. 10.

3. Optical character recognition is a way of taking a printed document or a digital image of a document and converting it into text, so that it can be edited or re-used or "read" by another computer.

4. EFILEIL ELEC. DOCUMENT STANDARDS, r. 3a-g (2022).

you were done and convert it to 12-point. But what if you had used additional font sizes: headings and so on? It is time to talk about one of the most powerful tools in Microsoft Word and a concept that, once you get it, can help you with efficient re-formatting in a variety of circumstances.

Styles and Stylesheets

I have worked with lawyers for decades and helped them with technology. Both in law firms and in all of the other organizations I have worked in, the ability to easily re-style a document is perhaps the most overlooked function in Microsoft Word. A vast amount of time is wasted by staff and professionals who do not think about how their document formatting will matter until after the document is finished. If more than one person is working on a document, you may find that one person indents text by hitting the space bar five times while another person uses a tab. Each of those choices complicates managing the document itself if changes need to be made later, especially if you have specific formatting requirements.

Enter styles. These are elements of a style set, a look-and-feel set of rules that describe how content is formatted, that you can apply to a Microsoft Word document. Microsoft Word style sets are accessible on the Ribbon under the Design tab. Style sets are just a starting point for your document, a collection of styles that someone has created in advance and that you can then edit yourself and save for your own re-use.

Here is the secret: as you create your document, apply a style set to it. Do not worry too much about how it looks at this point, the style set does not really matter yet. With your selected style set, work through the document and apply it in a consistent manner. Do not go through your document, apply a style, and then manually change the look and feel of the styles that you do not like. This can feel wrong when you are doing it, but there is a more efficient way to manage a style set. Instead, use the style set as it is designed, even if you find it ugly, even if it does not comport with the court rules or other formatting with which you must comply. You will fix that before you are finished.

Complete your document and now assess what needs to be fixed. Instead of highlighting the text on the screen, see if you can edit the appropriate style to create the look, effect, or format that you desire. For example, this book was written using Microsoft Word. As I went through, I would add headings over each section like the one above. I knew what level of hierarchy it should be in the book's structure. I clicked on the Home tab on the Ribbon, selected Styles, and selected the right Heading: 2, 3, or 4. I did not use any additional headings past Heading 4 although I could have. As I applied each heading style, it reformatted the line of text that was there. The font size changed, the color or spacing altered, and the resulting text looked different from the text around it, the regular text or *normal* text as it is termed in Microsoft styles.

I did not need to use the Heading styles. There is nothing magic in the actual formatting of each one. I could have, as I moved through the book, just highlighted the heading text and selected the new font size, made it **bold**, and manually adjusted the spacing around the heading. I could then repeat those steps for each heading as I created it. There are dozens of headings in this book, though. What if I did one incorrectly, and so it no longer signaled to the reader where they were within the document? Or what if I changed my mind, and I needed to change some of the Heading 3s to Heading 4s or I wanted to make them easier to distinguish by making one heading larger or the other smaller? I would have had to locate each of those headings, by sight, and repeat the multiple adjustments to each one, one-by-one, until I had made them uniform again.

The reason I used styles is because they are tied to a style definition. The style definition describes all the components of the formatting and look of the style. When you click on the Style option on the ribbon and apply a style, it places a style code around that text (almost always text that is contained within a paragraph marker). The style code is invisible to you, but the effect it has should be visible.

I can move through my document adding styles to distinguish the elements of my document. Some of these will not be exactly the way I want them to be, but I still will not make manual changes. What if I want the Heading 4 headings to all be centered? I could apply the style and then manually center the heading. But that is almost as bad as manually applying all of the formatting.

We have a style definition for that Heading 4. That means that the style definition is defining the heading as being justified to the left or right. If I want to move all of my Heading 4 headings to the center, I do not center them individually. I edit the style definition. As soon as I click *ok* to save the modification, all of the headings in my text that are styled as Heading 4 will reformat themselves to be centered.

You can perhaps see how easy it is, then, to change the entire document text from 11-point font to a 12-point font, without impacting other font choices on headings and the like. I open my Home tab on the Ribbon, click on Styles, and modify the Normal text style which usually applies to any regular text. I change the font size from 11pt (which is what it will be set to) to 12 pt, save the modification, and the entire document's *normal text* will reformat to the new font size.

This can be a very hard habit to unlearn if you are accustomed to formatting as you move through a document. The "wrong" formatting can be a distraction to just drafting your document. But you really want to just type and not focus on the formatting until either (a) you are finished with the document or (b) you have already created the styles and you can apply them as you move through your document. This brings me back to style sets.[5]

Stop me if you have heard it already, but this is another opportunity for templates. The first time you need to prepare a court filing, you can format it to the court's standards: margins, heading sizes, font sizes, the works. Once you have finished that document, you can *save your style set so that you can re-use it in the future*. The next time you are creating a court document for that court, instead of manually formatting as you go, you select the style set you saved and apply it to the entire document. Now, as you type your new pleading or filing, you can apply the styles knowing that you have already ensured they are compliant with the court's rules. If someone sends you a draft document—say a co-counsel or inside counsel—and you need to reformat it, you can also apply a whole style set to someone else's document to quickly reformat it from top to bottom.

Practice Pointer

You may be asking how this is different from a template. In general, a template is itself a document: an email, a meeting object, a Word document. A template may also be styled in a specific way. It will usually also contain text or other information that is required each time the template is invoked. A style set, on the other hand, is just the formatting and look-and-feel. It can be added to any document after it has been created—unlike a template, which is used at the start of your writing—and it can be applied to someone else's document, which a template cannot.

5. Style sets appear on the Design tab of the Microsoft Word Ribbon. They are adjacent to Themes, and they may be confused with themes because of their impact on the document. Style sets are more likely to be of value to you as a lawyer because of their impact on words and formatting, as opposed to color and font choice design elements.

Remember that I did not apply a Heading 1 throughout the document. This is for aesthetic as well as practical reasons. In the world of formatting, a Heading 1 is your overall title. There should only be one Heading 1 on your document for accessibility reasons. Heading 2 is the next most common level, and then you create a hierarchy with each higher numbered heading.

It is important that you use them in this order. Not only does it mean that your document is internally coherent from a formatting standard, the headings are used in other ways. For one thing, your headings will create an outline format for your text. You can view it in Microsoft Word's navigation pane under the View tab on the Ribbon.

If you save your document as a PDF, your headings will be saved out to the PDF, creating a hierarchy in the PDF document as well. PDF readers usually have a navigation pane as well. This will allow the reader of the PDF to get the same heading structure that you created in the Word document, rather than having to scroll through an endless document looking for specific information.

People who use assistive technology to help them *read* the document—converting it into audio or otherwise making it readable—will also benefit from the use of consistent headings. Their assistive devices or apps will use the headings to help orient their reader. If you use headings in an inconsistent manner, this benefit is lost.

What do I mean by an inconsistent manner? Let's say you like the style or formatting of Heading 3 but you want your Heading 2 level headings to look that way. Some people will apply the Heading 3 style because it looks right, even though, from the perspective of the document's structure, the text it is applied to is a Heading 2 or Heading 4. This prioritizes the look of the document on paper at the expense of the structure of the document and the ability for people to navigate it. This confuses the purpose of styles with simple formatting changes. Screen readers and PDF users will end up with an unintelligible hierarchy. If you decide to reformat your document for consistency, you may find that the use of styles in this manner has undermined any benefit in efficiency.

Avoid this by applying the styles in the hierarchy in which they are intended. If you do not like how Heading 2 looks and would prefer that it look more like Heading 3, you can edit the style. Open up Heading 3, figure out what you like about it, then open Heading 2's style definition and modify it. Once you save the modification, the new style will appear throughout the document. Now, of course, Heading 3 and Heading 2 may be indistinguishable, but you can fix that the same way: modify Heading 3's style and save the new definition.

The benefit of styles is that they allow you to quickly and efficiently reformat Microsoft Word documents. Often, once you have figured out the styles you want to use, you can save them in your basic blank Microsoft Word template or save them as a style set.[6] If you can build this habit, you will save untold amounts of time over the lifespan of your law practice.

Precedents and Work Product

An under-appreciated form of automation is the work product you create. As soon as that first prospective client contacts you, you start to create documents and information that you can build on. In some cases, deadlines will require you to just complete the document as fast as you can.

Other times, you will have a bit of time to think about the document as you create it. This is an investment that is worth making whenever you can. As you create that letter, be thinking about how you will re-use it in the future. When you start to deal with what are essentially form documents, like contracts or letters to opposing counsel in real estate transactions or court filings, start to notice which documents re-use the same language or content.

These documents are sometimes called precedents, which are distinguished from court precedent but with a similar meaning. They are existing creations on which you build your new creation. The term is useful as it distinguishes these documents from forms, which are also re-usable documents but often connote a fixed format and content.

What lawyers may often do is to just find that document—"Get me the letter I sent to opposing counsel in the Bark, Bath, and Be Gone matter"—but that itself involves retrieval issues. Is that an open or closed file? Where is the letter, and how was it saved? Hopefully, after considering your document management strategy, it would be relatively easy to find it. But you do not need to go through a retrieval process every time you want to re-use your work product.

Large law firms have staff called knowledge managers who may perform this task, but it can really be done by anyone in a law firm. Once you gener-

6. Whenever you modify a Microsoft Word style, it will ask you if you want to save the change just to the document you are working on or to save it to the Normal.dot (dot is the filename extension for Microsoft Word templates), in which case the modification will be available on all new documents you create from that template. The Normal.dot template is the one that is used if you open Microsoft Word and create a blank new document.

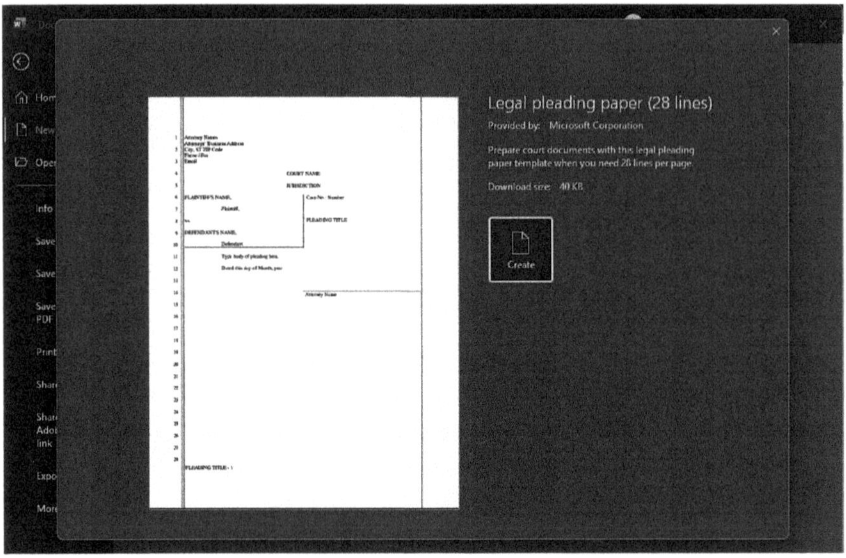

Figure 7: Microsoft office template for pleading paper

ate a document that contains key information—a legal standard, a contract clause—you can start to save those elements into templates. These templates will represent a starting point for you as you practice and will incorporate the best examples of your writing and work.

You are not the only person creating templates, either. You should think of them every time you are starting to create a document that you have never created before. An excellent example is a pleading. How do you get it to look the way it does when you see it in a legal research tool: each line has a number, there is a specific formatting to the information about the parties and the court (called the case style), and so on.

You can absolutely craft your own version. Or you can look for an existing template. This may be something a colleague has, perhaps a lawyer who started practice just before you did. In the case of pleading paper, it is such a commonly requested template that it is easy to find. Courthouse law libraries will often provide a free template for self-represented parties. Microsoft Office provides templates too. While many of them are business-oriented and not tailored to law-specific functions, they happen to have pleading paper already designed for lawyers. Click on File, New, and in the template search box, type *pleading*.

If you download the template, go ahead and make it your own. It will only have generic information in it. You can add your own contact information or otherwise tailor the document before you save it. Then save it as a template (.dotx) instead of a normal document (.docx). That way, you will see it among your templates in the future, and you will not have to try to remember where you found it.

There are extensive collections of digital templates for law practice in practically every practice area. While you will need to customize them to your client's needs, there is no reason to try to re-create the wheel every time you have a new document to draft. Look for templates and prior work product. Once you have found a suitable document, you will still need to perform legal research to update any citations or statements of law that it contains. But it will allow you to slingshot ahead of where you might have been drafting from scratch, saving you or your staff time.

Automation in Microsoft Word

We touched on automation a bit above when discussing calendars. There are perhaps even greater possibilities for automation within Microsoft Word and your document creation than in any other application you will use for law practice. Some of these add-ons (or, in Microsoft parlance, add-*ins*) can be found for free and some will be purchased from the developer.

Microsoft operates an app store of add-ins for its products.[7] While it is a resource for add-ins, Microsoft is not the developer for each one. Like a mobile phone app store, you may find some that require additional software or are from developers you will need to do some additional research on. Just like a dedicated software app, your selection of an add-in should consider who made it and for how long they may continue to support it. There is a filter for "Compliance and Legal" and a second filter for "Legal" that will surface over 100 Microsoft Office add-ins geared towards lawyers. Keep in mind that Microsoft Office is a productivity suite and the problem you are trying to solve might be one that impacts professionals well beyond the legal profession. If you filter on "Legal" and do not find what you are looking for, drop the filter and see if someone has developed the add-in you are looking for in a different context.

Unlike Microsoft Outlook, which primarily has Quick Parts to create minor automation, Microsoft Word has an extensive collection of automation tools. Many of them require you to design your document using standard

7. https://appsource.microsoft.com/en-us/marketplace/apps.

approaches, like style sets, for these automation tools to work properly. For example, once you have applied heading styles throughout a document, you can click on the Insert tab and add a Table of Contents. This will draw all of the headings together and build the table of contents for you. As you edit your document, adding or removing the headings, the table of contents will continually update. Like other parts of Microsoft Word, the table of contents is itself built around styles, and so it can be re-styled and customized for your particular purpose.

Tables of Authorities and Built-in Features

Some parts of Microsoft Word have been developed specifically for lawyers. These features have ebbed and flowed over the years as Microsoft's interest in the legal profession has waxed and waned. There used to be dedicated tools to create pleadings, for example. Microsoft led a legal advisory council that created a Microsoft Word Legal User's Guide in 2000, which was available for Word 2003 well into the next decade.[8] They also created specialized tools for legal assistants and other law office staff.

One obvious lawyer-specific feature that remains is the Table of Authorities tool. There is a good chance that you have already experienced this tool in law school. It will be used to generate the table of authorities required for many appellate briefs, both in law school and in law practice. For example, the Federal Rules of Appellate Procedure state that an appellant's brief must contain:

> Rule 28. Briefs
>
> (a) Appellant's Brief. The appellant's brief must contain, under appropriate headings and in the order indicated:
>
> (1) a disclosure statement if required by Rule 26.1;
>
> (2) a table of contents, with page references;

8. *Microsoft Word Legal User's Guide*, MICROSOFT OFFICE UPDATE (last visited Apr. 13, 2001), http://officeupdate.microsoft.com/legal/ [https://web.archive.org/web/20010413163649/http://officeupdate.microsoft.com/legal/]. Devoted legal fans have kept this project alive long after it was dropped by Microsoft. A lawyer in Wisconsin has updated and expanded the original. Charles Kyle Kenyon, *Intermediate Users' Guide to Microsoft Word*, INTERMEDIATE USERS' GUIDE TO MICROSOFT WORD (last visited Apr. 21, 2025), http://addbalance.com/usersguide/ [http://web.archive.org/web/20250421193413/http://addbalance.com/usersguide/]. Microsoft itself hosted a copy of the guide at least until 2014, according to the Internet Archive's Wayback Machine.

(3) a table of authorities—cases (alphabetically arranged), statutes, and other authorities—with references to the pages of the brief where they are cited;[9]

If you have not used it yet, it is worth taking a look at because it is a model for a number of the other Table features in Microsoft Word. These should not be confused with tables, however, which are ways to organize information in columns and rows. Tables with a capital T include Tables of Contents, of Authorities, of Figures, etc.

This approach is the same one described above with styles. First, put your content into your document. For a table of authorities, this would be all of your citations to statutes, cases, and other references you are including in your appellate brief. Make sure you have done any citation checking you need to do—especially if you have used any generative artificial intelligence tool—to confirm that the citation is correct *and* that the citation is properly formatted for the court or law professor or whoever will be reading it.

Once you have your citation set, you can apply the coding Microsoft needs to understand how you want to treat it. If we were trying to apply formatting to the citation, now is when we would apply a style. Since we want to add this citation to a Table of Authorities, we need to mark the citation as an entry for that Table.[10] You will go through your document, marking each item that you want to be included in the Table. Once you have completed your document and marked every citation, you can return to the References tab on the Word Ribbon and use the Insert Table of Authorities command. It will create the Table where you have placed your cursor, so check the appellate rules again to see if it needs to go in a certain place within the brief, at the front or back, for example.

The Table of Authorities function is a great example of a very narrowly designed, specific tool for one document. It is the sort of function that takes something that can be labor intensive, especially as you may not create a Table of Authorities more than once or twice a decade, and automates it. It saves you from having to remember how to create them. Instead, you can create

9. FED. R. APP. P. 28.

10. As of writing, switch over to the References tab on the Microsoft Word Ribbon and click the Mark Entry button on the Table of Authorities section.

your brief in the manner that is familiar and automate the actual creation of the Table.[11]

Some functions in Microsoft Word have been adapted by lawyers to do more than they were probably intended to. These *hacks* allow you to create what are essentially simple replacement programs. We looked at the use of auto-correct above as one example. This is perhaps the easiest way to complement your use of templates. A template will be an entire document that you use as a starting point. Sometimes, though, you just need a specific turn of phrase or a regularly cited piece of information. Since auto-correct is supposed to replace one piece of text with another—the design was to replace incorrect text with corrected text, like *teh* to *the*, but it does not have to involve incorrect text—you can use it to create small text snippets.

Quick Parts and Auto-Text

Unlike Microsoft Outlook, though, which has limited automation when it comes to text, auto-correct is just a starting point. Outlook's Quick Steps pale in comparison with the Quick Parts functionality in Microsoft Word. Quick Parts provides a tool called auto-text, which is designed to allow you to save longer bodies of text and recall them quickly without having to retype them.

Here's an example. This is the start of the standard for summary judgment provided by the United States Equal Employment Opportunity Commission in one of the motion templates they provide for free for self-represented parties and lawyers on their website:

> Summary judgment is appropriate if the pleadings, answers to interrogatories, admissions, affidavits and other evidence establish no genuine issue as to any material fact, and the moving party is entitled to judgment as a matter of law. See 29 C.F.R. § 1614.109(g); see also Murphy v. Dep't of the Army, EEOC Appeal No. 01A04099 (July 11, 2003) (noting that the regulation governing decisions without a hearing is modeled after the Federal Rules of Civil Procedure, Rule 56).

11. It will come as no surprise by now that Microsoft Word has a specific formatting style for Tables of Authorities. This means that, like any other part of your document, you should not manually format it until you have seen whether you can conform the style to the formatting you desire. If you can get the style to format your Table the way you like, you can then re-apply the style in this or future documents.

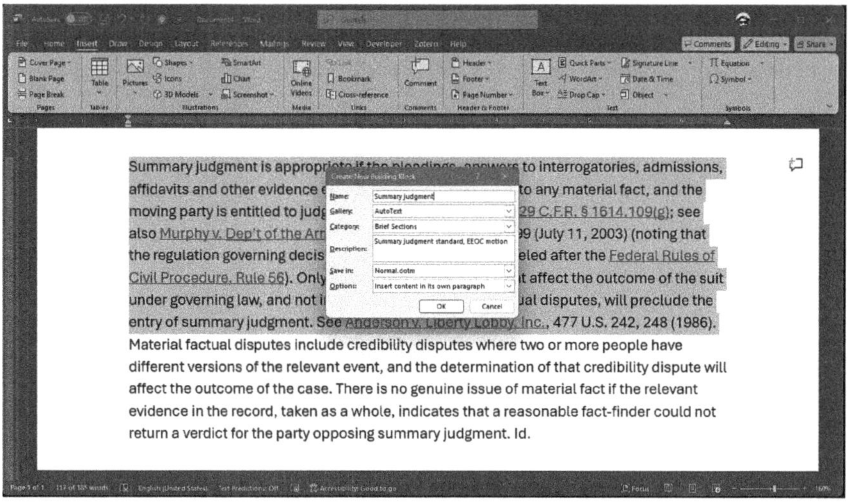

Figure 8: Quick Part auto-text with clause drop down

I can now highlight that paragraph and add it to my Quick Parts. When I select the option to add it to Quick Parts, I get a long list of types of parts to which it applies. If I click the first one, for auto-text, I can further categorize or describe the text I am saving.

As you can see above, I can create groups of auto-text elements so that, as I am creating new documents, I can avoid retyping them each time. In this case, I have placed the summary judgment standard in a category called *brief sections*. I could just as easily create a group of auto-text contract clauses for, say, apartment leases. I might start with a template lease that provides most of the standard clauses and those required by law. Then I could use auto-text to insert additional clauses based on the client's requirements or the particular property involved.

A Header Hack

Another way lawyers use Microsoft Word in ways that it wasn't intended was by leveraging the Header and Footer parts of the document. You are familiar with their normal use: they provide a uniform set of information at the top and bottom of the page, often with page numbers and headings or corporate branding for a consistent appearance.

If you recall that pleading paper template mentioned above, though, you can see how Microsoft and lawyers will use the header to place information

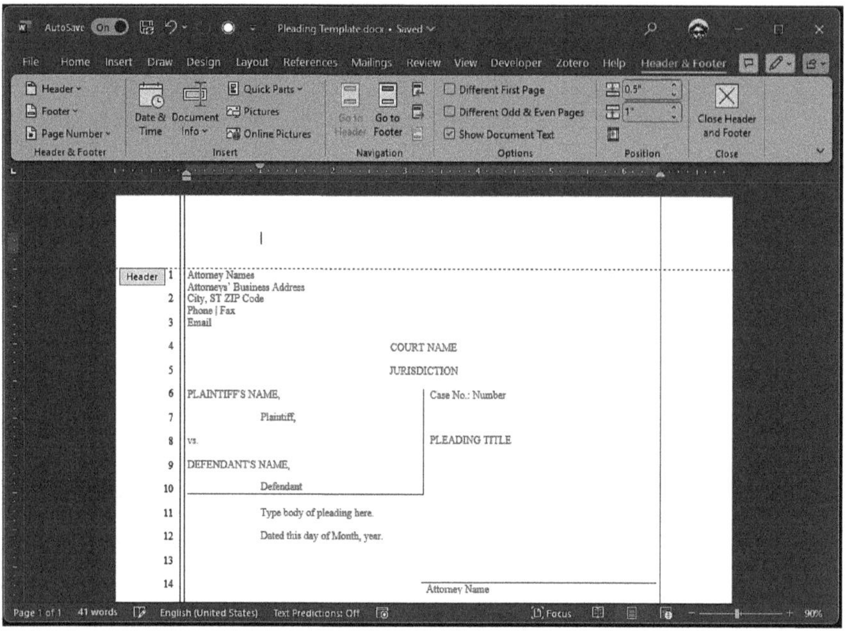

Figure 9: Header used for pleading numbering

below the text of the document. If you open up that pleading template, whether you download it from Microsoft or have created your own Word template, you will notice that you cannot edit the numbers on the left-hand side nor the double line that separates them from the text.

This is because they have been placed in the *header* part of the document even though, counter-intuitively, they run down the left side of the page. But if you double-click in the header space (or use the menu to access the header), you will see that the body of the pleading document is greyed-out. The line numbering is now dark and editable, as you can see above.

Another common use of the header in a Microsoft Word document is to place a phrase describing the stage of the document—draft, final, and so on—so that it appears below the text. This use of the header for watermarking is so common that there is now a function in Microsoft Word (under the Design tab on the Ribbon) to insert a Watermark. If you use this function and click to edit the header, you will notice that all that Microsoft Word has done is inserted a pre-designed element under the header. You can click into the header and edit it directly or create a custom watermark.[12]

This is not an obvious way to use Microsoft Word. As you come across documents, you are likely to see other examples of how you might want to adapt your own. If you can, see if you can get a copy of the Word document format version of the document to see how the original author created it. When that fails, consider looking at some of the features in Microsoft Word that you may not have used, or used in that manner, and see if one of them will help you adapt your document.

Hotkeys and Macros

You will already be familiar with the hotkey or key combinations in your commonly used applications. CTRL-P to invoke a printer. CTRL-F to find a word within a web page or document. CTRL-A to select all objects on the page, and CTRL-C to copy them and CTRL-V to paste them. Microsoft Windows is replete with hotkeys, and you will find that almost everything in Microsoft Windows can be done from the keyboard. In some cases, the hotkeys have been defined for you (like CTRL-P), but you can also create your own world of hotkey combinations.

Some hotkeys will only work within the Microsoft desktop apps. For example, if you are in Microsoft Excel, and you want to insert a row, you could hold down ALT, hit I, and then R. This hotkey will fail if you try the same combination in the Excel web app. If you start to rely on hotkeys for accessing common functions, you may need to ensure you are in the full application on your desktop.

Hotkeys will invoke an existing function on your application. This is because a hotkey has to be assigned to something that exists. What may not be apparent is that hotkeys can be assigned to small programs known as macros that you create within Word or PowerPoint or Excel.

12. Be judicious in what you use as a watermark or how you use this feature. A lawyer commissioned a purple dragon watermark and included it in their court filings, much to the frustration of the court. Nate Anderson, *Don't Watermark Your PDFs with Purple Dragons in Suits*, Ars Technica (May 1, 2025), https://arstechnica.com/tech-policy/2025/05/dont-watermark-your-legal-pdfs-with-purple-dragons-in-suits/ [http://web.archive.org/web/20250519155622/https:/arstechnica.com/tech-policy/2025/05/dont-watermark-your-legal-pdfs-with-purple-dragons-in-suits/].

Macros were once considered our allies, helpful applications, and then they became the enemy. A macro, put simply, is a small program that you can invoke to do repetitive steps. In word processors, they can be used to apply a specific set of formatting or other functions to avoid you having to do them yourself.

Before the turn of the century, lawyers were able to purchase collections of word processor macros for WordPerfect.[13] Microsoft Word had a macro capability as well, but it was not as easy to use as WordPerfect—speaking as someone who has developed macros in both—and eventually became a security threat.[14] Over time, the macro functionality has been hidden under the Developer tab on the Ribbon, and the Developer tab is hidden unless you turn it on in Microsoft Word (and other Office applications). Additionally, Microsoft Office now has a function called the Trust Center. It will allow law firms to disable macro usage across all documents to ensure that someone does not open a file sent to them by email and unwittingly run a macro exploit.

This is too bad because the macro still has a role to play, particularly in a small law firm or solo law practice where there may not be staff who can do technical programming. Macros can be complex, but they do not have to be. You could have a macro that looks through a document and does a find and replace for the 10 words you are most likely to have misused (statue instead of statute) but that will not be flagged by a spellcheck. Like the Quick Parts in Microsoft Outlook, they can provide a way to daisy-chain a number of discrete steps into a single process.

For example, let's say you have a number of steps you take with your documents that are repetitive. You have already created Quick Parts for them, or they are otherwise automated with a hotkey combination within windows. Or they might be something that can only be accessed part-way by a hotkey function. A macro can stitch together multiple hotkeys and intermediate stages so that you do not have to repeat all of the steps.

13. There appear to still be some purveyors of macros for lawyers and for WordPerfect, but they are probably a relatively niche product.

14. In fact, Microsoft Word had its first macro virus in the mid-1990s, well before it saw broad adoption by the legal profession. Lawyers may have noticed macro viruses as they started to migrate from WordPerfect (later known as Corel WordPerfect) to Microsoft Word. *20 Years of Macro Malware: From Harmless Concept to Targeted Attacks*, TRENDMICRO (July 31, 2015), https:/www.trendmicro.com/vinfo/us/security/news/cybercrime-and-digital-threats/20-years-of-macro-malware-from-harmless-concept-to-targeted-attacks [https://web.archive.org/web/20250222035437/https://www.trendmicro.com/vinfo/us/security/news/cybercrime-and-digital-threats/20-years-of-macro-malware-from-harmless-concept-to-targeted-attacks].

The easiest way to create a macro is to just record the steps you are already taking. Once you have recorded the macro, it will play them back to you in the same order. If you do not like the outcome, you can re-record and overwrite the macro until you have it working the way you want. Similarly, if you create a macro and decide to customize it, you can simply re-record it.

You can also edit it if you know the scripting language that is used in Microsoft Office. There are some parts of the legal profession that believe every lawyer should know how to code. But I do not think that is a normal part of law practice, and I would expect few lawyers to know how to make these edits. I would just say that there are lots of programming and developer resources available for free on the internet. If you decided this was an area you wanted to explore, it would be easy to do so.

As a simple example, I have created a macro that uses some built-in functionality in Microsoft Word but that requires me to take multiple steps. Once I have started recording the macro, from the Record Macro option on the Developer tab on the Ribbon, I invoke the Insert tab. From there, I select the Insert Signature block option. This opens a dialog box asking me for information about the signer—name, title, email address—and, when I confirm the choices, it inserts a signature block in my Word document. I then move my cursor back to the left and use a Quick Part auto-text I created earlier that uses a stock sentence related to an engagement letter. I stop recording the macro and I'm finished.

The resulting macro looks like this:

```
Sub AddSignatureBlockEngagement()
  ActiveDocument.Signatures.AddSignatureLine _
    "{00000000-0000-0000-0000-000000000000}"
  Selection.MoveLeft Unit:=wdCharacter, Count:=1
  Application.Templates( _
    "C:\[path to my folders]\AppData\Roaming\Microsoft\
    Templates\Normal.dotm"). _
    BuildingBlockEntries("Engagement Letter-Signature").Insert
    Where:= _
  Selection.Range, RichText:=True
End Sub
```

There are three components. The first is the AddSignatureLine request. Then you can see, just below it, that there is a Selection.MoveLeft for the count of

1 character. That is when I move my cursor to the left. Below that you can see where it opens the Building Block Entries (a description for the group of elements that includes Quick Parts auto-text) and inserts the one called "Engagement Letter-Signature."

This is what it looks like on the page:

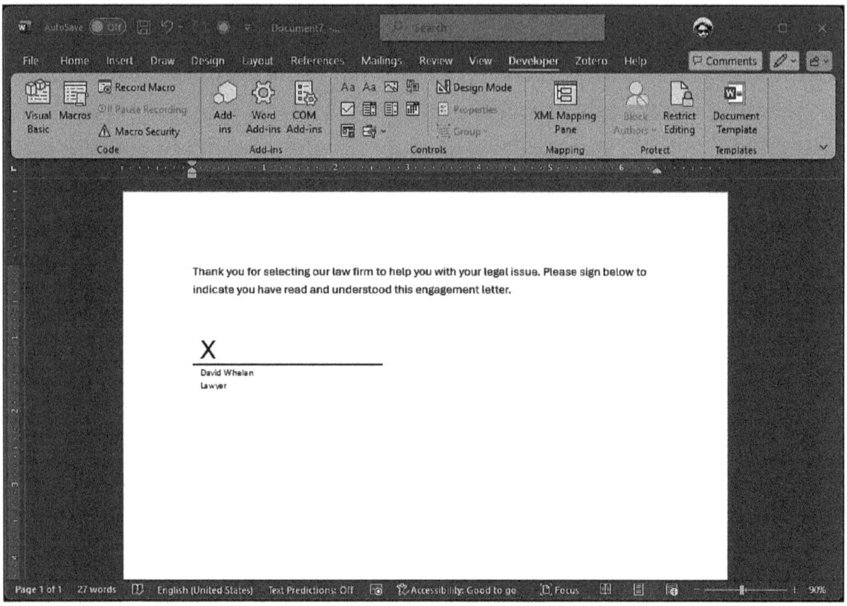

Figure 10: Signature block

Once I had completed the macro, I might change my mind and realize that, if I did the Quick Part first, I would not have to move my cursor to the left of the signature block. I can re-record the macro to make that change. In other words, although you *can* edit the script of a macro or even paste in a macro you have found on the internet or received from a colleague, you do not need to. You can record the steps you are already taking within Microsoft Word and save them as a macro. Once they exist as a macro, you can apply your own hotkey combination to them and re-use the macro in the future.[15]

15. I would be leery of pasting in a script that you received from an unknown source. The whole point of Microsoft Office's Trust Center is that you will be prevented from running unknown macros. It is far safer to use the macro feature, if you use it at all, for (a) internal documents only (since external recipients may also block macros and (b) for stitching together functionality already in Microsoft Word.

My recommendation is not that macros will make sense in every law practice nor, especially, that lawyers need to know how to code them. They are an excellent example of how you can stitch together small automations and functionality quickly so that you reduce the number of steps you have to repeat and create a way to avoid having someone skip a step in your process.

As you create documents in law school, start to think about where you are doing repetitive activities and consider how you might automate those. Consider the variety of options you have to automate this key part of law practice. Perhaps more than any other area of law practice technology, document automation within Microsoft Word offers a great deal of scope for making very small time-saving changes to your work.

Chapter 8 Exercises

A. Create a macro in Microsoft Word that will generate a case style in the form of your state court system. You can write the programming code or use the Developer macro recording function to create your macro. You can create a short video showing the macro working or print off the code for your instructor.

B. Create a Quick Part in Microsoft Outlook, or with Microsoft PowerAutomate, or use a similar automation tool (like Zapier or IFTTT) in another personal information manager that has email and calendaring. Create a rule that triggers upon the arrival of information, writing new information to your calendar.

Chapter 9

Document Management

Your intake process is now complete. You have gathered information from the prospective client. You have analyzed your ability to take on the case, performing legal research and perhaps even some legal analytics to help you decide whether to accept, reject, or refer this case. You have cross-checked your client data for conflicts of interest. You have generated your engagement or non-engagement letter, and you have sent it. You now have a document, and you will need somewhere to store it, as well as the other information you have gathered so far through the intake process.

The best time to start thinking about how to manage your client files is at the beginning of your legal career, before you have created too many of them. Document management is a key method of managing your client files throughout their entire life cycle, from the day you meet your prospective client to the day you close the files related to their issue and store them. The more you consider your approach beforehand, the less likely you will have to recreate your processes later on and apply a new process retrospectively to existing documents and client matters. Even something as small as how you name files or a numbering system can become a bigger issue the longer you practice. You may have heard of the Year 2000 problem, where computers had been programmed for much of their existence in the 1900s with dates ending in two-digit years. This meant that "00" could mean either 1900 or 2000 and caused a lot of uncertainty as systems were remediated to account for a four-digit year. A bit of planning now to accommodate that sort of change—when you reach your thousandth client, for example—can make a difference.

Just as with every other part of law practice technology, there are professional rules that you need to keep in mind. Perhaps the most important of these is the lawyer's duty of confidentiality to their client.[1] This has almost certainly already been drilled into your thinking throughout law school. As you create new documents related to your client's matters, you will need to manage who has access to them. These documents, whether they represent the work product that you keep as part of your law practice or the documents that belong to the client that you hold for them during your representation, will make up the client file, and you will need to keep them for the life of your representation of the client on the matter.

Some documents may have to be kept well past your actual representation of the client, the period in which you are in regular contact or consider the client's matter "open." Wills, for example, are documents that may only have legal import *after* your client's death. Your need to retain that will does not necessarily end on the day that they sign the document you have drafted for them. You do not need to hold *all* documents for your clients forever, but you will need to communicate to them what you are and are not keeping for them and for how long. You may also have professional obligations that require you to retain documents for a specific period of time after your representation ends. If you offer your clients a method of retrieving their client file, even if you are printing it off for them, you want to be confident that you have given them everything they are entitled to receive.

Think about the documents you currently have under your control in your own life. How many of these are even a handful of years old? Perhaps you still have notes or essays you wrote during your freshman year in college. For those that are more than a few years old, when was the last time you tried to open them and use them?

A more mundane question is *where are they*? Can you find and retrieve a document you created or received from five years ago, and how long would it take you to do that? How do you organize your personal files so that you can find them as quickly as possible? Are they all stored in one place, or are your documents stored in a Google Drive, and as email attachments to Google Mail, and on your computer's desktop, on your phone or tablet, and in other locations? I expect the answer is that your personal documents are spread across a number of devices and locations and that it might be a bit daunting to have to find any given document if it is more than a few years old. This would not be unusual for many lawyers as well.[2]

---

1. A.B.A. Model Rules of Professional Conduct, r. 1.6 (Am. Bar Ass'n 2025).

2. RELX LexisNexis used to conduct an international workplace productivity survey that included lawyers among its audience. The last one I have been able to find was in

File Formats

We will get to organizational challenges in a moment. Even before that, an issue that will only increase over the lifetime of your law practice will be the retention and retrieval of documents that were made in earlier versions of the current software you are using or in which they were made. Lawyers and courts who created documents using early word processors like WordPerfect 5.1 or even Microsoft Word 6.0 may find that their documents will no longer open twenty years later. Unlike a paper book that might be accessible and understandable after hundreds of years, our digital file formats are much more at risk of becoming inaccessible within the lifetime of a typical lawyer's practice. File formats change and, by the time you or your client need to access them, there may not be conversion tools to make them accessible. Twenty years may seem like a long time, but it is probably only the halfway mark for most lawyers who practice their entire working life.

While portable document format (PDF) files may create a greater expectation of document accessibility, printing or saving a document into a PDF format generally means that you risk losing functionality within, or even descriptive information about, the document.[3] This loss will impact your document templates, those efficiency tools discussed above in the context of email and calendaring. In a matter of a decade or so, we have seen widespread file format changes as Microsoft created a new, open document standard. Doc-

---

2010. Even then, it showed that 90% of respondents from the United States said that the inability to access the right information at the right time was a huge time-waster. LEXISNEXIS, INTERNATIONAL WORKPLACE SURVEY WHITE COLLAR HIGHLIGHTS 20 (2010), https://www.multivu.com/players/English/46619-LexisNexis-International-Workplace-Productivity-Survey/flexSwf/impAsset/document/34ef84f1-beaa-4a48-98c5-0ea93ceae0cb.pdf. 92% indicated they had to search for an old email or document at least once a week. 55% indicated that they needed to recreate a document because a previously created version could not be found. While we have seen substantial improvements in the speed of technology since that 2010 survey, the underlying processes are part of the problem: if information is not well organized, it will be hard to find and retrieve. Even fifteen years later, I would expect many of these numbers to be very similar to what they were in 2010.

3. You will sometimes see PDF referred to as Adobe PDF, as if it was a product name. It was an Adobe proprietary format until 2008, when it became an open standard. When you see references to PDF documents requiring the Adobe Acrobat Reader, there is a good chance that any PDF reader will open and allow you to view the PDF. Similarly, all modern web browsers will render a PDF so you can read it within a web browser. There are some limited times, especially with court documents and forms, where they are designed using Adobe proprietary tools, and those may require an Adobe PDF reader to allow the completion of the form.

uments lawyers created in the past few decades may already be inaccessible depending upon what software was used to create them and their ultimate file format, because they can no longer be opened and read, even if they have been safeguarded and stored.

The longer those digital files are stored, though, the greater the concern that not only the file format will change but that the medium on which they are stored will no longer work. Storage drives fail and, even when they do not fail to be accessible due to a physical fault, the data on them may become corrupted and made unretrievable. Later on, we will take a look at data backups and business recovery, but the issue of document retrieval goes well beyond tornados, fire, and theft. You may need to open a document in a client matter from only a few years ago. How do you ensure that you can do that at the moment that you need to in the future?

You can see why some law firms resort to paper as a means of managing documents and making them accessible. But paper has its own challenges, especially in relation to the cost of storage and the speed of retrieval. Whether you manage your documents in a paper format or a digital one, you, as a law student about to graduate into the legal profession, may have to manage those files for the next 50 years, the life of your law practice. The time to start thinking about that file retention and planning for your document management strategy is at the start of your practice. You have the fewest documents at this point, and so a change will not require much retrospective reconfiguration.

One approach is to focus on editable formats for the lifecycle of the client matter. These are often counted in months or years. The likelihood of substantial file format changes without good conversion options in that period of time is small. In the case of Microsoft Office, when you open an older format Microsoft Word document (in the .doc format) in a newer version of Word, it will prompt you to save it in the newer file format (.docx).

In the worst case, where you have an older file format and no way to open it, there are document conversion utilities available that may be able to solve the problem. These are one-and-done utilities that can convert large numbers of documents from one format to another. Keep in mind that converting a format does not necessarily preserve everything that was in the original document. The layout, formatting, and other content may change. Things like images or figures that rely on specific functionality in the original program may be lost. The file itself may be accessible, but it may not look anything like the original.

You can maintain this approach—using editable formats of whatever documents you are creating—until you close the client's matter. At that point, it makes sense to print or convert every document to a long-term format, like portable document (PDF). In fact, PDF supports an archival version (PDF/A) that attempts to ensure a long access period.[4] The drawback to PDF/A is that it flattens the document in ways that may not be helpful if you or your client needs to use the document in the future.

For example, if a Word document has a hypertext link that can be clicked and goes to a website, the website address to which that link goes may not be visible in the document. It may appear as a piece of text that is underlined and in a different color. If you save your document as a typical PDF file, that hyperlink is usually retained and will continue to work when clicked within the PDF.[5] However, if you save a document in an archival format such as PDF/A, the conversion removes external references like hypertext links. It will also remove interactive functionality like scripts that may have been embedded in the document.

Due to the increased use of hypertext links in court documents—briefs you submit, possibly even letters and other documents sent to the court—as well as in routine business communications, including emails and texts, the best avenue will be to preserve those links so they work. Otherwise, you may lose important context if all you have is an underlined line of text and no retention of the destination it was supposed to go to.

What Is a Document?

This may be obvious, but you should also consider what a document *is*. We may default to thinking about a document as something we type up and perhaps print out or upload to a website, things like homework or a court filing and so on. But the concept of a document can extend beyond those stereotypical digital files and includes emails, text messages (SMS), chat and video call

4. *PDF/A*, WIKIPEDIA (last visited Aug. 29, 2025), https://en.wikipedia.org/wiki/PDF/A.

5. When I say the link will work, I mean that the function of clicking the link will work, and it will try to send the reader to a website address or wherever the link was designed to go. There is no guarantee that the destination will exist for the lifetime of the document and the link.

transcripts, and other communications. It can be important to consider the broad range of documents because you may need to store these digital objects as well, whether you consider them traditional documents or not.

In particular, communications like text messages may not be exportable or downloadable, depending on the device and app you use. You will want to consider how you will retain them and manage them as part of your client file or, perhaps, avoid communicating in formats that you cannot export and retain. Similarly, emails can often be exported as an email file (the format may be .eml or .msg). However, remember that each format you use creates the need to have an application that can open it after it has been saved. At the end of a case, you may export the emails—perhaps with attachments still in place—but, once exported, you are committing to keeping an app that can open them.

The best approach may be to print off the emails, as pieces of paper or PDFs, along with their attachments so that you reduce the number of file formats you have to manage. PDFs would have the advantage of being easier to find and retrieve, and storage costs would probably be less over the length of your career. Thinking longer term, it will also reduce the number of file formats your clients will have to negotiate if they are trying to work with their client file after your representation is over.

Folders and Files

It has been decades since the first lawyer used a computer to manage their documents. In that time, new methods of organization have appeared—labels and categories were referred to above, things like *folksonomies* that create a make-it-up-as-you-go personalized tagging system, under email and calendar organization—but files and folders remain a common and reliable method of organizing documents. It is a simple way to organize digital files and, because it can mimic a paper filing system, it can enable the person using the files and needing to retrieve them quickly to create a single process that works no matter what format the file is in.

The concept is simple. A folder is a container that holds multiple things. A paper folder can hold a variety of documents, and it can contain a label to describe what's inside. Similarly, a digital folder can contain a wide variety of digital files. Like a paper folder, it can also contain folders that themselves contain additional digital files.

There is a lot of easy-to-find advice about using folders in a law practice to manage your client files. It centers around creating standard, consistent naming conventions (sound familiar?) and a hierarchy that makes things easy to find once they have been stored. The simplicity of the folder-and-file approach makes it relatively easy to move folder-based file systems from computer to computer or storage device to storage device. While there is still the file's format to consider, folders and files can generally be moved between operating systems—Windows to Macintosh OS to Linux and so on—more easily than database-driven storage systems that may rely on additional software or functionality.

The hardest part may be to choose one approach. You have not yet opened your law practice, and you do not have your first client yet. How can you choose without more context?

The great thing about folders and files is that they can be used in any information organization, including that of a law student maintaining class outlines, notes, papers, drafts of memos, and so on. In law school, you might create folders based on the course name or the year in which you took it, or, if you are taking multiple classes in a specific substantive area, by topic. I use the class name and year in my own folders to distinguish the classes I teach and when I taught them.

The practice of law is centered around people with legal issues. You will be representing people, either as individuals or as representatives of entities. An organizational structure that takes this people-centric approach will be durable and can work in practically any practice area. The first step is to create your naming convention for the first level of your hierarchy. People's names will often be distinguishable by their last name first, so perhaps start there:

- Able, Michael
- Baker, Samantha
- Charles, Pat

Then consider how you will add in organizations, where the individual you are working with is the representative:

- Able, Michael
- **American Standard Pie Dishes, Inc., The**

- Baker, Samantha
- Charles, Pat
- **Christmas in July, Inc.**

Notice that there are some words—referred to as *stop* words—like the, an, and a.[6] In particular, consider how to handle *the* in your folder and file scheme. You may want to move those stop words to the end of your names or omit them altogether, unless they are integral to the organization's name.[7]

What Is in a Name?

Early personal computers had name length limitations. In general, you could create a file name that had eight characters and then a period and then a three-character extension that explained what the file format was. This meant that, in a law firm, you often had to truncate common words and you might end up with a lot of files that looked the same:

- complain.doc
- motsummj.wpd
- dinterrg.doc

The files were distinguishable because of the folders in which they were placed. A file that was mis-filed into a different folder might be copied on top of the same-named file belonging to a different client. It is one reason that you should consider being as detailed as possible in your filenames. A detailed filename is unlikely to be duplicated and cause a file to be overwritten by mistake due to a shared name.

This limitation has fallen, although there are still limits to how long a filename can be. As you start to think about how you are going to organize your

6. Stop words are words that are frequently ignored in keyword searches too, so no matter how you deal with them, they may not be used when you go seeking a file. The question you should ask yourself is whether you will remember that the stop words like *the* have been removed or displaced for easier alphabetical organization. *Stop Word*, Wikipedia (last visited Aug. 29, 2025), https://en.wikipedia.org/wiki/Stop_word.

7. For example, The Ohio State University has a trademark in the word "the." *Ohio State University Trademarks 'The'*, N.Y. Times (June 23, 2022), https://www.nytimes.com/2022/06/23/us/the-ohio-state-university.html. Sometimes a stop word will have meaning to your client's brand, so you should keep that in mind when you are interacting with them. If you drop off a stop word to make your files easier to navigate, you will want to add it back in any letters or correspondence you send them.

documents, consider how your naming convention will impact your ability to retrieve the documents. If you found those example names above confusing or short on information, think about what would make your filenames more meaningful:

- 20250304 Complaint.docx
- 20250402 Defendant's Answer and Counterclaim.docx
- 20250414 Motion for Summary Judgment CV-124019.docx

You should definitely use full words or, so long as you are likely to remember them, clear abbreviations such that, when you are trying to find information, you are not having to guess at how you named a file. You might include information like the date of the document, which would allow you to sort your files based on date order. You might include the case file number given by the court so that, if a document is accidentally placed in the wrong folder and you are naming files with client numbers, it will be visible because the file number will be different from adjacent files.

The filename is not your only organizational tool, though. You can also use folders to organize your files, to keep files belonging to different clients separate as well as to distinguish between types of documents within a single client matter. For example, a simple set of folders might be:

- Able, Michael
    - Correspondence
    - Evidence
    - Pleadings
    - Research

Ideally, the folder structure you create would *be the same* across different clients. In that way, you could improve the likelihood that, if you are looking for an original letter or a draft of a document filed with the court, you would know in which folder it is likely to be found. You do not need to be foolishly consistent. If you engage in both litigation and transactional work where there is rarely a pleading, you do not need to create an empty *pleadings* folder for the sake of adhering to a standard.

The other thing to consider with your folder names is that you may want them to be briefer than your filenames. Since you are likely to have a standard convention for the names of folders, a shorter name or abbreviation may be a better choice. This is particularly true because, in the Windows-based system which will be the most common in law practice, there is still a limit on how many characters can go into a filename *and* the folders in which it sits. If the file *path*, which is the combination of filename and folder names, is more than 260 characters, the file may become irretrievable. For example, any file that is placed inside Michael Able's pleadings folder:

c:\users\wheland\documents\able michael\pleadings
--------10--------10--------10--------10--------10 = 50

cannot be longer than 205 characters because the folder names in the path consume 50 of the available 260 characters. There are ways to work around this limitation, but you may find that overly long filenames and folders cause problems for you in the future when you are attempting to backup and recover files or move them to a new storage device or even send them to colleagues as email attachments. In some cases, you can rename a file in such a way that, while it is accessible where it is placed, it cannot be moved or backed up to a new storage medium.

I would recommend finding a balance, naming your files as clearly and completely as you can using a mixture of words and abbreviations. You are unlikely to create a file name that is over 200 characters long. At the same time, if you can find ways to shorten your folder names to save space, it cannot hurt. You will need to balance the technological limitations of your systems with the need to be efficient at finding and retrieving information.

Metadata

One reason that you do not need to overthink your filenames and folders is that they are utilized in just one retrieval method, browsing. Folders and files allow us to browse through our information quickly and visually, and thus well-thought-out filenames can make retrieval of those documents more efficient. Whatever document management system you end up using, however, whether it is the folders and files of a Windows computer or an online document manager or a Microsoft SharePoint installation, you will almost certainly also have access to a text-based search that can look beyond just the outwardly visible filenames and folder structure. This means that your filenames and folder-naming conventions can focus on improving how browsable the folder system is. They will not act as the only method for finding and retrieving files.

Search will not be hindered by short or abbreviated filenames so long as you are able to search the contents of the files you are storing and organizing. While Windows does not, by default, turn on indexing for the contents of files, you can enable that. Online file storage systems will generally index the contents of files by default. If you are uploading and storing your files on Microsoft OneDrive or Google Drive, your searches may be able to retrieve documents based on their contents without you having to specifically make that configuration change. Some documents like PDFs may not be searchable while others, like Word .docx files, are usually fully indexed when uploaded to common cloud storage providers.

Neither retrieval method—search nor browse—is superior to the other in all cases. You will have a personal preference for how you access your files. You may prefer to browse than to search, or to start with one and use the second as a fallback. Perhaps the system you use has a really good search feature that is superior to its browsing feature, propelling you to always use search. The thing to keep in mind is that you will usually be able to use both methods to access and retrieve the documents you create. This means you should think about both the filenames and folders and also the text you expose to any search functionality.

There has been something of an alternative third path opened up with the appearance of Microsoft SharePoint and its attempt to move away from traditional folder-based hierarchies. In fact, in early implementations of SharePoint, document creators were warned not to use folders because of the filename and folder character limitation issue mentioned above. Microsoft SharePoint has a 400-character limit for folders and files, and so it can lead to the same limitations and problems caused when storing files on a local Windows computer with its 260-character limit.[8]

The solution for SharePoint implementations was to use the information about the file itself, the file's metadata, not just the contents of the file, in order

8. It has some other peculiar limitations as well. For example, a SharePoint document library can have up to 30 million items in it. *SharePoint Limits*, MICROSOFT 365 (last visited June 7, 2025), https://learn.microsoft.com/en-us/office365/servicedescriptions/sharepoint-online-service-description/sharepoint-online-limits [https://web.archive.org/learn.microsoft.com/en-us/office365/servicedescriptions/sharepoint-online-service-description/sharepoint-online-limits]. However, if you attempt to retrieve more than 5,000 of those items at a time, you will be blocked. The items will exist, but SharePoint expects that any search or browse will use metadata filters to limit the number of possible matching files. *Overview of Large Lists and Libraries*, MICROSOFT (last visited Aug. 29, 2025), https://support.microsoft.com/en-us/office/overview-of-large-lists-and-libraries-e2ea4d5d-ec23-4171-95c4-c7f5b5dbfd8a.

to get around the character limitation's impact on folder-based organization. In other words, you could describe the document with a keyword and find that document even if that keyword did not appear within the document itself. For example, you might create a letter on one day and put that creation date in the metadata. The letter itself might be finalized and mailed two days later. The date in the actual letter document, visible to the reader, would be the day it was sent rather than the creation date when you started and named the file, but you can now search on either piece of data.

If you open a Microsoft Word document and click through to the Info screen, you can see the properties for the document. Document properties can include a hyperlink, information about the author, who the author's manager is to help orient yourself within the organizational hierarchy, keywords or tags that apply to the document but that may not be part of the document, and so on. PDF documents contain much of the same types of document properties but can also track information like copyright and embed a long description of the document, like an abstract.

Document properties are data-about-data, otherwise known as *metadata*. They are typically something that is invisible to the person reading or interacting with the document but can be visible to a search engine or computer system. Metadata can be used to enhance and organize files without (or as well as) a folder-based system. In addition to its filename, examples of document metadata can include:

- Dates saved by your word processor, including creation date and last modified date
- The author of the document. If you use a template, the author of the template may be added to the authors of the document
- The file's size and how much space it takes up in storage
- Time spent by anyone working on the file
- Word count, which can be a useful productivity tool but which also may be an important piece of information if you are filing a document with a court that has a word count cap.[9]

9. This may seem minor, but Microsoft Word was redesigned around legal issues related to word count. Lawyers were having filings rejected by the court because Microsoft Word did not always show the words in the footnotes as part of the overall word count; it depended on where you looked within Microsoft Word. But the courts did count footnotes. Now, when you look at Microsoft Word's word count, you can see both and use the one that is appropriate to your situation. See Vermillion v. Corazon Health Inc.,

All of this metadata will be created automatically by Microsoft Word; other word processors will create similar metadata. You can supplement this default metadata with your own. For example, Microsoft Word supports the addition of keywords. You can create a document title that does not appear in the document itself and is also not the filename for the document. Let's take our engagement letter. It can have three different ways of being named, all at the same time:

- **Filename on the storage medium**: 20250303 Letter – Engagement – American Standard Pie Dishes.docx
- **Title inside the document properties**: Engagement Letter to Lucille Berry, President, American Standard Pie Dishes, March 3, 2025
- **The "regarding" line in the body of the actual letter**: American Standard Pie Dishes Engagement on Hole-in-One Dish Matter

Only the last one would be visible if this letter were printed out. But all three can be used to find and organize the document. A search that uses an index that includes the text of this document could use any of the information in any of those three names. Metadata provides a lot of versatility in how you can enhance the information that describes the document.

Your only limitation is really the types of metadata fields that your technology supports. Microsoft Office applications use a standard template for document properties, that extends across all of its applications (Word, Excel, PowerPoint).[10] These are essentially fixed fields. The exception is in the Advanced Properties. In there, you can create your own metadata terms.[11]

---

906 F.3d 696 (7th Cir. 2018), http://media.ca7.uscourts.gov/cgi-bin/rssExec.pl?Submit=Display&Path=Y2018/D10-24/C:18-1517:J:Easterbrook:aut:T:op:N:2239288:S:0 [http://web.archive.org/web/20240831082502/http://media.ca7.uscourts.gov/cgi-bin/rssExec.pl?Submit=Display&Path=Y2018/D10-24/C:18-1517:J:Easterbrook:aut:T:op:N:2239288:S:0].

10. Microsoft Office products—Word, PowerPoint, Excel, and so on—also support a more extended set of metadata in the Advanced Properties menu. *View or Change the Properties for an Office File*, MICROSOFT (last visited May 28, 2025), https://support.microsoft.com/en-us/office/view-or-change-the-properties-for-an-office-file-21d604c2-481e-4379-8e54-1dd4622c6b75#viewcreate16 [http://web.archive.org/web/20250528140226/https:/support.microsoft.com/en-us/office/view-or-change-the-properties-for-an-office-file-21d604c2-481e-4379-8e54-1dd4622c6b75#viewcreate16]. You would want to adopt a specific process to ensure that these advanced data elements are used by everyone in the law practice and in a consistent way, since they are not obvious when looking at a document's properties.

11. Microsoft SharePoint supports extensive metadata, including what is called managed metadata. This is far beyond the scope of this coursebook, but large law firms

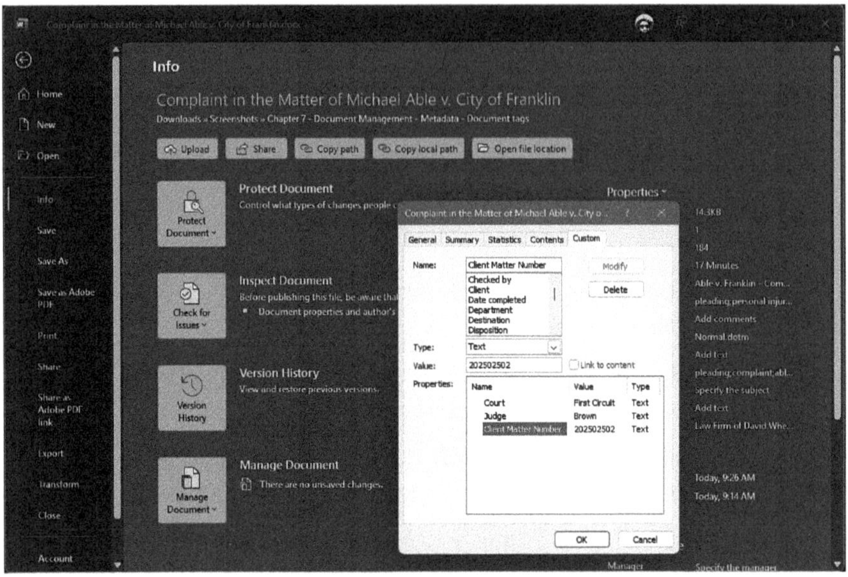

Figure 11: Microsoft Word pleading.dotx advanced metadata properties

You can create new metadata on the fly, but the better way would be to create your document templates—for a brief, motion, letter to a client, letter to a court, billing statement, and so on—and place the custom fields inside that template. In that way, you can ensure that each document created using the template will have access to the same fields. It also saves you and your staff or other lawyers from having to create them from scratch each time you create a new document and minimizes the risk that someone will forget to include one.

Here is an example. I created a blank pleading template. It might contain the case style and the basic components of the pleading but otherwise would be empty of client- or case-specific information. When it is invoked, it would create a new barebones pleading template that someone could then fill out without having to format from scratch.

Before I saved it, I entered the Advanced Properties area and selected the Custom Properties tab. I added three new metadata elements: court, judge,

will likely use managed metadata—as a way of turning the metadata into a controlled vocabulary—in ways that smaller law firms will not. *Introduction to Managed Metadata in SharePoint*, MICROSOFT (last visited Aug. 30, 2025), https://support.microsoft.com/en-us/office/introduction-to-managed-metadata-in-sharepoint-b324aebd-67ab-45a8-933d-ceedb2d909ea.

and client and matter number. The template shows them populated, but the populated field just shows an example of what should be there. Each one would be modified by the document creator.

The custom properties can have very simple validation. You can have text, a date, a number, or even a yes/no checkbox. By selecting the most appropriate one, you can improve the likelihood of the right data going into the field. For example, if your client and matter number is always numbers, then selecting the number type when you create your metadata property can help to enforce that the field will only accept numbers.

You can start to imagine how you might be able to use this. Wouldn't it be great to have all of your documents searchable by client matter without having to put those numbers in the documents' filenames? Or to be able to find every document filed with a specific judge or in a specific court, so that you can quickly re-use successful arguments or find a legal research starting point that you had already developed?

You may also start to picture some of the risks it could create, since you may not see all of the data that the document contains if you are only looking at the "print layout" view of the document, the way it looks when it is printed. Metadata travels with the document, so when you re-use a document or create a second version of it, the original metadata is brought forward as well. There are obvious risks in re-use, where you intermingle client data or you retain strategy or details from an earlier version of a document. Imagine sharing a contract with an opposing party who can see the different iterations of your strategy as you made changes to the document?

You should also be thinking about your duty of confidentiality. Metadata is a primary source of risk when you are communicating with others about your client's legal work. If you are sharing documents in their own formats, you can perform some clean up in advance. Microsoft Office products, on the same information screen as the metadata itself, will have an *inspect document* feature. This will allow you to scrub the metadata from a file being sent outside of the law practice or even to another lawyer within your firm, if there is an ethical wall of which you have to be mindful.

The risk that metadata poses to professional responsibility for lawyers is such that there is a large marketplace of redacting and metadata scrubbing tools. In larger law firms, through their document management processes, metadata may automatically be wiped clean as part of any document being saved. Microsoft Outlook and Exchange email systems can be configured to warn if attachments are sent that contain personally identifiable information

(PII) like credit card numbers. They can also warn if a document is being sent outside the law firm, to remind a lawyer or staff person to check for metadata or other inadvertent information sharing.

Some of this is harder to accomplish in a solo practice or small law firm, where document management systems may not be used, due to cost or complexity. If everyone is using shared storage, on an internal file server or on a shared cloud storage provider, then the lack of automation will need to be made up with increased process and oversight. The good thing is that most metadata can be added once, when the file is created, and can be removed once, when the document is finalized and distributed to outside recipients.

Keep in mind, though, that once it has been scrubbed and the document is saved, that metadata is gone. This is particularly challenging in our always-connected, cloud-based law practices and legal organizations. If you open a document from Microsoft OneDrive or SharePoint, it will often be set to auto-save your changes back to the storage location. When you scrub the metadata from that file, that change will be saved back to your default location too. You would need to ensure you have version controls on so that you could return to a previous version if you needed to access a copy with the metadata still intact.

There are a few ways to work around this sort of issue. The first is to create a final copy without the metadata. For example, once a document is entirely finalized, save it as a new document, perhaps adding "final" to the filename. Then scrub the metadata from that *final* file. Now you can save it a final time with a name that shows it is the same as the final document but that is metadata-free. You can also use Microsoft's version control, available on both OneDrive and SharePoint (although it may need to be turned on), to return to a previous version of a document. You could return to the pre-scrubbed version in this manner. I think using versioning is a rather convoluted approach and that having a standard approach to creating a final document will be easier to adopt and to teach others.

An easier method is to avoid creating duplicate versions of your editable document. When you are ready to send it out to someone else, print it to a portable document format (or save as PDF). This will eliminate much of the metadata you would not want to share—like tracked changes or comments and revisions you and your staff made to the document—while still retaining some of the basic metadata (author, title, creation date). No method is entirely foolproof except to print off a document in a paper format, which will strip away all of the metadata. Although you could still print comments

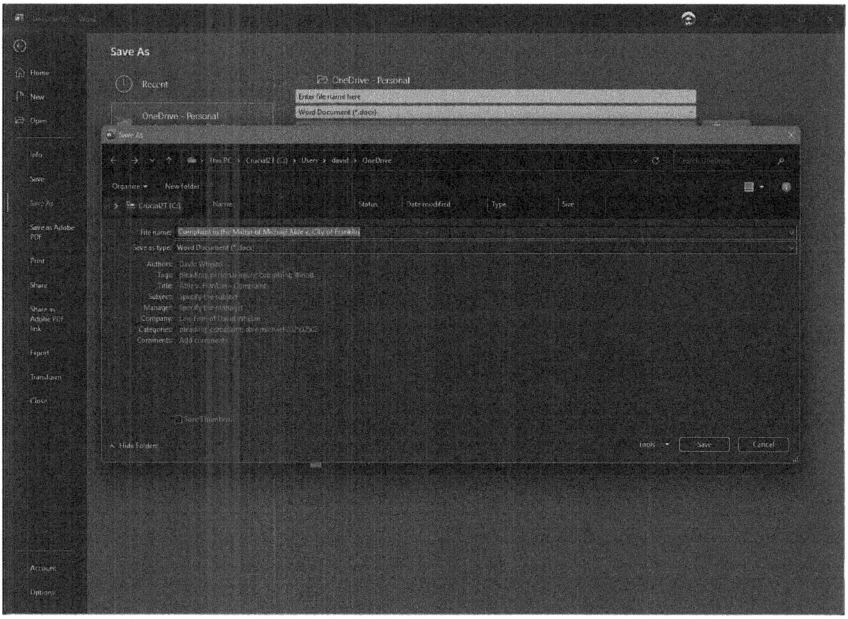

Figure 12: A screenshot of Microsoft Word's save screen

and revisions, you would most likely see them upon reviewing the paper document.

A best practice for you as you start to create and manage documents is to start to practice adding this metadata to each document as you work. It is a habit—although if you are using a document management system, it can be enforced by the software so that you cannot save a file without adding the required metadata—that you can build as you start your law practice. When you get ready to save a document in Microsoft Word, you can start to apply tags and a clear title to the document.

That is the baseline, though. If you click on the Microsoft Word File tab and look at Info, you should be able to access the broader array of metadata properties. This is where you can place additional information that will help you to organize and retrieve the document in the future. This will take some planning.

As with tags and labels, discussed above under emails and calendaring, you will want to have a controlled vocabulary so that everyone is using the same keywords. Some personal choice can come into these tags as well. You may use a particular keyword to describe a document or type of matter or stage of creation of the document. If someone else uses a different word, it will not create a conflict. Keywords and tags in documents can support multiple entries. Each person who touches it can add tags that help them retrieve the document in their own manner. A balance of personal keywords and shared ones is possible so long as documents can be found and retrieved efficiently.

Storage Locations

This chapter has mostly focused on process and metadata. That is because your document management is mostly about process and metadata, enabling storage and retrieval of documents. Indexing and searching the contents of files will be the easy part; it is the extra metadata layer, in filenames and folders and within the document, that takes planning. It is important to think about how you will organize it—using files and folders or tags and metadata—and how you will retrieve it. These choices will lead you towards the technology that is most suitable to your needs.

Document management is an area where cloud computing has leveled the playing field. Cloud storage providers like Microsoft and Google have enhanced what might otherwise be a barebones storage tool with more versatile document management capabilities. Since they are likely to use it as a storage location, a solo lawyer may be as likely to use Microsoft 365 and OneDrive for document management as a large firm lawyer is. OneDrive is a consumer-oriented storage product, but Microsoft has been increasingly blurring the line between it and SharePoint, which is the more likely storage option at the largest law firms if they are not using a law firm-specific document management product. A Microsoft 365 user may click on their OneDrive app icon and be taken to a MySharePoint site with some of the features of both OneDrive and SharePoint, like a SharePoint lite.

The common theme we have seen in other areas continues here, though. Solo practitioners are much less likely to have dedicated document management and retrieval software—beyond what they get with their Microsoft Office subscription—and large law firm lawyers have almost fully adopted it.[12] The cost and complexity of a dedicated application may not make sense in a

12. Am. Bar Ass'n, 2023 Legal Technology Survey Report: Law Office Technology 28, question 23a-I (2024). 39% of solos responded that document or records management software is available to them while 96% of survey respondents in firms with more than 500 lawyers had access to it. Notably, nearly 29% of solos say they personally use document management software, while there is a much bigger drop among large law firms, where only about 80% of lawyers actually use it themselves. *Id.* at 36, question 23b-b.

solo or small lawyer practice. The lack of the existence of a document management app does not mean that solos and small firm practitioners are not engaged in the process and metadata aspects of document management.

A solo practitioner may also use a simpler file storage system than a large law firm is likely to have and yet have a very similar experience. Consumer-oriented networked attached storage (NAS) can act as a simple file server for a law practice of any size.[13] Large law firms may prefer to use file servers, large storage computers with redundant storage disks, instead of the cloud for reasons of security or isolation or business recovery. The fundamentals for the technology—creating a standardized file and folder structure, using consistent naming conventions and metadata—will be the same no matter how complex the actual implementation is.

Document management systems are one of the earliest law practice technologies that has existed. Even before practice management applications, document management systems were being adopted by and designed for lawyers. This is understandable given that, while the contents of the documents that lawyers create are often unique to the legal profession, the need to manage documents is universal to any business that creates them.

File names, folder structures, naming conventions, controlled vocabulary, use of metadata—all of those are challenges that any business might face. Similarly, the cultural challenges of ensuring that everyone engages with documents in a consistent way, both in the creation of the document and the cleaning of it before it is shared, are common across many types of businesses.

This can mean that, while there are document management applications that have focused on the legal profession over the years, there is a broader marketplace of products available. You might consider document management applications used by other types of professionals or organizations when you are building your selection list. These products will provide features that go

13. It is not always clear what people mean when they use the term "server." For our purposes, a server is a computer that has been designed to provide a particular function. It uses the same components as a desktop computer in most cases—at least one hard drive for storage, RAM memory for operations, at least one central processing unit CPU), and so on—although usually more of them than a typical lawyer's personal computer and it will normally use a variant of a common operating system, like Windows Server or a version of Linux. In this case, a file server acts as a high-availability computer for lawyers and staff to quickly access the entire organization's shared files and folders. The design of the computer and the additional components will make it faster at delivering its specific function, like serving files or serving email, than a normal desktop computer would if it was trying to perform the same task.

beyond the mere document storage that you can do on OneDrive or Google Drive. It is in those extra features that you may be able to find opportunities to work in a more secure fashion or find productivity gains.

Workflows and Automation

One example is the use of the document workflow. This is an automated process that can emulate parts of your manual process. We will look at document automation further on but, as it is a key part of document management, we can take a sneak peek now. Let's look at an example of how a simple document workflow might be designed.

In our example, your first year in law practice has been financially and professionally successful, and you have so much business you have hired a staff person to help you. They are now creating the first draft of your letters, using a template and merging data from your client records. When they have finished the draft, they email you to let you know. This is a manual workflow: staff person creates, email sent, you review and revise, you may email back to the staff person, repeat. It can create a lot of emails, creating productivity challenges that offset the benefits of offloading the drafting of letters.

You can create an automated workflow that eliminates all of those emails. Instead, once the staff person has created the letter and saved it, the workflow that the letter drafting is a part of will cause you to be notified. This may be as an email, but it does not have to be. Also, unlike having to manage emails that are largely just prompts to look at the document, you can usually see a workflow's progress from being initiated to completion. If you are wondering where a document is in process—who is currently working on it, for example—this can be visible in an automated workflow in a way that is not when people are communicating via text or emails as the process wends along between inboxes.

The challenge with a workflow is that you need to have an application that will support it. This is not the sort of thing that is available out of the box, so to speak, with Microsoft Word or OneDrive. A law firm that wants to use workflows will need a specific application that supports them, in order to create them but also to have them fire off when the tasks in the workflow occur.

Again, because so many people need to manage documents, it is unsurprising that there are a number of ways you can find to automate document management processes. A simple approach would just be to drop a file-in-progress into a specific folder. When you saw a new file there, you would know it was ready for you to work on it. This is a digital equivalent to a paper-based inbox or incoming mail tray. You can ignore a letter or document until it appears in that tray.

Cloud computing provides some interesting intermediate approaches that do not require more complicated software to create a workflow. The goal is to find a tool that, when one action occurs, it then causes a second one to occur. In programming terms, this is often referred to as an "if-then" statement or "if this, then that." That also happens to be the name of one of the workflow tools—IFTTT—which, along with another product called Zapier, have been developed to create workflows. For example, our new staff person could save the file in a specific folder on your shared OneDrive storage. If you have given access to a workflow tool that is monitoring that folder, it can initiate the next step in the workflow: send you a message? Add something to your calendar so that you have a document review scheduled? Workflows do not need to be simple communication replacements. You can have them take on additional functionality in your process.

If this sounds a bit like artificial intelligence, that is understandable. The edges of automation and AI are blurry, and you may have options to have an AI agent act in a way that is similar to a more methodical automation tool. The main difference is that an automated workflow is designed to follow very specific rules, and some AI agents may be susceptible to creating their own interpretation of steps.

SharePoint used to have a built-in workflow process, but it is most likely that any SharePoint installation you use now will have dropped that internal functionality. Originally called Microsoft Flow and now called Microsoft Power Automate, it functions very much like Zapier or IFTTT. From a lawyer's perspective, it has the added benefit of not requiring you to open remote access to your client files via a third-party product. It is not free, but it comes with most business- or enterprise-level Microsoft 365 licenses. This is one place where using a consumer or *home and family* version of Microsoft products will exclude you from functionality. While consumer-oriented software can be attractively priced for a sole practitioner, it is usually better to license the business-specific versions of an application to ensure you get all of the features and functionality that are likely to help you practice law.

By now, it will be unsurprising to learn that Microsoft Power Automate provides a wide variety of templates. Just like templates in other areas of your law practice, they are pre-designed workflows. You can customize them, but they are designed to be used without a lot of technical knowledge. There is a whole category devoted to approval processes, which could get you started when you and your staff are working on drafting a letter or other shared document.

These workflow templates can allow you to start to blur the lines between your different office systems. You may have received emails from the opposing counsel and the court with files included as attachments. There is a Power Automate workflow to move Outlook email attachments to a Microsoft One-Drive or Google Drive storage account.

Microsoft SharePoint is not a document management system. But you can manage documents on it, and it is an excellent document manager, with a bit of planning and maintenance. There are also other popular applications used by large law firms for document management, including NetDocuments and iManage.[14] They all do far more than simply manage documents, but you will need to evaluate whether that functionality is necessary for your law practice. The reason that lawyers at all firm sizes, including solos, would consider a dedicated document management application is that it eliminates the need for you, as the lawyer, to create all of the manual processes, metadata functionality, and workflows. You are exchanging your time to create and maintain those systems with the money required to license someone else's work.

This exchange—time and money—is the most common one within the practice of law when it comes to technology. As a law student, it is too early to know whether you need the power and complexity of integrated systems like practice management or document management. You may decide you want to create your own processes, to learn how you practice law best, before engaging with technology that may require you to work in a very specific way. It is one reason that I think law practice-specific software remains relatively unadopted in the vast majority of law firms, which are solo and small law firm practices. Solo lawyers may find that their manual or slightly automated system is *good enough* such that the cost required to move to a more sophisticated system may be outweighed by the lack of true need.

---

14. A quick look at International Legal Technology Association (ILTA) surveys over the years will show that the same product names continue to appear, year after year. When you are considering a document management application, it will be relatively easy to identify and evaluate contenders focused on the legal profession.

Planning for the End

All good things come to an end. So does a client's matter and your representation of them. As you start to think about how you will manage documents as they are created, also be considering how you will archive them or store them once the client matter is closed. Your document management strategy, which will include all of those other documents like emails and text messages and perhaps even voice mail recordings, needs to be flexible. You should be able to export or otherwise move closed files out of your primary document management system, whatever it is.

One reason for this is to keep your open matters in as uncluttered a system as possible. As you add more data to a database or file storage system, it can take longer to search and retrieve. If you are moving closed files out once the client's matter is resolved, you are helping your systems operate at their most efficient. Since documents can be a significant part of the client's digital file, decluttering your document management system should make working with your open matters easier.

You can always keep your closed files on hand. They do not need to disappear to offline storage. You may want to access them if a client calls up with a question or you may find that you left work product in the client file and want to retrieve it to create a new template. Whatever the case may be, it is worth thinking about how the information you are putting onto storage media and into folders, or into a document management platform, will get back out of it again once your representation of the client is over. Skip to the last chapter for more on closing your case files.

Chapter 9 Exercises

A. Create a new document in Microsoft Word that you will turn into a template or precedent. After creating the document, and before saving, edit the full properties of the document to add useful metadata about the document's purpose or qualities. Remember that these are to describe the document *in the future* to eliminate the need for new document creators to have to re-key it. Save the file as a template file (.dotx). Open the template so that it creates a new document (.docx) and view the metadata. Use the Protect functionality to purge the metadata from the new document (.docx) before saving it.

B. Create a list of metadata that does not exist in Microsoft Word's default document template but that you think would be useful to help you organize documents. As a starting point, think about your law school classes: how would you segment your documents: by class? By professor? By year? By document type (outline, memo, and so on). Note the similarity with practice document metadata. If it is a court-related document, what data might help you describe the court or the process? If it is a transactional document, what data might help you distinguish it from other, similarly named documents (like contracts, or real estate transactions, or types of trusts)?

C. Create a simple two-step workflow using Power Automate or a similar process trigger tool (like Zapier or IFTTT). You can design it yourself, customize a template, or use the AI functionality to describe your desired workflow and have it automatically generated. Test it and tweak it until it works the way you expect it to and can be repeated. For the purposes of this exercise, try to focus on something related to documents: moving them, approving them, notifications, etc.

Chapter 10

Communications

You will have spent most of your time in law school communicating, one way or another. Sometimes you will have done it orally, but, by and large, you will have left a huge number of written communications—your course memoranda, your essay exams, and any number of postings to your law school's learning management system and emails to your classmates and professors. Communication is a key part of law practice as well, and your professional obligations will require you to think about it differently from how you may have up to now. Perhaps the most vital communication tool in the modern law practice is the venerable email.

The Model Rules of Professional Conduct discuss communication very directly in Rule 1.4.[1] It is not just that a lawyer must communicate, but they should do so in a timely manner, they will need to be consultative, and perhaps key, they will need to keep the client informed. It may surprise you, but failure to adequately communicate is a top reason for complaints against lawyers. You will want to consider how, when, and what you communicate before you start your law practice. These are both habits for you but also a matter of setting—and meeting—expectations for your clients.

1. A.B.A. Model Rules of Professional Conduct, r. 1.4 (Am. Bar Ass'n 2025).

Technology Overtakes In-Person

Law practice is about helping people or their organizations solve legal issues. Despite this being a people-centric profession, lawyers are reporting that they are engaging in less face-to-face contact than they are technology-enabled contact with their clients. While all lawyers are meeting with their clients face-to-face, not even half meet with them regularly in-person.[2] This number is over 50% for solo practitioners but drops below 25% for lawyers in the largest law firms. Instead, email and telephones (and voicemail) are the dominant communications methods.[3] Lawyers are far more likely to use telephones for voice calls than to use them for text or simple messaging (SMS).[4]

Practice Pointer

There can be a strategic reason to using voice instead of a text-based record of a communication. Unlike an email or SMS text message, a voice call is usually not transcribed or recorded. To that extent, it can provide a way of communicating with a client or someone else without leaving the same sort of trail of information that a "document" might. At the same time, if you use phones for calls with your clients, be aware of your surroundings and theirs to ensure that, while the call itself may not leave any traces, people who can hear the call at either end are not ending up with privileged information.

This shift reinforces the perception—and possibly the reality, in some law practices—that time is of the essence in client communications. Since you do not need to wait for a meeting with someone but can engage in asynchronous communication like texting, it can feel like communication is both fast and

2. Am. Bar Ass'n, 2023 Legal Technology Survey Report: Marketing & Communications Technology 75 question 71a (2024). 45% of lawyers responding to the survey met face-to-face regularly with clients.

3. *Id.* at 75, question 71b-c. 86% of lawyers regularly communicate by telephone and voicemail and 92% regularly communicate by email. There is not a substantial difference in law firm size in telephone or email usage.

4. *Id.* at 76, question 71g. 18% of lawyers report using text messaging regularly with clients while 19% never do. Text messaging is more common in solo practices than it is in large law firms, but only 23% of solos report regularly texting clients (only 7.5% of large law firm lawyers do).

requires immediate responses. This can quickly become a time management issue and use up resources, like your attention, that you need to focus on your exercise of professional judgment and expertise.

Like so much of law practice technology, the technology is really the easy part. It is functionally easy to send an email or text message and perhaps easier to receive a reply. There are processes to consider, though, to help you to use email and other online communication tools effectively. The more you think about these in advance of starting law practice, the better able you will be to select technology that fits and supports how you want to practice law. Law schools will say they teach students to *think like a lawyer* and part of that is to be deliberative. Apply this sense of deliberation—thinking about what your client is asking and responding to that question, which may require legal research or other analysis or even just some time to think it over—despite your technical ability to respond immediately.

A good starting point is to be clear about how you plan to communicate with your clients and when. There is a view that lawyers need to be available around the clock to deal with client matters, but I think that is perhaps not as true as it is a perception. In light of data around poor lawyer mental health—greater than average substance abuse and suicide for starters—it is worth considering how you will balance your work, one part of your life, with the other important parts of your life.[5] This is particularly true in law firms where there may be an expectation of around-the-clock access, perhaps as a part of "paying one's dues," that can lead to burnout. Consider when you will be available, and how, and to whom. Once you have determined what works best for you, be clear in how you communicate that to your clients and be consistent in your implementation.

---

5. One in 5 lawyers reported problematic drinking and considerably higher mental health issues. The research also found that, unlike other professions, these issues were higher in early career lawyers than in lawyers who had been in practice longer. Patrick Krill, Ryan Johnson & Linda Albert, *The Prevalence of Substance Use and Other Mental Health Concerns Among American Attorneys*, 10 J. ADDICTION MED 46 (2016), https://journals.lww.com/journaladdictionmedicine/fulltext/2016/02000/the_prevalence_of_substance_use_and_other_mental.8.aspx. 8.5% of lawyers in a second survey reported suicidal ideation, double that of the general working population. Patrick Krill, Hannah Thomas, Meaghyn Kramer, Nikki Degeneffe & Justin Anker, *Stressed, Lonely, and Over-Committed: Predictors of Lawyer Suicide Risk*, 11 HEALTHCARE 536 (2023), https://www.mdpi.com/2227-9032/11/4/536 [http://web.archive.org/web/20250610215121/https://www.mdpi.com/2227-9032/11/4/536].

Email

Email has been a central communication tool for the legal profession since the early 2000s. It is probably hard to imagine a time when lawyers did not use email. It has become more and more central to our communication but creates new challenges in how we use it as new automation and artificial intelligence is added to our email systems.

Email technology is perhaps the most generic application that a lawyer will use. Unlike a lot of other tools that lawyers use in practice, though, it has two components. One is the email client, which allows you to compose and send emails and to receive and process them. The other is the email server, a computer that manages the delivery and receipt of emails in the background and the place where your email lives and is stored. If you have heard the term *client-server* networking, email is a good example of it. You need both components to use email.

Clients and Servers

A server can support a wide variety of functions. Remember how we discussed document management? That involves storing your documents on a file server, whether you create your own folders or use a document management system. A server is just another type of computer, compared to a desktop or laptop, and is configured in a way that allows it to provide this background functionality.[6]

An email server, then, is a computer designed with the goal of sending and receiving email. It will use email server software (the most common product name for email servers in law firms is Microsoft Exchange, but it is not the only email server). In a sense, it provides a workflow: it watches for when you click the send button on your email client, and then it goes to work. It ensures the email can be sent, then it transmits it. If there is a problem with the transmission, it will alert you (often by a returned email). If it reaches the destination, it will take note of that. If you have enabled a request for a "receipt"

6. Server computers used to primarily mean a piece of hardware that looked like a desktop computer or a near variation. Most larger or more complex organizations that use the term server now are likely to be referring to *virtualized* servers. You may have multiple virtual servers running on a single physical piece of equipment. It can be easiest to think of a server as a physical object when learning about which device does what in your law practice, but you should not assume that it will be in reality.

that your email has been viewed—and your recipient allows that receipt to be transmitted—you may actually know when it has been opened. Any responses to your email will be received by it and placed in the appropriate inbox, where you can retrieve and use them in your email client.

Your email server will probably be invisible to you. Servers tend to be high-risk, highly technical resources and are supported by dedicated technology staff. If you join a law firm with an IT staff, they will manage that part of the email process. If you start a solo practice or join a small firm, the email server is likely to be provided to you by Microsoft, in the case of a Microsoft 365 license, or Google, through a Google Workspace license. If you have a website, you may also have an email server built-in to your subscription (since the website will use a domain name just the same as your email address). In all of these cases, though, the lawyer is rarely the person monitoring the availability of the email server and ensuring it is updated and secured.

An email client application is what enables you to work with the email you send and receive. It is different from other applications you use—like Microsoft Word or Excel—in that you need the special functionality of the email server to use email at all. If you create a spreadsheet in Excel, for example, you can save it to your OneDrive or to a USB flash drive or somewhere else. The file will open again in Excel or a compatible viewing application without any additional software; you do not need a spreadsheet server. Email clients will only work with a server that knows how to, and is configured properly to, send and receive email.[7]

Unlike a word processor, which requires some format compatibility to open a file created in a different program, email clients are largely interchangeable. This is due in large part to the fact that email servers use a few basic protocols (IMAP, SMTP, and POP3) to send and receive email. As long as your email client supports the protocols that your email server uses, you can use it for sending and receiving email.

7. Email servers increasingly need to be configured to interact with each other in a secure and authentic manner. Email configuration involves functions like SPF, DKIM, and DMARC to authenticate that the server that appears to be sending the email is actually the sending email server. *What are DMARC, DKIM, and SPF?*, CLOUDFLARE (last visited June 2, 2025), https://www.cloudflare.com/learning/email-security/dmarc-dkim-spf/ [http://web.archive.org/web/20250602234845/https://www.cloudflare.com/learning/email-security/dmarc-dkim-spf/]. Incorrectly configured email servers may cause your email to appear as spam to the recipient's email server, resulting in your email being rejected before it is even delivered to your recipient's spam folder.

Even if you decide to license Microsoft 365 for the office suite and the email support, you do not need to use Microsoft Outlook as your email client. Microsoft offers hosted email through its Microsoft 365 and Exchange services but the email server will talk to a huge number of email clients. Outlook? Check. Thunderbird? Check. K9 Email? Check. Decide to use an Apple Macintosh? Apple Mail, Canary, and many others work fine with Microsoft email servers. Some lawyers use a distribution of Linux. They also will have no problem sending and receiving email (and many email servers run on Linux even if you are sending your email from a Windows computer using Microsoft Outlook).

If you have an email client that you are comfortable with, there is no particular reason for you to switch to Microsoft Outlook. Many lawyers will use Microsoft Outlook by default, merely because their law firm uses it or they have paid for it as part of the license that gets them access to Microsoft Word.[8] It is just as common to use one email application on your desktop or laptop, like Microsoft Outlook, and a different one on your phone or tablet. Again, this is because email applications are looking at your email server and, so long as the client supports the server's sending and receiving protocols, there is no issue of app compatibility.

If the selection of the technology is not a particular issue—and it shouldn't be, as email clients tend to be free-to-use and easy to install—then the use of it by lawyers can be the tricky area. In particular, you want to make sure that what you are sending and to whom you are sending it is correct.

Email Recipients

The first place that you should focus in your email is what is also generally the first line of the email: the TO line, the person or people you are sending the email to. Many email applications will look at your contacts list and suggest possible matches. As you type, it may pop in a full email address. If you are not careful, you may find that you have selected or accepted a suggested address that is, in fact, the wrong one.

8. Until recently, Microsoft confusingly had more than one version of Outlook (Outlook v. Outlook Classic, which had different feature sets) and, in the past, has included default mail applications like Outlook Express and Microsoft Mail on their Windows platforms that lack a lot of the functionality of the full Outlook email client. When you are considering your email application, be sure to open it up and confirm that it is Microsoft Outlook, if that is what you are hoping to use.

Microsoft Outlook calls these suggestions *auto-complete*, and it is a feature that is worth disabling. It is a small thing to have to open up your address book—you can double click on the TO line to open your contacts—and manually select the address you need. It is better to do this than to have the alternative occur. Lawyers have violated confidentiality by sending emails to the wrong person and have also ceded lawyer-client privilege. Once the cat is out of the bag, it is hard to put it back in.

Practice Pointer

Some lawyers will use a signature block that suggests that the email is confidential and can only be used by the person for whom it is intended. In fact, according to an ABA survey, a confidential message in an email is the leading—66% of respondents—security precaution lawyers take when sending privileged communications.[9] Email signature blocks are not a way to mitigate the risk of sending the email to the wrong recipient. For one thing, most confidentiality blocks are placed below the confidential information, so it has been exposed before the warning is visible. Secondly, there is no way for the lawyer to enforce that confidentiality. The best way to avoid having a breach of confidentiality is to not send the communication to the wrong person.

One approach that can help is to leave the addressing step for last. Skip over the TO lines—and the CC and BCC if they are available—and type in your Subject line. Then type your entire email, focusing on the actual task at hand. If you have files to attach, attach them. Once you are finished, return to the TO line and select the correct recipients. This will mean that you are not thinking about your email content while trying to locate your recipient. You can select your contact with a clear head.

9. Am. Bar Ass'n, 2023 Legal Technology Survey Report: Marketing & Communications Technology 74, question 70 (2024). 66% of all respondents said that they "rely on confidentiality statement in message body" when sending confidential or privileged information. 24% of respondents rely on the use of "Confidential" in the email subject line. Only 44% indicated they used encryption and 25% used passwords, which are actual security precautions. 8% took no precautions.

Also, consider when you can and cannot use BCC in your emails.[10] If you are emailing people in government, you may have limitations on what you can and cannot send as a BCC. For example, if you are working with a public agency's governance board, emails to the board may create a risk of violating an open meeting statute. You might use BCC to ensure that everyone gets the message but that, if someone decides to reply to it, the reply goes only to you and does not violate an open meeting requirement.[11]

Professional Email Addresses

You may wonder how you will get your own email address with your firm name in it. It is usually as easy as selecting and registering a domain name. This is the part of an email address that follows the "@". A domain name is an inexpensive investment in your law practice, and you can acquire it even before you graduate and head out to practice. Common ".com" domains can be registered for about $10 a year. There are also more unusual top-level domains (.com, .edu, and .us are examples of top-level domains) that you can choose from to append to your own domain name: .lawyer, .abogado, .law, .esq and so on.[12] Each of these will have its own cost and cachet.

Different domain names will cost different amounts of money and some will only be available from certain domain name registrars. This may guide where you register it and what your ongoing cost will be.[13] When you are selecting a domain registrar, look at what privacy options are available. You will need to provide information about your street address and a phone number as part of your registration. Normally, this information in the domain name

10. BCC stands for blind carbon copy (CC stands for carbon copy), an archaic way of making duplicates of a paper message by putting a piece of carbon between two pieces of paper when the original document was typed. A BCC is "blind" in that the recipient in the TO line will not know it was sent to the recipient on the BCC.

11. Also keep in mind that someone who is BCC'd on an email that has recipients in the TO or CC line can reply to those recipients. An alternative to using BCC is to forward the message to the recipient you would otherwise BCC. In that way, they will not unwittingly respond to parties who themselves will not know that the BCC recipient also saw the email.

12. The Internet Assigned Numbers Authority (IANA) maintains a list of current approved top-level domains. http://web.archive.org/web/20250612081905/https://data.iana.org/TLD/tlds-alpha-by-domain.txt.

13. If you are considering a domain name that is managed by a foreign country—like .ly for Libya or .tv for Tuvalu or .io for British Indian Ocean Territories—consider the fact that the country can change its domain name registration policy and cause you to lose your domain name.

registry is publicly available. The *whois* protocol allows people to look up domain names and learn information about how it is registered and to whom. If your registration details are not private, anyone using whois can see them.[14]

Domain names are cheap to acquire, but they are a lifetime commitment. While you can acquire multiple domain names, once you start using one for your law firm, you should be planning to use it for a lifetime. Imagine, for example, that you register the domain name *mcguintylawyers.esq*. You practice under that name for a decade, and then you decide to use your law degree in a different way. Perhaps you are elected or appointed as a judge or you join a company as inside counsel or in the C-suite. If you let that domain name registration lapse, it can be registered by someone else. At best, it will be unavailable if you decide to return to private law practice. At worst, a new owner can undermine your law firm branding by presenting itself as you and causing people with links to your website or who are looking for a lawyer to be tricked and exploited.

We are still in the early days of domain name lapse issues with law practices. Lawyers who started practicing at the start of the internet—who could register the first domains—are still practicing. When you consider the current cost of domain names (a dot.com domain is roughly $10–15 a year) and the likely practice lifespan of a lawyer (let's go with 50 years), the cost to maintain a domain name is a pittance compared to the professional risk of letting it lapse. Once you register a domain name, if you use it even once for your law practice, set it up to auto-renew, and keep it active for the lifespan of your law license. Who knows, if it is a particularly novel one, you might be able to sell it with your practice when you retire.

Once you have a domain name you want to use, you can assign it to your email provider (like Microsoft 365 or Google Workspace) or you can license an email hosting service. We will discuss websites below, but if you have a website host, it will often provide free email hosting, and you will use the domain name for both the website and your email system. If you do not have a website host with email, you can have your email hosted separately. In either case, your domain name will be used for your email addresses on that server.

Email is such a common and easy-to-use tool that we might forget that there is a cost to send and receive each one. It is not an individual cost, but

---

14. There are many domain name registrars. I use Cloudflare for my domain names because they are inexpensive and because privacy is part of every domain name registration. When you shop around for a domain name registrar, watch out for privacy being sold as an add-on.

each email has to traverse the internet, landing on other email servers and being sent to and arriving from an email server at either end. Each of those email servers costs money to run. Your email costs will reflect the choice you make as to who will host your email and where.[15]

Phones and Texting

Your phone may not even strike you as a technology choice. We have grown so accustomed to having them available, and the ability to communicate with them now that they are mobile, that they may not feel like a law practice tool. We have moved beyond the stage where law firms prohibited lawyers and staff from using their personal devices, requiring two devices or going without. While many law firms do not have a specific personal device—or "bring your own device"—policy, most allow them to be used.[16]

The commonplace role of phones can belie their value and also some of the security risks that they raise that will impact a lawyer's professional obligations. If your phone has access to your law firm's billing system through an app, can someone who gains control of your phone pay themselves from your bank account? Mobile phones can be secured in many ways without any additional technology. You can place a PIN or other entry restriction on accessing your phone. You can encrypt the storage (or have it automatically encrypted by the phone without your intervention) on many phones. In this way, if a phone is lost, the ability to use it or to use what is on it can be made more difficult for unauthorized access.

15. You can host your own email server and run Microsoft Exchange on it. It will take time and expertise to do it in a way that is secure. It will be the rare lawyer for whom this will make financial or professional sense. If you decide to host your own email server, be sure to hire technical expertise to maintain and monitor it for you.

16. Am. Bar Ass'n, 2023 Legal Technology Survey Report: Technology Basics 41, question 33; *Id.* at 43, question 36. Nearly 30% of lawyers reported that their law firms had a personal technology or BYOD policy. This was understandably lowest in solo practices (13%) and highest in large law firms (77%). 84% of law firms responded that personal devices were allowed, either with or without approval. Solos were much more likely to allow personal devices without restrictions (44%) while large law firms predominantly required restrictions on personal device use (74%).

> **Practice Pointer**
>
> Biometrics and passkeys are two other ways of limiting access to a device. When you consider how to restrict access to your portable device, consider that you may need to enable access to it by a trusted third party in the event you are incapacitated. A biometric, attached as it is literally to your person, and a passkey, that may be locked to a particular device, may create obstacles for people to help you—and your clients who are relying on you—should you be unable to manage your law practice due to illness or death.

Law firms can also use endpoint security. Endpoints can be mobile phones, tablets, laptops, and desktop computers, anything that can run the security software and has access to the law firm's confidential or private information. Endpoint security will be covered more extensively later on, but it is part of how law firms can balance the risk of allowing personal devices with the firm's and lawyers' obligations to protect client information.

Phone selection is another technology choice that really has no preferred outcome. It does not matter if the phone is made by Apple or runs the Android operating system. It may need to have certain specifications or be recent enough to run some law practice or business apps, but this is unlikely to substantially narrow your ability to select a phone. As many productivity and law practice software applications provide a web-based interface, often a mobile-friendly one, the phone need only have an internet connection or a sufficient data plan and a compatible web browser to be able to access common law office resources.

You will probably need to replace your phone every few years, just as you will your laptop or desktop computer. Hardware is improved over time, of course, but beyond the productivity benefit, the companies making the phone operating systems stop updating older versions. In order to ensure your phone remains safe to use with confidential and private client information, it should be able to receive security software updates.

Lawyers use their phones for voice calls more often than they do texting. Keep in mind that, when you are talking on the phone, you may be disclosing client information in a location that makes it possible for other people to hear what you are saying.[17] You would not be the first lawyer to violate confidentiality in this manner, by talking on a phone in a public space or in a shared space like a train, but you do not want to be the next one.

If you plan to use your phone for texting with clients, you will need to think about how you can keep those texts as part of your client's file. This can be a challenge depending on the applications you use for sending text messages. These texts are no different from emails and may contain similar information: photos, links, and other content. If you decide that you are going to communicate with your clients by way of texting, you should have a plan for how you will retain the texts outside of the phone. This may involve being able to export them or back them up.

Similarly, you may want to consider how to keep voicemails. In the past, a phone call from a client might have gone to a person and been transcribed then sent to the lawyer as a phone message. You may want to use a digital version of that system to create a text-based record of a phone message to store with the client file. Automated voicemail transcription may not be overly accurate, however, so you may also want to consider using a voicemail service that sends you a recording of each voicemail. That file can then be saved with the client's other files as a record of what they asked so that you can be sure you are responding, when you email them or call them back, to the specific issue they raised.

You may also want to consider using an internet-based phone system to provide you with additional functionality. For example, a voice-over-IP (VOIP) phone can allow you to have voice mail delivered to you as an email, which you can then make accessible to other people in your office using, for example, an email forwarding rule, so that calls are responded to regardless of your availability. You may be able to have voice mail auto-transcribed so that, if you are in a meeting, you can get the gist of a message without having to listen to it in its audio format. Voice over IP can sometimes provide you with phone access, using a facility's wi-fi network connection for example, when you may not have good phone reception where you are. If nothing else, a VOIP number can act as a backup to your primary number and an alternative to giving out your personal phone number. These features can provide

17. There is also the risk of shoulder surfing, something you may have done without any particular ill-intention. But when we hold our devices to access information on them, someone sitting next to us in a courtroom or on a train may also be able to see what we are doing on the screen. *Shoulder Surfing (Computer Security)*, WIKIPEDIA (last visited Aug. 30, 2025), https://en.wikipedia.org/wiki/Shoulder_surfing_(computer_security).

additional options when you want to balance your need to focus on the task at hand while also being responsive to client or other emergencies.

Social Media

Social media may not feel like a communication in that you may not always be responding to or interacting with an individual. In fact, you may be using it as a marketing tool and trying to communicate with a larger group of people but in a single direction, as a broadcast. Whatever the case may be, it remains a communication medium and requires some thought as to how you will use it.

Unlike one-to-one communications like an email or a text message, most social media will be one-to-many. It is a broadcast medium, and, even if you are replying directly to someone's post, you are often doing it within an online community, publicly. Even a private direct message could be forwarded or shared beyond your intended audience. This should guide the kinds of information you share and the things you say. Social media misuse is an area where lawyers have been disciplined, and you will need to tread carefully.

This is particularly tricky because there is no specific professional rule about social media. There is, however, a rule against communicating with a represented party.[18] There's a rule about confidentiality, which can sometimes extend to not disclosing your success after a courthouse win. What about rules or norms related to the decorum and impartiality of the tribunal and how that might constrain what you can say about a court or a judge?[19] Let's not forget what are essentially advertising rules limiting false or misleading claims.[20] This is not to suggest that a lawyer would say or do any of these things. But of all the communications tools that are available to a lawyer, social media and social networks may be the place it is most likely to unintentionally occur.

The most common social medium is email, and you will most likely find yourself invited or added to an email discussion list with other lawyers. This can be a small community, or it can be a large slice of your professional association or other organization. Your email client will be the technology that most likely directs your interactions, unless it is web-based.

18. A.B.A. Model Rules of Professional Conduct, r. 4.2 (Am. Bar Ass'n 2025).

19. *Id.* at 3.5(d).

20. *Id.* at 7.1.

Social media apps will be specific to the platforms they are designed for. In most cases, the app is designed by the platform provider and so there is no selection process. If you sign up for an account on the social media platform, you use the app and website provided. This is less true with some social media—including the various components of the Fediverse, like Mastodon and Pixelfed—where there are a variety of potential clients that you can use to access the social media content and interact with it.[21]

As with email, the process involved around social media selection is both far more important and requires far more thought than the technology. In many cases, you will not have an app choice, but you will need to come up with a way to identify yourself. Your social media handle will define you on that platform. You should be very deliberate in choosing your handle so that it reflects your professional profile. Although it may seem unfair, once you have joined the legal profession, your social media profile will be difficult to separate into personal and professional spheres.

In fact, as a law student, there is no better time than the present to start to think about and clean up any social media accounts that may not present you in a professional light. A law student in Canada used the handle "Oliver Klausoff" (which is usually interpreted as meaning "all of her clothes off" since that was not the student's real name) and this account remains active despite the fact that he is now practicing law under his actual name. Social media is something you will need to monitor and manage over the lifespan of your legal career.

Just as with domain names, mentioned above, you will need to consider your career lifespan when you create your social media accounts. Once you have created an account, you will need to maintain it for the life of your law practice or risk someone else assuming it and impersonating you. Lapsed social media handles are perhaps worse than other forms of online profile masquerading because it will be hard to distinguish the social media you shared

21. Fediverse, short for federated universe, is a nickname for a decentralized set of technologies that have gained some attention recently as internet users departed well-known commercial social media platforms. These technologies tend to be open source, meaning anyone can run their own social media server. They use a set of protocols that allow each social media server to interact with as many or a few other servers as they want to. This means that a microblogging server might connect to—or be federated with—an image server even though those two formats would normally, in a commercial platform, be isolated. The social media network consists of all of the interconnected or federated servers. There is no central platform.

when it was owned by you and what was shared after you ceded the account. As social media platforms start to initiate inactive account timelines—X considers an account inactive after 30 days and may delete it—you may find that you need to limit how many social media accounts you create and use for your law practice.[22] Otherwise, you may find yourself with an unwieldy number of platforms to maintain and keep alive.

There are many more considerations to using social media, but they have more to do with the content and less to do with the technology. You will want to look at your lawyer regulator's guides and educational materials to prepare for using social media during law practice. Like email, you will want to have a plan for how you will or will not interact with people online who are seeking legal advice.

Websites and Marketing

A website is not required for your law practice, but it is likely your clients will expect that you will have one. There are people who will argue with that statement, but the reality is that lots of lawyers do not have websites. Nearly a third of solo lawyers responding to a 2023 ABA survey indicated that they did not have a website.[23] This may reflect that solo lawyers often do not have marketing staff or a marketing budget.

It may also reflect that many law firms are powered by referrals from friends, family, and clients, and a solo lawyer may not need to seek business via the internet.[24] A lawyer can be found in a number of ways—bar association directories, lawyer referral services, online lawyer directories that prepopulate information without a lawyer seeking inclusion—online without having to take any steps. You may prefer to invest your time in maintaining

22. *Inactive Account Policy*, X (last visited May 16, 2025), https://help.x.com/en/rules-and-policies/inactive-x-accounts [http://web.archive.org/web/20250516182402/https://help.x.com/en/rules-and-policies/inactive-x-accounts].

23. Am. Bar Ass'n, 2023 Legal Technology Survey Report: Marketing & Communications Technology 12, question 11. While 87% of lawyers responded that their law firm had a website, only 65% of solos did. This number jumps to 89% of law firms with two to nine lawyers and approaches 100% at the largest law firms.

24. If you have a profile on sites like Avvo.com, Findlaw.com, or Martindale.com, you may be as findable as if you had a website. It is not the same as having your own domain and website but you may find that it is enough to be findable.

and contributing to your LinkedIn profile or other online marketplace, particularly if you are seeking business clients who are on the same platform. This *brochure-ware* or business card information may be enough for a lawyer to be found by prospective clients.

Practice Pointer

There are some activities a lawyer may need to engage in even if there is no measurable outcome. Marketing is one of these, and you may feel that having a website is a cost that you are unable to measure your return on your investment. Despite this, you may find that clients will have a negative perception of you if you fail to have even the most rudimentary, brochure-like website. Additionally, if you already have a domain name for your email, a website is a natural addition. If you plan to use online intake forms or other automation that is unrelated to marketing, having a website can provide an anchor for those sorts of activities.

While the website is not your only marketing avenue, let's look at marketing—the broad concept—in connection with websites because some of the things you will want to do with your marketing are easiest to explain in the context of the web.

Website Hosting and Design

A website comes with a cost, but it does not have to be a large one. You will probably want to hire someone to design your site and to populate it with information. You can do it yourself—it is usually not technically difficult—but this is one of those areas where the technology is relatively distant from the practice of law. You could invest time in learning how to do it yourself, but you are likely to take far more time than an expert would, and you will have fewer opportunities to maintain and upgrade your knowledge. Even if you have someone create your site for you, you may want to maintain the content on it yourself. Many websites are built on content management systems (CMS), and these can be designed so that you or your staff can easily add, edit, and remove content to keep your site fresh.

WordPress is perhaps the most common CMS for websites, and it is said to power about 40% of *all* the websites on the internet.[25] It is a free-to-acquire, open-source application that is available in practically all website hosting companies' offerings. You can run your own web server—like the email servers, mentioned above, a computer dedicated to delivering a website or web content—but you are likely to spend more in time lost to law practice billing than you will gain by avoiding an annual hosting fee. Website hosting for a simple law firm website can be found for $150–300 a year, depending on your requirements and preferred services. It is a relatively inexpensive way to market your services, and a WordPress site will come largely ready to be found by the internet search engines.

Practice Pointer

I have worked at a number of organizations that were paying far too much for a brochure-ware website. If you find that your hosting prices are going up and you do not require a lot of functionality or support, then you should shop around. Like you will with your desktop or laptop, it cannot hurt to move websites to save money. It is extraordinarily easy to migrate a website—especially if you use a CMS like WordPress—in a couple of hours from one provider to another. When you sign up with your website host, look for a multi-year agreement to keep your annual price down. At the end of the agreement, compare other multi-year offerings to ensure your website costs are still appropriate. Website hosting is fungible, and there is no reason to be locked in.

If you are investing in a website for your law practice, you will want to be conversant with search engine optimization (SEO) concepts. This is a large, consultant-driven market that you do not need to engage in, but you still may want to understand so that you know what it is they are selling. For the most part, search engine strategies revolve around tailoring your content to appear higher in the search results. This can involve how you create and present your information as well as buying advertising or keywords from search providers

25. *Our Journey to Powering 40% of the Web*, WORDPRESS (last visited May 31, 2025), https://wordpress.org/40-percent-of-web [http://web.archive.org/web/20250531093228/https://wordpress.org/40-percent-of-web/].

that cause your website to be a preferred result. The common rule of thumb is that, if you are not in the top 10 results, your website will not be visible to people who are searching.

This depends heavily on the keywords people use to search. It depends also on what weight the search engine provider gives to elements of your website. In the past, things like the speed with which your website loaded, the quality of the content on your website, and the links to and from it would matter.[26] Many of these things are within your own power to manage. But there will be a point where the investment exceeds the return.

The increased presence of artificial intelligence in web search engine results, sometimes to the point of moving traditional search results much further down the search engine results page (SERP), means that SEO is in flux. Companies like Google who have been leaders in web search are now investing heavily in an AI-based search interface.[27]

You may wish to experiment with SEO—and its related activities, including buying ad words from providers like Google—but I would encourage you to put up your website and give it some time to work on its own. The search engines, AI and otherwise, will still crawl your website and index your content whether you pay for or engage in search engine optimization. SEO is a place where you can pour in a lot of money without really knowing whether it is making any difference to your law practice's bottom line. You need to find ways to measure any investment in SEO.

Conversions and Measurement

If you decide to do marketing, a website can provide an anchor for your efforts. For example, say you want to use your customer relationship management application or even just a simple mail merge of your Microsoft Outlook contacts. You would like to send them all an email with a *call to action*, a link to click on or activity you want them to take like attending an educational event you are presenting at. You want to measure those emails and those click-

26. A list of the most important things Google considers when it returns search results. *Automatically Generating and Ranking Results*, Google Search (last visited June 9, 2025), https://www.google.com/intl/en_us/search/howsearchworks/how-search-works/ranking-results/ [http://web.archive.org/web/20250609151158/https://www.google.com/intl/en_us/search/howsearchworks/how-search-works/ranking-results/].

27. *Supercharging Search with Generative AI*, Google (last visited June 5, 2025) https://blog.google/products/search/generative-ai-search/ [http://web.archive.org/web/20250605113100/https://blog.google/products/search/generative-ai-search/].

able links to see if they are having any impact on your client base. If no one is reading them or clicking the links, then perhaps you need to rethink your marketing, both methods and content.

Email marketing technology can be licensed with a simple subscription. Companies like Constant Contact and Hubspot will provide you with templates and help on the analytics related to email marketing. They can measure if an email is opened or not and can customize your links so that you can tell if they were clicked or not. These analytics are not foolproof. The methods they use can be blocked by the recipient, so, like anything to do with marketing, you will not get an exact number for these sorts of interactions.[28]

The other thing you can do with emailed links is customize them so that, if the link goes back to your website, you can view it in your own website analytics tool. You can add customized text to a URL called a UTM code that allows you to send information about where the link was clicked to your web analytics program.[29] For example, let's say my law firm had a new resource about a change in the law, called "Statute Changed to Increase Fees." The URL or website link to that might look like:

> https://ofaolain.com/statute-changed-to-increase-fees

If I send an email out to my clients with that information, and they click on it, those clicks will be recorded in my website analytics program. But I will not be able to tell those clicks from people who have seen it in a search engine or, if I post it on my social media platform profile, who click from there. I can change the link in the email—and on social media and anywhere else I post it—to give me more information when the link is clicked:

> https://ofaolain.com/statute-changed-to-increase-fees?utm_source=email&utm_campaign=blogpost-fees

28. Many email marketing tools assume that the person receiving the email will view it as a web page. This allows the marketer to hide things—invisible image pixels or embedded tracking tags—that will alert the marketer to whether the email is opened and viewed. If it is opened, the pixel or tag, which resides on the remote server hosted by the marketer, will register the action in its analytics program.

29. This is an explanation of what the UTM codes are, where they came from, and how to use them. http://web.archive.org/web/20250611102346/https://www.searchenginejournal.com/utm-codes/370088/. There is no "right" way to use them. If you use them differently from this description, they will still work. Your results may just look different; the URLs will not break or cause the visitor any problems.

http://ofaolain.com/statute-changed-to-increase-fees?utm_source=Bluesky&utm_campaign=blogpost-fees

All of those links will work exactly the same. So long as that blog post or web page exists, the web browser will ignore everything after the question mark. But my website analytics will record the *utm_source* and *utm_campaign* information to help me distinguish each visitor. I can then run reports to see who clicked on the link, whether they came from email or Bluesky, and what the campaign was called. All of this can be done manually: you do not need an SEO expert or even a special application to work with UTM codes.

You will need website analytics. Google has a free application called Google Analytics, which is a good start. The only drawback to Google Analytics or its commercial alternative Doubleclick is that you may not have full control over what your visitor data is used for and, because of those privacy concerns, some website visitors will be blocking Google's website analytics products. This will mean that their visit to your website will not be recorded in your website analytics. Your website host may provide some free website analytics or you can install an open-source application like Matomo, which will run on your own domain but provide you with an experience more like Google Analytics.[30]

These clicks are known as conversions: someone has seen your marketing collateral and interacted with it.[31] Your goal when you engage in marketing is often to create a high rate of conversions. The idea is that, the higher your rate of conversions, the more likely you are to be hired to take on a legal matter. Or, if you are sending out a link to current clients, to be retained or sought out for a new matter.

Do you remember when we discussed your initial intake process for prospective clients and discussed asking them where they heard about your law practice? This is why. You are running a business when you have a law practice, and you want to understand how people are finding you. This will help you spend your marketing resources in the right places and identify places where you may want to try finding clients.

You will have seen lawyer advertising. You may also have noticed that, for the million-plus lawyers that are in practice, not all of them take out billboard

---

30. Matomo is an open source, free-to-acquire website analytics platform. https://www.matomo.org. You can pay for premium support and resources, but the basic functionality, including support for search tags and utm codes, is available in the free version.

31. *Conversion Marketing*, Wikipedia (last visited Aug. 30, 2025) https://en.wikipedia.org/wiki/Conversion_marketing.

ads or bus wraps or even glossy ads in publications. You do not need to do just what you see other lawyers do. Ask your local bar colleagues how they find clients—and how clients find them—and emulate those lawyers who are successful. Whatever marketing you end up doing, be sure to consider how you are going to measure the results. Every website, every email you send (and the time your clients spend looking at it and the resources you highlight for them), every networking event, they all come with a cost to you. Sometimes it is an actual cost and sometimes it is an opportunity cost, because you do one thing and forego doing an alternative.

Be Found

If you are going to invest in a website, at the very least, make it easy for the search engines to find you the first time. Once you have, you can sit back and see how they treat your website. You can also watch to see if your prospective clients are arriving through your website or through other means.

You really only need to submit your website URL to two search engines: Google and Microsoft Bing. Most other search engines use one or the other of those two as their foundational index. You or someone on your staff—or your website consultant—can create an account with Microsoft Webmaster Tools and submit your website URL.[32] There is a simple validation process to overcome and then Bing will start to index your site. Google has something called Search Console. Similar to the Bing Webmaster Tools, it is where you can submit your website and manage information about it.[33] While you can connect a Google Analytics account to Search Console, you do not need to use Google Analytics in order to use Search Console.

There is far more to website analytics and findability than we can cover here. Things like site maps (not the kind your visitor can see, the kind that the website search crawler uses) and so on are things you can dig into on your own. More likely, you will hire someone who will look at these things for you.

32. https://www.bing.com/webmasters/. If you already have a Microsoft 365 account or an Outlook.com email account, you can use that account to sign in.

33. https://search.google.com/search-console/.

Chapter 10 Exercises

A. Complete a phishing test like this one from the United States Federal Trade Commission's Cybersecurity quizzes: https://www.ftc.gov/business-guidance/small-businesses/cybersecurity/quiz/phishing.

B. Learn how to look at message headers in Outlook and Gmail. Are there differences between whether you can see them on mobile apps compared to desktop apps? What are the red flags you should be looking for? What other tools can you locate that help you to determine email validity, including DKIM and DMARC lookup?

Chapter 11

Accounting

Law school prepares you for a lot of things related to law practice, but it tends not to prepare you to deal with money. This includes pricing strategies as well as keeping track of your time and billing for your work. A law practice needs revenue in order to exist. One major gap in preparing law students to practice is in the area of accounting. In particular, there is inadequate preparation related to the specific professional obligations lawyers have to manage the money their clients provide them before the lawyer has earned it.

If we turn to the Model Rules again, we find a specific rule dealing with the safeguarding of property. Rule 1.15 deals with the creation and maintenance of a trust account to secure client property. There are very specific rules around putting money into and taking money out of a trust account. Trust accounting is an incredibly important ethical obligation and a common reason for lawyers to be disciplined or disbarred.

One reason that accounting may not be taught in law school is that it is its own profession. It is a complex set of rules and obligations and so, while you can license accounting software like Intuit's QuickBooks or Sage50 Accounting, you will still need to educate yourself in how it all works. The technology will not provide you with the processes, including things like internal financial controls, all by itself.

Practice Pointer

No matter how you decide to solve your accounting needs, you should get a working knowledge of accounting. What is a Chart of Accounts, what is a profit and loss report, and so on. You do not need to master accounting, but a conversational knowledge will help you work with accountants, whether they are your clients or you are theirs. Your knowledge can act as an extra check on whatever processes govern the flow of money through your practice. A lack of knowledge will not be a reasonable defense against financial misconduct. It will also provide you with background necessary to work with corporate, government, and business-owning clients whose legal issue touches on their financial operations.

If there is one obvious area where a lawyer should not merely license software, it is accounting. As soon as you are ready to start practicing in your own law office, seek out professional accounting help. This may take the form of an accountant who handles your financial books virtually. This may be someone you know and trust in the town where you are practicing, or it may be a recommendation from an accounting software provider.[1]

You might also hire a person to manage your books as a part of your law firm staff, either a dedicated bookkeeper or someone who has that as part of their duties. This might give you more latitude if you have a particular accounting software product you want to use, as you can match an employee with experience to the product that they know how to use.

Common accounting applications have strong integrations with banks and other payable and receivable tools. For example, you can connect your bank account or even services like PayPal to your accounting application to automatically record income and expenses that are moving in and out of those accounts. If your law practice is primarily using payment methods other than paper checks, this can automate a lot of the information gathering that an accountant or bookkeeper would need to manage the money flow. They can then process that information and provide financial reporting for you. They may even be able to help you file your law firm's taxes.

A trust account is a separate account from the one you will use to manage your law practice's operational finances. You will create it directly with your financial institution or by working with your jurisdiction's lawyers' trust fund. They can help you find a bank or institution that can create an IOLTA ("interest on lawyer trust accounts") account that will help you comply with your professional obligations.[2]

1. For example, Intuit has the Quickbooks Pro Advisor, https://proadvisor.intuit.com/app/accountant/search?region=US.

2. Lawyers cannot keep interest from their client's money—money that is not owed to the lawyer—and so that interest is transferred to the state lawyers' trust fund, if the money is

Although it is a different type of account, it still needs to be managed with accounting software and, most likely, professional assistance in the form of an accountant. Not only will having a professional's help improve the likelihood that your accounts will be in good order, it gives another layer of internal controls to have someone other than you—the person who is likely to move or request to move client's money from the trust fund to the law practice's operations account—managing the reporting and recording of those transactions. When it comes to financial management, the more people involved in oversight, the better. This can be hard in a solo practice where it may just be you on your own. If you hire an accountant or bookkeeper to help you, you can increase the odds that processes are properly followed as you can act as a check on them and vice versa.

Accounting Integration

It may seem like a lawyer does not have a particular interest in accounting software given that the recommendation is to use an accountant. But that wouldn't be entirely true. An accounting software package does not exist in isolation. It is merely the way you are recording your income and expenses. Your income involves payments you receive from your clients and others, based on invoices you have sent them. Those invoices will be based on the time you have billed or the agreements you have with particular clients on how you will be paid for the professional work you are performing: how much, when, and under what conditions.

In other words, your client's data is at the heart of all of this. The decision you make about your accounting software may drive a number of other decisions for your law practice. To start, you may need to use an accounting software application that is preferred by your accountant or bookkeeper, because of their expertise with one program or another. In that case, you may not select the accounting application so much as default to one. When you start to look at other software, especially law-specific software like practice

held in an IOLTA account. If it is not in an IOLTA account, any interest needs to be payable back to the client.

management applications, this accounting software choice may drive that selection decision.[3]

You do not need to have an integrated accounting system but, if you decide to attempt integrations—particularly if you are going to use practice management software or a time and billing application—then your accounting application will be a key component. It can simplify your ability to see which clients have or haven't paid, to automate distribution of invoices (and potentially be reminded to follow up on unpaid bills), and more. Accounting and bill paying applications will frequently have the ability to synchronize client (or payor) data so that you do not need to duplicate names and addresses in each system.

Practice Pointer

Another reason that the selection of your accounting system may not be as determinative is that, for the most part, you are dealing with data. It may be a large amount of data, but it is still mostly numbers and adjacent information. This can be easy to export and import into a new system if you decide to change. Unlike some systems where linkages between data may be difficult to export or migrate, accounting systems are frequently designed with the expectation of bringing in old accounting data when you subscribe to a new product.

It is incredibly important to keep this data up to date in your accounting or payables system. Otherwise, you may be sending out invoices to old client addresses or inaccessible email addresses without realizing it. This can slow down your ability to receive payments for services while also causing potential issues with clients who may not realize that they owe you something. When you think about your law practice's customer service, and your firm's reliance on referrals and goodwill, you want to avoid having a client receive overdue notices because of administrative data updates related to housing and email address changes.

3. At the time of writing, many of the well-known law practice management applications had integrations with well-known accounting packages like Intuit Quickbooks and Xero. You may not find that you need to prefer your selection order—accounting first, or practice management first—in that sort of situation. Although your accountant or bookkeeper will likely have a say in the decision as well.

Electronic Billing

In the early days of law practice management, electronic billing meant emailing a PDF of an invoice to a client, who would then send a paper check in the mail. Increasingly, electronic billing is truly electronic both ways and reflects a quick way to invoice a client and to have them pay you. Technology can remove the friction and delay that lawyers have experienced in the past in trying to secure their practice revenue.

Nearly 80% of lawyers have electronic billing at their law firm, with solos having the lowest adoption.[4] The electronic billing applications vary from integrated practice management products to common accounting platforms.[5] There are accounts payable applications that a law firm can use as well, that enable both electronic invoicing and payments but can also deliver an electronic invoice for a paper check. Some of these systems can also be used by you to pay bills owed by your law firm to others. As you are considering your accounting software, look at what options it provides for integration with accounts receivable and accounts payable billing platforms. The greater your ability to integrate systems, the fewer chances you or those who you hire to help you will have to make mistakes or have to manage duplicate information.

There is no shortage of other payment options, applications like Zelle or Venmo. The important thing to keep in mind is that, if your clients are paying you money via an electronic system, the money is going into the correct bank account. Money intended for your trust account should not flow first into your operations account. You will need to balance the convenience to your clients of using multiple or varied payment platforms, and the efficiency and expeditious payment to your law practice, with your professional obligations.

4. Am. Bar Ass'n, 2023 Legal Technology Survey Report: Law Office Technology 30, question 23a-o (2024). 62% of solos had e-billing software at their law practice while 94% of large firm lawyers reported having it at firms with 500 or more lawyers.

5. *Id.* at 42, question 23c.

Chapter 11 Exercise

A. *This exercise does not require you to transfer any money or link up accounts.* Choose one or two of your online accounts where you do transfer in or out money—paying bills, receiving income—and identify tools they provide that allow you to track the flow of money. For example, can you see both the order for the purchase at an online shop and see the purchase show up in your bank account? How long does it take? How do you monitor whether the things that were purchased are received? Some financial services offer a hub where you can integrate all of your payment accounts. What are the possible downsides of centralizing this sort of access?

Chapter 12

Securing Your Practice

Your law practice is now up and running. You have completed your intake of your first client, you have started to do legal research, bill time, and create and store documents. Now you need to start planning and preparing for how to keep your law practice running from day to day. This is known as business continuity, and it is a process of building in resilience, and fallbacks when things fail, so that your ability to practice law and represent your clients is not impaired.

We will touch on a lot of different aspects of business continuity—security, disaster recovery, and so on—below, but an important place to start is with your ethical obligations. In particular, Model Rule 5.3 and your duty to supervise non-lawyers you employ.[1] This was the area that gave a lot of lawyers fits when cloud computing first came out: how do you supervise people you are hiring to manage your client records and information when it is in the cloud?

This issue has not gone away, and you will need to consider who has access to what client data when you start to store their information in systems. But it is not limited to the cloud—and never has been—and you will need to consider this with your physical computers and other equipment. For instance, a strongly recommended practice is to remove a storage backup of your practice data so that it is in a physically different place from your office, in case your office is damaged or destroyed. How you store and manage access to information that is stored *just in case* is as important as how you store and manage access to the information you use every day.

1. ABA Model Rule 5.3 requires that a supervising lawyer make reasonable efforts to ensure that the non-lawyer's conduct is compatible with the lawyer's, or the law firm's, professional obligations. A.B.A. Model Rules of Professional Conduct, r. 5.3 (Am. Bar Ass'n 2025).

Confidentiality and Security

Once you have confidential or personally identifiable information from a client, you need to secure it. Papers need to go into a filing system, digital files need to be on secured devices. You do not want to leave files open on your desktop, whether it is your physical desktop and file folders or your desktop computer.

Most of the tools available for securing your law practice data are within your control. As you think about your professional obligations, remember that the ethics rules tend to require you to take reasonable steps. There are many unreasonable steps you could also take: drive out to a data center and, if it is possible, test its security by trying to access it without authorization.[2] Many of these are not only not recommended, but they are not necessary if you are taking reasonable precautions.

Any device connected to the internet, including a lawyer's phone or laptop or "smart" devices in their office, bring with them a potential risk of data loss. Even if a device were not connected to the internet, there is some risk of data on it being lost, if only through something as common as device failure. But the modern law practice relies on internet-connected devices, whether it is your phone or your laptop or your entire law practice. You cannot eliminate all risk of client data loss and breach of confidentiality or other critical information. You can act reasonably, though, and take proactive steps to minimize the risk that *you* are the cause of whatever loss may occur.

Passwords, Passphrases, Passkeys

The very first step is to ensure you are using passwords on every device or application that involves client information. This will come as no surprise, but it remains a weak security link because people tend to have bad habits when it comes to passwords and personal identification numbers (PINs). In particular, passwords tend not to be very strong, and they tend to be used repeatedly.

This is no surprise to anyone who follows mainstream news. There is a permanent tension between securing information and accessing information. On

2. This may sound like it's a joke. It's not a joke. If you look for firms providing *penetration testing* services for law firms, you will find consultants who will do this at your law practice. They will call your staff or test your doors or otherwise poke and prod at your systems and physical structures to see if there is a way in or if anything is exposed that shouldn't be.

the one hand, we try to be efficient. We want to start up our computer quickly, get to work, complete tasks, and all with as little friction as possible. On the other hand, everything that we can access quickly and efficiently can be accessed by other people just as quickly and efficiently if they have the right keys.

What if you put your client files up on a website with no username or password, so they were accessible to anyone who had or could find a link? This might fail the *reasonable* test and result in lawyer discipline or loss of lawyer-client privilege if, as in this case, the defense lawyers were given the link and able to access the file that was not meant for them.[3] Why risk sharing files without securing them? Because passwords for multiple people to access secured data can be hard to implement and sharing secured information can be even harder since you need to create and communicate access information securely.

There is a great deal of free advice on how to create passwords. The most important technology you can use is a password manager. Ideally, this is an application that is designed specifically to help you create and manage strong passwords. The goal is to help you create a unique, strong password for each resource so that you are not tempted to use a password more than once. If you are able to use a password manager, you can ignore a lot of advice about password creation—how many characters, how many numbers or letters, and so on—because that logic will be built into the password manager application. Your use of the password manager and the intention behind it (unique, strong passwords) may be the single most important technology you can implement in your law practice.

This is not to say that every password manager is the same. Obviously, an application whose sole purpose is to hold passwords will become a target for people whose business is to exploit passwords. Online password managers like LastPass have themselves been breached, with password databases being stolen and, in some cases, broken.[4] When we talk about the tension between

3. Harleysville Ins. Co. v. Holding Funeral Home, Inc., No. 1:15CV00057, 2017 U.S. Dist. LEXIS 162058 (W.D. Va. Oct. 2, 2017). This case was a shambles, with the defense getting an unsecured link to the plaintiff's files on a cloud storage service, then themselves providing the plaintiff with an unsecured copy of their privileged work product. I would not rely on this analogy—that the link to the unsecured file was like burying a briefcase in a large forest—instead of using passwords.

4. LastPass security incident Karim Toubba, *Notice of Security Incident*, LastPass (Dec. 22, 2022), https://blog.lastpass.com/posts/notice-of-recent-security-incident [http://web.archive.org/web/20250611155703/https://blog.lastpass.com/posts/notice-of-recent-security-incident]. $5 million stolen from LastPass users' blockchain accounts. Danny Park, *LastPass Threat Actor Drains $5.4 Million in Crypto from Over 40 Victim Addresses: Zach-*

security and access, this is part of the balance. An online password manager can be a decision to balance security and access, because an online service can be accessible from multiple devices and synchronized across multiple devices. On the other hand, if your password manager and password vault are internet accessible, then the same things that limit your access (your master password) may be the only things limiting other people's access too.

One alternative is to keep your password manager entirely on your devices offline. You can install the password manager on each device—laptop, phone, tablet, desktop PC—and then synchronize the password file among them. You can do it manually, depending on how often you update your passwords, or you can store your password file in a secure cloud location like your Microsoft OneDrive or Google Drive account. So long as your password for your online storage is unique and different from your password manager password, even if someone were to get your password file, they would still need to crack it open.

This can provide its own friction, though, and it can be frustrating if the synchronization does not work smoothly. You may find that one device has a newer or older password file than another computer. If this is too much complexity for you, using an online password manager may be the simplest approach. An online password manager can also mean someone to whom you delegate access would not need to have your devices in hand.

Practice Pointer

Everyone dies. The one thing you want to avoid is creating problems accessing your law practice files, your bank accounts, and so on if something should happen to you. In addition to your law practice, you may have family—a spouse, children, parents—whose lives will be much easier if they can access your passwords if you are incapacitated or killed. When you think about your password manager, consider how someone else might access it if you are unable to.

XBT, The Block (Dec. 16, 2024, 11:44 PM), https://www.theblock.co/post/331118/lastpass-threat-actor-drains-5-4-million-in-crypto-from-over-40-victim-addresses-zachxbt [http://web.archive.org/web/20250508023340/https://www.theblock.co/post/331118/lastpass-threat-actor-drains-5-4-million-in-crypto-from-over-40-victim-addresses-zachxbt].

The increased security applied to Microsoft Office apps in recent years has meant that the latest version of Microsoft Excel can actually be a decent password manager. It is a simple way to secure passwords, and it does not require an extra piece of software if you are already using the Microsoft Office suite. In the same way you use a master password for a password manager, you would password protect your Excel password spreadsheet. For this to work, you need to ensure the spreadsheet is in the latest Excel file format. Earlier Excel formats will not provide enough protection.

A lawyer who used Microsoft Excel as a password manager would still need a tool to generate new, strong passwords for you, something that most password managers have built in but that are not a part of Excel.[5] But once you have created your passwords and have entered them into your spreadsheet, you can use your Microsoft OneDrive synchronization to make the Excel workbook available on multiple devices.

Your password vault should be secured, however. For these reasons, saving your passwords in your web browser can leave them at risk. Google Chrome and Microsoft Edge support the saving of passwords, but they will also allow you to export your passwords as a spreadsheet or data file. If someone can access your computer and your web browser and guess your browser password if one is required, they can export your entire password vault.[6]

Passwords as a Selection Criterion

Ideally, you will use a password manager and be able to forego thinking too critically about how to create new passwords. At the same time, there are password security standards that go beyond personal choice and collegial recommendations.[7] These standards can provide you with some guidance when

5. An online password generator I have used is Wolfram Alpha. https://www.wolframalpha.com/input/?i=generate+a+password. It can be configured to produce passwords of a specific length and complexity, and it will generate a half dozen at a time. There are also Excel spreadsheet templates that will generate passwords, so this may be a gap that can be filled within Excel.

6. I have done this myself, in a situation where a person had been detained in a prison and their passwords were at risk of being accessed from a separate endpoint. I was able to use their password—which had been written down at their desk—to access, export, and then delete their passwords from their web browser.

7. In particular, the National Institute of Standards and Technology (NIST, an entity of the United States Department of Commerce) standards guide many online organizations. They have a standard dealing specifically with passwords and multi-factor authentication, http://web.archive.org/web/20250615232325/https://pages.nist.gov/800-63-4/sp800-63b.html.

you are selecting a provider. If your cloud provider or application does not meet these standards, that should be a red flag. Some of the most common:

- **The website or organization requires you to change your password regularly.** This is an out-of-date practice and reflects an organization that does not stay current on changes in security.[8] Unfortunately, this may include a law firm or court that you go to work for. If it is a technology provider where you will be storing and accessing client data, you may want to shop around a bit more for someone with more current security practices.
- **You are only allowed to create a password of 8 characters.** Eight-character passwords used to be considered an acceptable number, but passwords tend to be longer now, often with as many as 20 characters. While there is guidance suggesting that the content of passwords be less rigorously enforced—how many upper-case, lower-case, special characters, and so on—be wary of sites that allow only 8 total characters.[9] Microsoft has done research into password lengths and has its own recommendations for Microsoft 365 administrators that are a good guideline for all sites.[10]

Of course, it is probably obvious that most of us cannot remember a unique, strong password that is 14- or 20-characters long for *every* website or application we use. That is the role the password manager fills. First, it eliminates the need to remember most of your passwords and second, it supports the

---

8. "Users tend to choose weaker memorized secrets when they know that they will have to change them in the near future." Nat'l Inst. of Standards and Tech, *Frequently Asked Questions, SP 800-63: Digital Identity Guidelines*, question B05 (Mar. 3, 2022) https://pages.nist.gov/800-63-FAQ/#q-b05 [http://web.archive.org/web/20250611145729/https://pages.nist.gov/800-63-FAQ/#q-b05].

9. "[R]ecommends against the use of composition rules (e.g., requiring lower-case, uppercase ...) for memorized secrets. These rules provide less benefit than might be expected because users tend to use predictable methods for satisfying these requirements." *Id.* at question B06, https://pages.nist.gov/800-63-FAQ/#q-b06 [http://web.archive.org/web/20250611145729/https://pages.nist.gov/800-63-FAQ/#q-b06].

10. Microsoft recommends 14-character passwords, without character requirements, and without periodic resets. *Password Policy Recommendations for Microsoft 365 Passwords*, Microsoft (Apr. 2, 2025), https://learn.microsoft.com/en-us/microsoft-365/admin/misc/password-policy-recommendations?view=o365-worldwide [http://web.archive.org/web/20250613114907/https://learn.microsoft.com/en-us/microsoft-365/admin/misc/password-policy-recommendations?view=o365-worldwide].

creation of sufficiently long and complex passwords to meet whatever security requirements of the resource you are using.

Unavoidable Passwords

Even in the ideal situation where you are using a password manager for all of your passwords, you will need to know and memorize your primary password, the one that allows you to access all of the other passwords. In addition, you will probably need to memorize your operating system password so that you can log on to your PC and access your password manager.[11]

You should not be using these two passwords anywhere else, but they should still be sufficiently complicated as to be unguessable. You should also avoid common mistakes connected to these key passwords:

- **Passwords should not be written down anywhere that is easily accessible.** As a lawyer, you need to consider the long-term resilience of your law firm. Pick a good primary password for your password manager, write it down, and then store it somewhere secure: your law firm's safe, a bank deposit box, somewhere you store other key documents (like your will) in case of disaster. *If you change it*, make sure to update this backup copy. But do not write it down and leave it accessible within your office or on your mobile device.
- **Passwords should not be shared.** You are the only person who needs access to your passwords. If you have a resource that someone else needs access to, give them their own account with their own password. They should manage it just as securely as you do. It is not uncommon in a law firm to have an account that only allows one username and password, whether it is for legal research or buying office supplies or other operational needs. In those instances, use a shared password manager to enable access by multiple people to that password without exposing your other, personal passwords.[12] This is

11. There are security tokens that you can use instead of a password. Your computer will look at the token, usually something you insert into a USB port or that can access your device using wireless technology like near field communication (NFC) to determine whether you have access to the account. Your work or employer may require this, but they are not universally supported so you will need to balance the use of hardware tokens with the many resources that can only be accessed with traditional passwords.

12. The open-source password manager Bitwarden has shared vaults. LastPass has shared folders. One benefit of cloud-based password managers is your ability to create

helpful both while people work with you at your law firm but also after they leave. If they have been using their own personal passwords, separate from ones used by the rest of the firm, then you can disable their accounts without impacting anyone else's access. You will also know which passwords they were able to access that so that you know to reset them.

Practice Pointer

As you are thinking about the technology you use in your practice, consider the concept known as the principle of least privilege.[13] This approach thinks about access to information—your documents in your document management system, your practice management data, your accounting—and limits access to just the data and functions that a person requires to successfully complete their job. It is often easier, in that it removes friction or obstacles, to give someone too much access "just in case." But each person should only have access, using their own username and password, to the parts of the law firm systems that they need for their work.

Passphrases and Passkeys

Passwords were the primary method of securing accounts for a long time. More recently, in response to poor password practices, there have been recommendations to use passphrases. These are complex word combinations that aim to be memorable but difficult to replicate with brute force.[14]

---

shared password vaults. Also, if someone leaves your law firm, you can retain access to their password vault after their departure.

13. *Principle of Least Privilege*, Wikipedia (last visited Aug. 31, 2025), https://en.wikipedia.org/wiki/Principle_of_least_privilege.

14. A brute force attack is one where the attacker repeatedly hits a resource, like a login screen, with new attempts until they are successful at guessing the password. *Brute-force Attack*, Wikipedia (last visited Aug. 26, 2025), https://en.wikipedia.org/wiki/Brute-force_attack. This is usually avoided by prohibiting multiple logins or locking an account after a certain number of incorrect logins.

On the one hand, a passphrase—one common reference point in discussions about passphrases is an XKCD cartoon that suggests *correcthorsebatterystaple*—is an easier way to memorize a strong password.[15] It can be true and still not be a good alternative to a password manager. There is a limit to how many passwords or passphrases a person can memorize. At some point, you will need to start recording these somewhere, no matter whether you use passphrases or traditional passwords. At that point, you may as well adopt a password manager whether you decide to use passphrases or not.[16]

An even more recent take is the implementation of passkeys. Unfortunately, there are two technologies that are referred to as passkeys. One is software-based (although it can use a physical storage device) and one uses a piece of hardware. Let's leave the hardware one for later, when we look at multi-factor authenticators, and focus on the software-based version.

This passkey is, in fact, a pair of keys. One is stored by the site or resource you are trying to access, and the other is stored to your device or passkey manager.[17] The intention is to eliminate the need for both passwords and multi-factor authentication. The implementation of passkeys appears to be inconsistent and confusing, and you might end up saving the passkeys to a device (like your laptop computer) that makes it unavailable on your phone.[18]

Both passphrases and passkeys are technologies that are attempting to overcome the widespread problems with weak passwords.[19] Passwords are largely a

---

15. Password Strength, XKCD comic, August 10, 2011, http://web.archive.org/web/20250614192904/https://xkcd.com/936/.

16. A password manager provider has done surveys that have found the average person has an increasing number of passwords. In 2024, the average was 168 passwords, up from 100 in 2020. Of those 168, about half (87) were related to their business accounts. Kamile Viezelyte, *Juggling Security: How Many Passwords Does the Average Person Have*, NordPass (Apr. 24, 2024), https://nordpass.com/blog/how-many-passwords-does-average-person-have/ [http://web.archive.org/web/20250605221119/https://nordpass.com/blog/how-many-passwords-does-average-person-have/].

17. This public-key-private-key arrangement is common in internet security and has been around for decades. *Public-key Cryptography*, Wikipedia (last visited Aug. 31, 2025), https://en.wikipedia.org/wiki/Public-key_cryptography.

18. See Bruce Davie, *Will Passkeys Ever Replace Passwords? Can They?*, The Register (Nov. 17, 2024), https://www.theregister.com/2024/11/17/passkeys_passwords/ [http://web.archive.org/web/20250609145131/https://www.theregister.com/2024/11/17/passkeys_passwords/].

19. It is estimated that billions of passwords have been exposed over the last few decades. In one breach, more than 184 million passwords were exposed. Matt Burgess & Lily Hay Newman, *Mysterious Database of 184 Million Records Exposes Vast Array of Login Credentials*, Wired (May 22, 2025, 6:00 AM), https://www.wired.com/story/mysterious

problem because of friction and complexity, though, and so new alternatives need to further reduce those obstacles. At this point, there does not seem to be a better alternative to passwords and password managers.

I have used a variety of password managers over time and have reluctantly come to the decision to use a cloud-based manager for myself. When I was managing just my own passwords, I used KeePass, which had Android and Windows clients. When password managers started to become more prevalent, though, my organization started to use a cloud-based password manager. Rather than using two different password managers that, as you can imagine, created more friction for me, I decided to merge my files and use the same application as my organization. You may find that your law firm drives your password manager choice too. Even though I use a cloud-based password vault, I tend to use local apps on my phone and computer for most of my access. I would make a password manager selection with a local copy in mind, just in case you need to access a local resource and the internet—and your password manager vault—is unavailable.

Security Questions

Security questions are an increasingly poor way to authenticate an online account. Unfortunately, despite the weak role they play, they continue to be used. Questions that ask "where were you born" or "what was the name of your first dog" or "what was your mother's maiden name" may contain information that you have shared online or that is otherwise discoverable with a bit of internet sleuthing or using methods like social engineering. There seems to be a relatively small number of questions that are asked by websites that deploy security questions, increasing the risk that a breach at one site might expose your answers—if they are truthful—to the same questions on other websites. As one group of researchers found:

> Statistical attacks against secret questions are a real risk because there are commons answers shared among many users. For example using a single guess an attacker would have a 19.7% success rate at guessing English-speaking users' answers for the question "Favor-

-database-logins-governments-social-media/ [http://web.archive.org/web/20250615144940/https://www.wired.com/story/mysterious-database-logins-governments-social-media/]. Mozilla Monitor, HaveIBeenPwned, and other sites have created data stores of email accounts and passwords so that you can search to see if your password was disclosed in any of those breaches.

> ite food?" Similarly, with a single guess the attacker would have a 3.8% success rate at guessing Spanish-speaking users' answers for the question "Father's middle name?" With 10 guesses an attacker would be able to guess 39% of Korean-speaking users' answers to "City of birth?"[20]

You may be disposed to giving *untruthful* answers in order to try to mislead someone who is trying to guess your answer. This approach to *security through obscurity* may make sense, intuitively, but it has been debunked as a safe way to approach security questions. It turns out, we humans tend to make the same untruthful answers and so it *increases* the likelihood that the answer will be guessed, where being truthful would have been far more secure. From the same group of researchers:

> These untruthful answers significantly weaken the potentially most secure questions. The security of these questions against extended guessing attacks is considerably higher, as they are very difficult to guess for users who answer honestly. However for certain combinations of language and question this degradation makes those questions even less secure that the one based on name and places. For example, 2.9% of the Arabic-speaking users used the same phone number as their answer and 2.4% of the Russian-speaking users.[21]

One way to manage security questions without falling into easily guessable answers is to treat them as passwords or passphrases. When you set up an account and it asks you to create security question answers, make your answers unique passwords or passphrases. Your password manager can generate additional passwords or you can create your own passphrases, using a tool or just thinking up unconnected groups of words. If you paste the security question and the password-as-answer into your password manager, you will not have to try to remember the answer. Like your password, you can cut and paste the password-as-answer if prompted for a security question. One reason to consider a passphrase—like milkindigocollateralfunicular—is that, if you have

---

20. Joseph Bonneau, Elie Bursztein, Ilan Caron, Rob Jackson & Mike Williamson, *Secrets, Lies, and Account Recovery: Lessons from the Use of Personal Knowledge Questions at Google* 141 (2015), https://static.googleusercontent.com/media/research.google.com/en/us/pubs/archive/43783.pdf [http://web.archive.org/web/20250519085103/https://static.googleusercontent.com/media/research.google.com/en/us/pubs/archive/43783.pdf].

21. *Id.* at 144.

to speak to someone in technical support and answer a security question, this may be easier to communicate than *33yUG9Zs4FmZSARL*.

The benefit to storing your security questions and answers with your passwords is that, if you are ever in a situation where you are incapacitated and someone needs to access your accounts for you, having the question and answer pairs in your password manager will help them overcome those prompts without trying to access your memory.

We referred to passkeys above and hardware versions that can store them. These keys can also be used to generate numeric codes and can provide a second authentication factor. A lawyer should use multi-factor authentication wherever possible, in addition to passwords. In that way, even if someone were to determine your primary password, they would still need to get an additional piece of information or, in some cases, access to a physical device. Let's take a look at multi-factor (MFA) or two-factor (2FA) authentication, two terms for the same concept.

Multi-Factor Authentication

Any time that you are using a password to secure client data, look to see if you can also add multi-factor authentication. These two steps—password and a second factor—are what I would consider reasonable for a lawyer protecting confidential and private client data. Anything short of this creates a potential risk that seems unreasonable, given the widespread availability of multi-factor authentication.

We use multi-factor authentication all the time, often without thinking about it. Any time you swipe or tap a debit card and provide a PIN at a point of sale, you are using multi-factor authentication. The card is one thing you have and the PIN is one thing you know. This is the way multi-factor authentication works in law practice technology as well.

The U.S. government agency tasked with cybersecurity says that MFA will reduce your likelihood of being hacked by 99%.[22] It can certainly make it harder to access an account—for you and for someone who is trying to make

22. *Multi-Factor Authentication*, U. S. Cybersecurity and Infrastructure Sec. Agency (last visited June 8, 2025), https://www.cisa.gov/topics/cybersecurity-best-practices/multifactor-authentication. [http://web.archive.org/web/20250608234504/https://www.cisa.gov/topics/cybersecurity-best-practices/multifactor-authentication].

an unauthorized access—and is another potential selection criterion when you are considering law practice technology, especially if it is cloud-based. If you are storing client information in an application or using a system for your law practice business operations, you should look for providers that offer multi-factor authentication.

The most common multi-factor authentication is probably the provision of a numeric code, often 6 digits although I have seen this number creeping up to 8 and 10 digits. You may have experienced this. You attempt to log in to your bank account or a government portal, and it asks you to authenticate yourself. You provide a username and password and then it prompts you to confirm this information with a code. In some cases, you will have given them a phone number, and the site will send you a text message with a 6-digit code. You type in the code from the text, or from an authenticator app on your phone, and you access your account.

It will come as no surprise, after the discussion of passwords, that even MFA is not the same in every instance. Some providers will only send text (SMS) messages with a code. Some providers will use a 4-digit code while others use 8-digits. Some organizations will require you to use their specific MFA mobile application or even a hardware key that generates the code that is so commonly used in MFA, the equivalent of your bank account PIN.

While it is better than nothing, text-messaging MFA is the least desirable method of authentication. Even one-time codes, generated by an app on your phone, are something you can disclose by mistake.[23] The best method is to use a hardware key that you place in or next to your device, using near-field communication (NFC), that transmits the authentication directly to the requesting application. In that way, if someone sends you a convincing email or text message and you are *phished*, you cannot accidentally divulge the last piece of information—in addition to your username and password—that someone would need to access your account.[24]

---

23. *Small Business Cybersecurity Corner, Multi-factor Authentication*, NAT'L INST. OF STANDARDS AND TECH. (last visited June 7, 2025), https://www.nist.gov/itl/smallbusinesscyber/guidance-topic/multi-factor-authentication [https://web.archive.org/web/20250607114023/https://www.nist.gov/itl/smallbusinesscyber/guidance-topic/multi-factor-authentication].

24. Phishing is a type of social engineering where a communication exhorts you to take an action, usually logging into an account to check on an issue which the communication suggests is an emergency. When you use the link or resource in the email or text message, you are taken to a mimic site where, when you provide your information, you are not logging in to your account but are instead divulging the information for someone else

You will not always be able to make a technology selection when it comes to multi-factor authentication. Many applications do not support the hardware option, and so using a multi-factor authenticator app is the next best option. In fact, you may not even be able to use an authenticator app with many banks and online services that only offer text messaging authentication. It is unfortunate, but the reasonable lawyer may be limited by the technology choices of the service provider in this instance.

At a minimum, look for the ability to use codes that you generate yourself, on an app on your own device or by way of a hardware key. This at least eliminates the possibility that the code will be intercepted due to an exploit like SIM swapping.[25] You will have a wide variety of authenticator apps available to you. Some of the things you will want to consider when selecting one:

- Does your law firm or organization use a specific app already? If they do, you will probably find it easier to use the one they have selected. This will ensure the greatest compatibility and the least friction in you adopting it.
- Does the authenticator app enable a backup of codes? Let's imagine you use your phone as your authenticator, with an app installed. If you lose access to that phone—it is stolen, lost, dropped in a sink full of water, dropped out of a window in a two-story building and the screen is smashed—then you may lose access to your codes. Think about how you will maintain a backup of those codes.

Most providers who offer this functionality will provide one or more backup codes to be used in an emergency. These are longer sets of numbers and letters that you are asked to save or write down. You can use these codes if you lose access to your authenticator app for some reason.

Since you can quickly accumulate a lot of these codes, consider how you will store them securely. Just as we discussed above with passwords, you may

---

to access your account. *Small Business Cybersecurity Corner, Phishing*, NAT'L INST. OF STANDARDS AND TECH. (last visited June 6, 2025), https://www.nist.gov/itl/smallbusinesscyber/guidance-topic/phishing [https://web.archive.org/web/20250606032016/https://www.nist.gov/itl/smallbusinesscyber/guidance-topic/phishing].

25. *What Is SIM Swapping & How Does the Hijacking Scam Work?*, MICROSOFT 365 (Jan. 5, 2023), https://www.microsoft.com/en-us/microsoft-365-life-hacks/privacy-and-safety/what-is-sim-swapping?msockid=3823184ec4716ad022b90e40c5136bbc [http://web.archive.org/web/20250617163641/https://www.microsoft.com/en-us/microsoft-365-life-hacks/privacy-and-safety/what-is-sim-swapping?msockid=3823184ec4716ad022b90e40c5136bbc].

want to have a Microsoft Excel spreadsheet to store them. If you are using Excel for your passwords, store these in a different password-protected spreadsheet. Some password managers, like Bitwarden, have a space within your password entry to store your one-time code (OTP or TOTP) as well. This can be helpful although it puts two of your important pieces of information together, and someone who is able to access your password vault will no longer need your authenticator device if you have stored your MFA backup codes there.

When we think about inefficiency, adding a multi-factor authentication process may be a perfect example of *more* friction. However, it is an essential additional layer of security. Also, one thing you may want to become accustomed to is going slowly when you are accessing your accounts. In this sense, more friction is a professional asset. In reality, we are not logging in and out of accounts all day long. We are often logged in once a day. If you are deliberate about each time you log in to your account, you are less likely to get buffaloed into a phishing or other error and inadvertently disclosing information or providing access.

Endpoint Security

In the beginning, there was the PC. It was perhaps the original endpoint but, before the internet and networks, it could easily be an island unto itself. Those days in law firms are long gone, and every device that enters a law practice—phones, tablets, laptops, desktops, servers, smart watches, even some appliances like video cameras and TVs—is likely to be connected to the internet or some sort of network. These devices are referred to as endpoints because they are the end of an internet connection. We communicate between endpoints with email or encrypt information transmission between them when we're in web browsers without really thinking about it. Each of these devices represents a potential security risk, though, and so your law practice technology should consider how secure the endpoints are to which you are connecting.

There is a limit to how much security you can demand of remote endpoints, devices that are outside of your control. Even if you license an application like a practice management system or cloud storage, you can generally only rely on what they *say* they are doing to secure their end of the interaction. In some cases, they may provide evidence of compliance with a standard such as International Standards Organization's ISO 27001, which provides guidelines on managing cybersecurity risk.[26] In others, you can see some information about how they secure their endpoints. For example, when you connect to another website, you can often look at the type of security they use to encrypt the connection. Click on the lock or shield icon next to their URL in your web browser to see information about an online provider's security.

Encryption in Place

One way to secure endpoints is to ensure that they are relying on encryption. There are two ways that encryption can help in a law practice. The first is when a device is turned off or not in use. Encryption is a technology that creates a wrapper around specific files, or a database, or an entire storage device like a computer hard drive. When your computer is turned off, you can use encryption to encase it in a protective, digital layer. If your computer was stolen or lost—you leave your laptop on a train, or someone breaks into your office and steals your computer with a hard drive in it—the encryption could inhibit the ability of someone to access the information on the computer.

Windows computers in law firms often run Bitlocker encryption. It is a simple example of how you might use encryption in your law practice. When you turn on a computer with encryption enabled, it first starts an application that is outside the encrypted drive. This will prompt you for a username or password. If you provide the right authentication information, it will cause the computer drive to be decrypted, removing the security layer. This will then start the operating system (Windows in most cases) on the lawyer's computer, and it will run and look like any other Windows computer.

At the end of the day, you will shut down and log out of your Windows environment. When the computer closes, it will re-encrypt your drive, reapplying the security layer. Until you provide the login credentials again to remove the encryption, the drive will be protected by the encryption.

You may notice that, while you are working on your device, even if it has encryption, it has to be decrypted for you or anyone else to use it. This means that, when you have decrypted your device, it is decrypted for *everyone* who can gain access to it. You should be thoughtful about this and use your operating system's lock screen and screen time out to automatically lock your PC

---

26. ISO is a non-governmental standards development body. *ISO/IEC 27001*, Wikipedia (last visited Aug. 31, 2025), https://en.wikipedia.org/wiki/ISO/IEC_27001.

when it is not being used. This will not cause your computer to be encrypted again, but it can make it more difficult to access the decrypted files.

Device encryption is not limited to computers. Your phone may support device encryption, that you can enable, or it may be fully encrypted. It will work just like a computer, though, which is that, when you are using it actively, the encryption is disabled, and the contents of the device can be accessed by anyone who has physical control of an unlocked device.

Practice Pointer

One of the simplest things you can do to secure your client's information and your law practice's business systems, like your bank account, is to lock your PC when you walk away from it. We often set our computers, if they do not default to it, to go to sleep after a certain amount of time without use. This window of perhaps 10 or 15 minutes is still more than enough if someone walks into your empty office and sits down at your computer. When you get up and leave your computer, hit the Windows key and L or the Apple key and Q to lock the screen.[27] Make this a habit every time you leave your computer. If you have a mobile device, set a PIN and have the screen time out automatically or have it lock when you press the power button.

There are some hybrid encryption options, where you create a secured vault on your device but your computer is not otherwise encrypted. Microsoft OneDrive has implemented a Personal Vault that is a specific location with an additional level of security applied to it. You can save files to your OneDrive, where they are encrypted in place. You can also drop them into your Personal Vault, where you will be prompted for an additional piece of information. This will mean that, even if someone gets access to your unlocked computer, they will still not have access to your Personal Vault.

27. This assumes that you have a login password set on your device. Every device a lawyer uses for law practice should require a PIN or a password for access. *Mac User Guide, Lock the Screen of Your Mac*, Apple (last visited Aug. 31, 2025), https://support.apple.com/guide/mac-help/lock-the-screen-of-your-mac-mchl8e8b6a34/mac. For details about Windows hotkeys including WIN+L, take a look at *Keyboard Shortcuts in Windows*, Microsoft (last visited Aug. 31, 2025), https://support.microsoft.com/en-us/windows/keyboard-shortcuts-in-windows-dcc61a57-8ff0-cffe-9796-cb9706c75eec.

This hybrid model can also be used with encryption applications that create hidden encrypted drives. One open-source app, Veracrypt, can be used to encrypt hard drives as well as portable storage, like external hard drives or USB thumb drives.[28] It can also be used to create a discrete storage container within a hard drive. The encrypted storage container looks like any other kind of file on your computer. Just like a OneDrive Personal Vault, you could create a drive called *Clients* and store your client matter files within the Veracrypt container. When you turned off your computer, it would be re-encrypted like a Bitlocker drive. But you could also close the container, re-encrypting it, while you were still working on your PC. This flexibility may be valuable to a solo lawyer or practitioner who may use their computer for both personal and professional activities.[29]

Encryption in Transit

Encryption is used throughout the internet. For a long time, encryption was a distinguishing factor. Some websites and internet resources used it, and some did not. This started to change in 2012, when a non-profit called Let's Encrypt was created. They developed a system where the security certificates used on the internet could be acquired for free. The elimination of the cost and complexity of security certificates has led to widespread adoption of secure web site connections.[30]

Unlike an encryption technology that you select for your computer or mobile device, internet encryption is something that has to be provided for you. You can make the choice to add encryption to your law firm's website, but other website owners will make the choice to provide encryption (or not) on their sites. You cannot force encrypted connections with servers that do not support it from their end.

You can tell if you are using an encrypted connection with a website by looking at the address in your web browser. The original website protocol meant

---

28. *Veracrypt*, WIKIPEDIA (last visited Aug. 31, 2025), https://en.wikipedia.org/wiki/VeraCrypt.

29. These lawyers may also be more likely to purchase a license to Windows versions, like Windows Home, that do not come with Bitlocker encryption. In that case, Veracrypt can be a free replacement for Bitlocker, used both to encrypt the entire computer as well as discrete encrypted containers on the computer.

30. *Let's Encrypt*, WIKIPEDIA (last visited Aug. 31, 2025), https://en.wikipedia.org/wiki/Let%27s_Encrypt.

that web browsers would connect to addresses starting with *http*. When a site is using an encrypted connection, called secured sockets layer or SSL, the http is appended with an "s" and becomes *https*. Web browsers have added other functionality to highlight whether you are on an encrypted connection or not. Some web browsers will show a shield or a lock when the connection is encrypted. Microsoft Edge will show a lock on a secured connection and a warning *Not Secure* next to the website address when the connection is not secured.

For some time, as this transition from http to https was occurring, security-minded lawyers could use web browser extensions or add-ons to force the use of https if it was available. Some websites would run a secure connection and an insecure connection in parallel. This functionality has largely moved into the web browser itself now. Google Chrome, Microsoft Edge, and Mozilla Firefox all support an *always https* option. Instead of dropping back to an insecure connection, which was often behavior the web browser addons allowed without giving you an option not to, a web browser with always https turned on will show an error message about an insecure website *before* you connect to it. You can then often choose to complete the connection, but it will not happen without your intervention.

Web encryption is important because, although it may look like you are connecting directly to a website, your connection is usually traveling through other computers. For example, a Canadian lawyer may access a Canadian website and think that the interaction is happening entirely in Canada. But there is evidence that about 64% of those interactions traveled through the United States even though both endpoints were in Canada, and another 9% traveled through a third country.[31] If your law practice is in the United States, you can be more confident that your traffic remains within the United States, but it will still be traversing multiple servers to reach you. The internet is a distributed network, and the requests your web browser makes are traveling through other people's computers.[32]

---

31. Bill Woodcock, Packet Clearing House, Results of the PCH/CIRA Study on Canadian Network Interconnection 10 (2016), https://www.pch.net/resources/Papers/CanadianInternet/Canadian%20Peering%202016.pdf [http://web.archive.org/web/20250305200615/https://www.pch.net/resources/Papers/CanadianInternet/Canadian%20Peering%202016.pdf].

32. You can get an idea of how your activity travels by using a network command like traceroute (tracert). On a Windows computer, open a command prompt window and type the command tracert and the website you are trying to reach (like nytimes.com or whitehouse.gov). It will show you a path and list of servers involved in getting from you to your destination. *tracert*, Microsoft (Jan. 11, 2025), https://learn.microsoft.com

Even though encryption technology is not something you can control, it is still something that will be a selection criterion for other technology you choose. There is no good reason to select a technology that you are going to use for your law practice that has not implemented secure socket layer (SSL) encryption. I would be wary of any device app or website that you are using that does not support encrypted connections.

This is easy to confirm, visually, in a web browser. It is much harder to confirm when you are using an app. Some apps will say that they use encrypted connections, but you may still need to investigate. For example, Apple iMessage users who send a message to other Apple iMessage users will be communicating with encryption. But an Apple iMessage user who texted an Android phone user would lose that encryption.[33] This would not be visible to the person sending the text or the recipient, although Apple is changing their app to support encryption to all recipients who have chosen to use Rich Communication Services (RCS).[34]

If your clients want to communicate with you via text, you may need to steer them to more secure communications options. Even if something is interoperable, where you can send a message from one device and app to a different device with a different operating system and different app, it does not mean that it is a secure communication. When you are identifying your communications tools, you will want to identify what will work for your secure communications and what will not.

/en-us/windows-server/administration/windows-commands/tracert [http://web.archive.org/web/20250510071246/https://learn.microsoft.com/en-us/windows-server/administration/windows-commands/tracert].

33. *What Is the Difference Between iMessage, RCS, and SMS/MMS?*, Apple (March 20, 2025), https://support.apple.com/en-us/104972 [http://web.archive.org/web/20250612194113/https://support.apple.com/en-us/104972].

34. Christian Zibreg, *Encrypted RCS Texting Between iPhone and Android Coming Soon*, iDownload (Mar. 17, 2025), https://www.idownloadblog.com/2025/03/17/apple-iphone-rcs-end-to-end-encryption-google-android/. [https://web.archive.org/web/20250610005347/https://www.idownloadblog.com/2025/03/17/apple-iphone-rcs-end-to-end-encryption-google-android/].

Audit Trails

Another technology that you will want to use as a selection criterion is the ability to audit access to your technology. This could be managed easily before the internet because most access was physical: someone had a key to a door or they did not. You may not always have known who had a key, or a lock might be picked for unauthorized access, but there was a need for physical access. Nowadays, someone can access your systems without you seeing any evidence of them, even if you are using the same systems they are. In some cases, this is planned. There are server applications that run all day long to ensure that your files are backed up and that email is being sent and received, and those server applications will have some privileges to access your resources. But what about everyone else?

When you are selecting a technology, look for ways to audit who is using it and what aspects of the tool they are using. If there is a need for a login for the system, make sure each person using the application has their own username and password. In that way, you will not see an action attributable to a username without knowing which person actually took the action.

Some systems, like Microsoft SharePoint will support an audit feature for their system, but it may need to be activated by you or your system administrator.[35] Microsoft Windows users can also turn it on for folders on their computers.[36] Once auditing is enabled on a folder or on a set of folders, your computer will record auditable events in a security log file. You can review this log to see who accessed what and when using Microsoft Windows' Event Viewer.

---

35. Microsoft OneDrive for Business has an audit feature. Microsoft OneDrive Personal does not, even if it is a paid license. *Microsoft 365 Reports in the Admin Center—OneDrive Activity*, MICROSOFT (Mar. 1, 2024), https://learn.microsoft.com/en-us/microsoft-365/admin/activity-reports/onedrive-for-business-activity-ww?view=o365-worldwide [http://web.archive.org/web/20250213140753/https://learn.microsoft.com/en-us/microsoft-365/admin/activity-reports/onedrive-for-business-activity-ww?view=o365-worldwide].

36. Right click on a folder and choose Properties. Select the Security tab and then choose the Advanced button. An auditing option will appear on the next screen, allowing you to enable auditing on all objects within this folder.

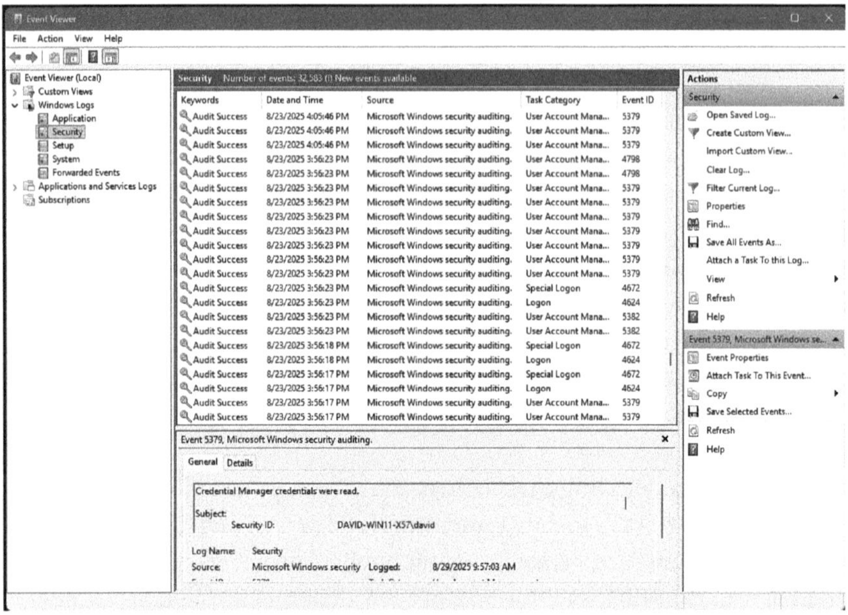

Figure 13: Example of eventvwr log audit success and failure

Patching and Updating

An under-appreciated part of technology purchasing is the ongoing maintenance that is required. This is particularly true for software, but it will apply to hardware as well. A solo lawyer may be able to get away with a consumer-oriented purchasing approach, where the cost is relatively low, and so it can be easier to buy a new piece of technology than repair an older one. Larger law firms will require more complex software or implementations if all lawyers and staff in the firm are using it. The thing to keep in mind is that whatever size law firm you are in, your technology is going to need to be updated regularly.

There is an inherent risk in these updates, but it is balanced against the risk of not keeping current. Microsoft is notorious for its Patch Tuesday, a term of art now for any regular software updates provided by vendors.[37] These updates can take a couple of forms. Some are software updates that bring new features to an application. Many updates will be much smaller, involving more discrete

37. Patch Tuesday's origins. *Patch Tuesday*, WIKIPEDIA (last visited Aug. 31, 2025), https://en.wikipedia.org/wiki/Patch_Tuesday.

software or configuration changes that make your software more secure or enable it to run with more stability.

The risk, of course, is that the update or patch will create new problems. It does not take much searching to find Microsoft Windows users who have updated their copy of Windows only to find that their computer will no longer start. These are usually issues that can be fixed, but it may require a lawyer to hire a consultant to resolve the problem, and they may interfere with your ability to help your clients.

This is one reason that larger organizations with information technology (IT) teams will test out new updates in advance of releasing them to others. Microsoft supports the creation of automation policies that allow IT to manage and push out updates. Some organizations will disable the automatic updating in Microsoft Windows so that they have the time to test updates. As the saying goes, an ounce of prevention is worth a pound of cure. If a software update is released to an entire law firm and it breaks every computer, this becomes a big problem. Not only will the law firm need to have its IT staff refocus their time on the emergency and away from other projects, but the lawyers' inability to access case files and client matter information will be impacted as well. This risk-balancing leans in favor of testing to avoid negative outcomes.

This is a harder balance to achieve with a solo lawyer or small law firm. If you do not have your own dedicated IT team, or someone who can do regular weekly testing for you, your choice is to enable the automatic updates or disable them entirely. You can pause them temporarily, but the value of this is questionable unless you are planning to do testing in the meantime. A choice to disable updates may seem like the easier one, but you have to remember that the update or patch you are avoiding is usually attempting to address a known problem. Some of these known problems are security risks that themselves will put your confidential and private client information at risk.

Practice Pointer

I recommend always using the automatic software update feature in your software or hardware unless you have a good alternative process. Most updates will have been tested and, in the case of things like an operating system update from Microsoft, will be released gradually. This means that they will often catch issues impacting certain types of computers before they release it broadly. While Windows offers an option for getting the very earliest updates, lawyers should steer towards the default update option. This more conservative approach will mean that, when an update arrives at your computer, it should be as thoroughly vetted as possible.

Whatever comfort level you have with your updates, there should be no question that you will want to receive them eventually. A common fact in stories about lawyers and others whose networks have been attacked and data extracted is that their systems were not maintained properly. A key element in that maintenance is making sure the software running on them is properly patched and current.

This is also reflected in how updates are delivered now. In the past, you might have had to seek out an update and patch your own computer. Or you would have updates available, but, by default, the auto-update feature would be turned off. Both of these created friction and the perception if not the reality that a bit of technical knowhow was required to be successful. It is now far more common for an application to keep itself up to date unless you disable the automatic updates. Windows is a prime example of this shift. The latest versions of Windows will not allow updates to be completely turned off:

> You cannot stop updates entirely—because they help keep your device safe and secure, updates will eventually need to be installed and downloaded, regardless of your update settings.[38]

This explanation by Microsoft misses one point that should be emphasized: if your computer is connected to the internet, then keeping it secure helps *other people* as well. Unpatched Windows computers and other devices can be exploited to attack third parties. They can be corralled into a loose collection called a botnet—managed by a bot herder—to take large-scale actions.[39]

---

38. *Windows Update: FAQ*, Microsoft (last visited June 23, 2025), https://support.microsoft.com/en-us/windows/windows-update-faq-8a903416-6f45-0718-f5c7-375e92dddeb2 [http://web.archive.org/web/20250623135752/https://support.microsoft.com/en-us/windows/windows-update-faq-8a903416-6f45-0718-f5c7-375e92dddeb2].

39. *Botnet*, Wikipedia (last visited Aug. 31, 2025), https://en.wikipedia.org/wiki/Botnet; *Bot Herder*, Wikipedia (last visited Aug. 31, 2025), https://en.wikipedia.org/wiki/Bot_herder. Unsurprisingly, there are cloud-based subscription botnets where you can pay a bot herder to take an action for you. These platforms, known as "Bots as a Service" (compare to Software as a Service), can be used to engage in large-scale attacks for a small fee and without the technical knowhow to create one's own botnet. *Bots-as-a-Service (BaaS): A New Era of Automated Bot Attacks*, Arkose Labs (Apr. 27, 2023), https://www.arkoselabs.com

When you patch your own systems, you are protecting yourself, and you are helping to protect the rest of the internet.

We have mostly been talking about endpoints that you would probably refer to as being a computer or computer-like: a phone, tablet, laptop, or desktop computer, or an internet server of some sort. But what about all of the other devices in your office that provide a utility function? How should you manage those devices and their updates?

Internet of Things

This collection of devices is commonly called the internet of things. They are devices that might traditionally have been entirely offline but, increasingly, are having additional features built-in, many of which rely on the internet. Home assistants like Amazon's Alexa and Google's Assistant provide options to create collections of inter-operational technology within your homes. Your refrigerator may have wi-fi connectivity so that you can download photos or synchronize a shopping list or play music from a streaming radio player. Your lights may have an internet component. If you have purchased surveillance technology like outdoor cameras or baby monitors or a camera-enabled doorbell, those devices are often able to be connected to the internet.

This collection of internet-enabled appliances does not even touch on the devices like your internet modem and possibly your wi-fi hardware, like a router, that are intended primarily to connect to the internet. The reality is that every lawyer's home and most of their offices will have devices that are internet-capable and possibly internet-accessible whether they are used in that manner or not.

This raises two issues. The first is that many devices that can access the internet can also be accessed *from* the internet. The second is that, to be internet-capable, it must have an operating system. This operating system will need to be updated and patched no less than your Windows laptop or your Android phone.

As you start to look around your apartment or your office or study space, you may start to visualize the scale of the problem. How many internet-enabled devices do you have within your living or workspace? How many of them do you know how to update or patch or even what version of Linux or Windows

---

/blog/bots-as-a-service-baas-a-new-era-of-automated-bot-attacks/ [http://web.archive.org/web/20250118211151/https://www.arkoselabs.com/blog/bots-as-a-service-baas-a-new-era-of-automated-bot-attacks/].

or custom operating system is running on them? How many of them provide you with information about whether they are secured or require an update?

The internet of things is an inherently thorny issue. As a rule, if you can access the internet with a device, the internet will be able to access your device as well, directly or by delivering files through your connection to it. This is most true when you access a web server and your computer downloads all of the files the server sends you. Some of those files will be visible to you, but many of them will not. Some of these invisible files make the page work more effectively, like a JavaScript file that enables a useful menu, or that make the page look more user friendly or modern, like a stylesheet. But you generally will not know what files are being downloaded out of your view.

As you think about the websites you visit, what other resources might you be using as a lawyer that are internet-facing? Perhaps your office uses remotely accessible resources like a client extranet or a file server so that you can access your files when you are away from the office. You may even be in an organization where you use a virtual private network (VPN) application to create a secure connection between your computer and your law practice.

Anything that is internet-facing, anything that you can connect to from outside your law office, is potentially accessible by anyone else who is also outside your law office. These devices are the most at risk. Let's take a look at an example.

There was once a lawyer who worked at home. They worked in a law office as well and sometimes traveled. When they were on the road, they would connect back to their law office by a virtual private network (VPN). When they were at home, they would also use a VPN to connect to the firm's systems, ensuring that no one could access their law firm systems except through a VPN.

Now, you might think that someone accessed the law firm's VPN server because it wasn't patched. In fact, they did not need to do that. This lawyer had an infant and had set up an internet-enabled baby monitor. The baby monitor shared the same wi-fi connection as the lawyer's computer, which was connected to the law firm's VPN. A remote user was able access the baby monitor and jump across the lawyer's home network to access the lawyer's laptop. Since it was logged in as the lawyer to the firm's VPN, the remote user could now access whatever the lawyer could.

The technology at fault here was the baby monitor. In order to deliver its functionality, it had an operating system and a wi-fi antenna. Despite the lawyer having thought through their technology choices and security—although leaving their home computer remotely logged in to the law firm's VPN exacerbated the problem—it was a small, consumer-oriented device that undermined their ability to protect their client's information.

The internet of things is focused on simplifying utility aspects of our lives: building a shopping list based on what's in our fridge, letting us see how our pets or children are acting when we're away, getting access to files that we forgot to put on our computer before we left our home or the office. At the same time, each of these things creates additional risk when they are brought into contact with our law practice technology. If the manufacturer of the consumer technology is not maintaining the hardware and software, and you connect the device to a network that also connects to your law practice, you may be at risk of breaching your client's confidentiality, having your client trust account drained, or other negative consequences.

The best solution is to patch and update all of these devices. The reality is that many consumer devices do not come with any plan or functionality to update them. They are as current as the day you bought them and cannot be made more current. They remain connected to the internet, sometimes without even having their default security configuration changed. Someone who can find those devices, and who knows the default username and password, can see if they are able to exploit that access.[40]

You might ask yourself, how would someone know?

Everything Is on the Internet

It is worth taking a moment to talk about how the internet works. Each device that is connected to the internet is given an address, known as an IP address.[41] When your phone is connected for data, it has an IP address. Same with your desktop or laptop computer when it is on wi-fi or a wired network

40. If you search the internet for "default password" and the name of a product that has a username and password, it is often visible as a search result. This has started to change. Two of the most common devices on a home or office network—the modem and the router, sometimes the same piece of hardware—now frequently come with a custom password on a label on the device. This makes it more difficult for you if you forget your password and cannot touch the device, but it means that no one can guess your default password.

41. There are two basic types. IPv4 has four sets of up to three numbers and looks like this: 192.168.12.240. IPv6 addresses are longer and contain colons instead of periods. Here's an example: 2345:0425:2CA1::0567:5673:23b5. We are in the middle of a transition from IPv4 to IPv6 because we ran out of (or exhausted) IPv4 numbers. Paul Wilson, *IPv4 Exhaustion and Address Transfers, and Their Impact on IPv6 Deployment*, APNIC (last visited Mar. 22, 2025), https://www.apnic.net/manage-ip/ipv4-exhaustion/ipv4-exhaustion-and-address-transfers/ [http://web.archive.org/web/20250322055109/https://www.apnic

connection. You do not have to be connected to the internet to have an IP address. Devices that are used just within your home or law office will have IP addresses too.[42] Pretty much every internet-connected device has a unique IP address. If they did not, the network—and the internet is just a really large network—would not know where to send information.

As the internet grew, though, it became harder to know all of the IP addresses you would need to remember. If you wanted to go and search the internet, you could go to 142.251.32.14. But it is far easier to know that number translates to Google.com.[43] We tend to use words like descriptive names or, as we referred to them previously, domain names, to access resources on our networks. They can be easier to remember. Even when we do not know, they can give us more information about what the network resource is: Bing.com and HPOfficeJet have more information in their names than 150.171.27.10 or 192.168.0.14.

These names, on the internet at least, are managed using a domain name system (DNS). This system is a large directory that connects IP addresses to, where they are known, domain names. When we type in a domain name like Tiktok.com into our web browser's location bar, our device sends a request to a DNS server who translates the name to the IP address—23.64.112.4—and forwards the request to the correct server.

The system works because sometimes our computers move and change IP addresses. If we know the domain name, though, the domain name owner can keep DNS updated on any moves. In that way, no matter what the behind-the-scenes IP address is, the DNS will forward us to the right location. If the domain name is sold and moves to a new IP address, we may not be able to tell by just typing in the domain name. This is one reason, as referred to above, that once you have a domain name for your law firm, you need to keep it forever.

There are network tools that allow you to look at who is using an IP address. This helps IT teams to diagnose what is causing a problem with someone's network-connected device. These tools can help you to find information

---

.net/manage-ip/ipv4-exhaustion/ipv4-exhaustion-and-address-transfers/]. However, you will still see both in use.

42. These are often called non-routable addresses because they are not intended to be visible to the internet. Because they are contained within a local network, there is no restriction on duplication. Your home and your law office could assign the same IP address to two different items—your toaster and your law practice's multi-function printer—but, because they're not connected on the same network, they will not be mistaken for each other.

43. Go ahead, try it. Paste or type that IP address into your web browser to go to Google's search engine.

about the IP address owner too. In particular, whois tools will often show information about the person or entity that manages an IP address or range of addresses.[44]

Why does all of this matter? Imagine that all of these IP addresses were instead phone numbers. What if I could create a tool that would automatically dial each phone to see if it was picked up? Or perhaps I could create an automated message to play if someone *did* answer the phone?

We know that is possible. The spam phone call is not a technological innovation. But there are people who do the same thing with the internet. It is possible to test every single IP address and see if something responds. If something is internet-accessible, there is a good chance that it will respond to a request. Just like telephones before caller ID, an internet-facing device may not know whether the request is coming from a friend or a foe. It will answer whenever it is called. Just as with spam calls, this information gathering can be automated so that the information is gathered without someone having to make each request.

The data from these interactions is recorded and stored in large databases. One of the best known is Shodan.[45] It is a search engine for devices that are internet-facing. It can search for resources that are on the internet but that are hidden—security through obscurity—because they do not have a domain name, just an IP address. A person can search for all kinds of information and filter it by IP address or country.[46] The real power of Shodan comes when you know that there is a weakness that someone wants to exploit. Sites like ExploitDB or CVE Details will list known vulnerabilities.[47] Once they have identified a vulnerability, they can return to a site like Shodan to see if there are any visible systems. For example, they might look up the common network

44. Two WHOIS searches I use regularly are at https://search.arin.net and https://whois.com/whois/. You can test them by first going to a web search engine and typing in "what is my IP address" to find out your own address (or use a service like https://whatismyipaddress.com/). Cut and paste your IP address into a WHOIS search to learn more about what your IP address says about your device. Or type in a domain name of a website and see what information you can learn about the domain name owner.

45. https://shodan.io.

46. A simple search like https://www.shodan.io/search?query=%22law+firm%22 will return all devices in the Shodan database where the host name includes "law firm." Some of the resources are websites. At the time of writing, one was an Apple TimeMachine backup, which suggests it might have contained law firm files.

47. https://www.exploit-db.com and https://www.cvedetails.com.

attached storage by Synology on ExploitDB and then go over to Shodan to see if any devices appear that might be impacted by the exploit or vulnerability.

This is not a recommendation to prod at other people's systems. Rather, it is a suggestion that you want to ensure that your personal and law practice technology resources do not become visible to others in databases like these. This requires you to patch and update and configure your technology securely. These are steps you will have to return to regularly over the lifetime of your law practice.

In particular, when it comes to the internet of things, be prepared to throw away devices that age out and are no longer secure and can also not be updated or be made secure. While I was writing this text, I noticed a law office that was running an Apple AirPort Time Capsule router, one that Apple discontinued in 2018. The Time Capsule is both an internet connectivity device and a storage device. It is the sort of internet-facing device that should be replaced when the manufacturer discontinues it.[48]

Remote Work and Cloud Computing

The issues surrounding securing your law practice technology from intrusion have only grown since the COVID-19 pandemic upended how lawyers work. We have gone from mostly being worried about things lawyers receive—viruses and malware, which could be disruptive but were not necessarily things that would bring law firm collapse—to exploits that include phishing trust account usernames and passwords or ransomware that encrypts every device. Now many lawyers are working from remote locations for some or all of the time, which may introduce new attack vectors (how secure is the wi-fi or internet connection you are using, are you mixing personal and professional activities on the same devices, and so on).

If your law practice was not considering hybrid or fully remote work before 2020, it almost certainly is now.[49] While the question leaves some ambiguity,

48. I was able to guess at the owner and emailed the lawyer who it belonged to. While somewhat taken aback, they appreciated the tip and knew the device I was indicating.

49. There is a shift among large law firms to return to a four- or five-day a week office-centric approach to law practice. Maria Lenin Laus, *Biglaw's Return-to-Office Trend: Why 4 Days a Week Is the New Standard in 2025*, JD Journal (July 13, 2025), https://www.jdjournal.com/2025/07/13/biglaws-return-to-office-trend-why-4-days-a-week-is-the-new-standard-in-2025/. Unless the law firm prohibits the use of devices outside the law

lawyer use of home offices has doubled both in solo law practices and large law firms since the pandemic lockdown.[50] Some practice areas, in particular criminal law, have always been a largely hybrid practice with a lot of time spent outside of the office, visiting clients at their location or working out of the courthouse. Remote work by necessity relies on internet technologies. These connections will enable you to access and update your calendar, engage in communications with your clients, staff, and other lawyers, and perform so many of the other operational functions of a law practice.

In many cases, working remotely does not require your law firm to expose its internal systems directly to the internet. Technology like VPNs can act as a gateway to the systems you need to access, for example. You can also secure internet-facing systems so that they are only accessible from specific IP addresses or devices. Another alternative is to license software that allows you to use it *offline* when you are away from the office. Neither your server nor your mobile app are connected and only synchronize when you return to your office. You can select technology that allows your law practice to remain secured away from the internet while you use internet-accessible technologies, secured by others, to run your law practice.

The easiest way to balance the risk with the need or benefits of remote work is to rely on systems where the internet-facing technology includes resources to maintain its security. This will result in a trade-off between hiring technology staff or consultants or licensing platforms that come with security support. For most lawyers, this will mean engaging with more, rather than fewer, cloud computing platforms.

Cloud computing is a huge area, and it is a marketing term that applies to a vast number of technology products, many of which are of little use to a typical law firm. As a technology selection criterion, it is not a very useful guide. The most common use of cloud computing is to access software hosted on servers that are not owned or directly managed by the law firm. But every layer of that software hosting—the physical servers that provide access, the management of the operating system or resources on the physical servers—is

firm, this shift will not reduce the potential risks that lawyers or staff may encounter while at court, in client spaces, or in shared public spaces.

50. Am. Bar Ass'n, 2023 Legal Technology Survey Report: Marketing & Communications Technology 12 (2024). Prior to COVID-19, 26% of solos reported that their home was their primary workplace and only 2% of lawyers with more than 500 lawyers did. Post-lockdown, 46% of solos reported that their home was their primary workplace and 25% of respondents from firms with over 500 lawyers did.

distinguishable as a "cloud" offering. Each layer can be licensed à la carte. A law firm would need to be large enough or have sophisticated enough requirements—such as developing its own software that it then licenses to its clients but runs on technology hosted in the cloud by a third-party—that are well beyond what a solo or small firm lawyer will need.

Some of these underlying cloud layers include Platforms-as-a-Service (PaaS), Infrastructure-as-a-Service (IaaS), or Data-as-a-Service (DaaS). Law firms might license services for other functions where it is not clear whether they are using Software-as-a-Service (SaaS), which is the most common cloud computing technology lawyers will experience, or a more refined *-as-a-Service* version of that function.

For example, Backup-as-a-Service (or Disaster-Recovery-as-a-Service (DRaaS) provides a redundancy using cloud technology. You might license a cloud-based backup service (or use Microsoft OneDrive or Apple iDrive for your primary data) like OpenText's Carbonite or Backblaze's eponymous product. These services can feel more like a Software-as-a-Service offering—simple web-based interface with a local application to manage the backup process—but may refer to themselves in marketing as Disaster-Recovery-as-a-Service. The latter category can include a vast array of redundancy services—including full backups of virtualized, in operation servers—that are far beyond what many solo or small law firm practices will need. The backup provider will themselves license cloud-based systems—Platforms, Infrastructure, etc.—to be able to deliver their products.

As you explore your options, you will notice that many of them will be internet- or "cloud-" based. Do not worry so much about how they are marketed or what label they use, and focus on the technology problem you are trying to solve. Whatever they are called, if they do not solve your problem, they are not the right technology for you.

These internet-facing services will be secured with a password and should also require multi-factor authentication, something that may not be possible with technology you manage on your own. Whether on the cloud or in your office, this is the baseline method to secure your law practice's confidential and private information.

A password and multifactor authentication can prevent unauthorized access through the front door. Unfortunately, not all unauthorized access attempts stop at trying the front door handle. When you run your own systems or servers on your law firm premises ("on prem"), you also take on the obligation to secure them against other types of lateral or backdoor entry and access. When you license a cloud-based product, they should be taking care of those issues for you. Cloud computing services will have a technology team and security measures in place to protect access to your information for you.

There was a time when cloud computing caused a great deal of concern within the legal profession. This came, in part, from lawyers assuming that the only way they could protect client confidentiality was to run their own servers and systems or that cloud-based systems would provide inferior security to an on-premises option. In fact, even when my book on practicing law in the cloud was published in 2013, many lawyers had been using cloud computing services for years. Cloud-based email, calendaring, and contact management was already the norm in many solo and small law firm practices. This acceptance of the cloud, whether an intentional technology selection or merely by default of what is easiest and, on the solo lawyer end of the profession, what is available to a consumer, has only grown over the last decades.

The selection criteria related to remote work is less about a specific product and more about how to maintain a secure connection to it while you are away from your law office. Each choice—cloud computing and on-premises software and hardware—comes with its own costs and benefits. Cloud computing can often have fewer up-front costs, but it can also provide less long-term flexibility due to vendor lock-in. If you run your own servers and secured connections for remote access, you will need to invest in all of the systems management that your cloud provider builds into their pricing.

If you do not think that you can maintain the systems and security necessary to expose your own law firm technology to the internet, you should think seriously about using cloud-based systems. You will not be alone. In fact, cloud computing is increasingly the default for lawyers. I think it is hard to argue that, nowadays, it is unreasonable from a professional competence standpoint for a lawyer to use cloud-based systems.

Solo lawyers and small law firms have often, out of necessity, used cloud-based solutions as they were sometimes the only realistic option other than to forego the technology. But we have seen larger law firms shift to a cloud-centric approach as well. The 2024 International Legal Technology Association survey showed that 43% of respondents were mostly in the cloud in their technology adoption, up from 24% in 2021.[51] Another 42% were considering cloud with every upgrade. In 2021, 28% of organizations responding to the

51. Int'l Legal Tech. Ass'n, 2024 Technology Survey Executive Summary 11 (2024).

survey indicated they were "considering" the cloud. That number had plummeted to 13% by 2024, a year in which only 2% still responded that they were not yet comfortable with cloud computing.[52]

An obvious benefit to cloud-based systems is that you can access the same system from wherever you are. You access the service, using an app on your phone or computer or via a web browser window, over the internet. The user experience or functionality may vary based on the device, but the role it plays in your law practice will be the same from whatever location you are in.

A locally hosted service or server would be different when you are in the office—perhaps using a piece of software that is unique to that application—and different when you are working remotely. If nothing else, there is a good chance you will need to use additional software like a virtual private network that creates a secure connection between your endpoint device and the endpoint that is physically within our law office.

Cloud computing can also achieve the setting of a software standard for a law firm. Even if your law firm prohibits remote work, if everyone is using the same cloud-based application, it provides the people supporting that technology with certainty about what people are seeing. If your law firm uses a mixture of tools, on-premises and in the cloud, it will increase the complexity when, more likely than not, someone needs to work remotely to support a client.[53] You may have already experienced this at your law school, where your university and law school may have provided *both* Google Workspace and Microsoft 365 or other duplicate sets of software. This duplication creates complexity for the user (which one do I use if I want to be sure I can collaborate with others) and for the technology staff who have to support each application. The attraction of cloud computing as a way to landing on a standard is pretty clear.

52. There is no reason to think this 2% of respondents are laggards. There are some law firms and law practices where there is a huge risk to their clients or their ability to manage compliance in the cloud. I believe there will always be some firms for whom the cloud creates more challenges than it solves.

53. There is a philosophical discussion in many law firms about whether remote legal work is appropriate, mostly from the perspective of the firm's investment in space and utilizing their employees' lives most fully for revenue generation. The reality is that lawyers have always worked remotely, even before the widespread use of the internet. Lawyers were using dial up modems over telephone lines in the 1980s and 1990s, connecting from courthouses and client conference rooms. Remote work will always be part of the law practice of any lawyer who considers their client's needs.

Redundancy

As your law practice grows, you will want to consider how you can create redundancy in your law practice technology. At the start, as you emerge from law school, this may require more of a financial outlay than you can justify. But, over time, it will be an area where you will want to make investments to ensure your systems are available.

In the past, redundancy has come in two key areas. One is in your law practice storage. It is imperative that the hard drives that keep your client data do not fail or, when they do, you have a copy that ensures the information remains accessible. Another is in your internet connection. It is common for organizations to have more than one internet service provider (ISP) or more than one connection with their ISP. It is not uncommon to hear in the news of an internet cable being damaged—someone who has dug through a buried cable or a fishing boat dragging a cable and severing one—causing a temporary internet outage. If your law practice relies on a single method of accessing the internet, an outage like this can take your law firm offline as effectively as a more malicious attack.

Redundant connectivity is much simpler in most locations now. If your land-based internet connection goes down, you will almost certainly have an alternative in your phone's data plan or over-the-air internet connectivity. You can tether your phone as a wi-fi hotspot to temporarily replace your connection to your internet service provider. You should plan for this sort of outage with your selection of a phone and telecom services. Your data plan will need to support tethering, and you should understand any costs associated with using your data in this way. But in an emergency, there is a good chance you could call your telecom company and upgrade your service to provide the access you need.

Storage redundancy has become sufficiently commoditized that a law practice can buy a device that is designed for redundancy. These are often referred to as network-attached storage (NAS)—since they attach to the law firm's network and provide storage—and come with multiple hard drive storage bays. Each bay can hold a hard drive, and your choice of NAS will determine how many bays you can use.

Storage redundancy uses a few basic models. One is to mirror your drives, which does exactly what it sounds like. You use one hard drive and a second (usually the same model and size as the first one) copies everything over. It becomes a mirror of the first drive. If the first drive fails, you can switch over to the second one. Since it is an exact copy, and it is in the same NAS device on your network, all of your systems should treat it the same way they treated the first drive. Once you order a replacement hard drive (or buy one in anticipation of a failure), you can pull out the failed drive and install the fresh one. At that point, the working drive will copy itself over to the new drive.

Practice Pointer

Test your backup. I cannot say this enough times. Once you have copied your files to the cloud or onto an external drive, look at them. See if you can recover or retrieve one file that was backed up. You would not be the first lawyer who thought they had backed up their files only to find out, when they needed them, that they had not. Systems will not always show an error when they fail, and I have worked at organizations that have lost years of data because the backup process looked like it was working and was not. Test your backup. Periodically, once you have successfully created a backup of your files, see if you can retrieve a file you've "lost" and see what happens. You should be able to recover a file from a backup.

A more complicated system is called RAID. A drive mirror is the most basic type of RAID, but a RAID array uses more than two drives and can be configured in a variety of ways.[54] Each additional drive increases the redundancy of your data storage.

It is common to supplement this sort of storage redundancy with a regular full backup of your data that is stored away from the working copy. You might use storage tapes, because they can hold a large amount of data. A solo or small law firm practice may use a cloud backup service, or they might purchase a few external hard drives. These are cases that have a small computer inside and hold a single hard drive, just like the ones in your computer or in a network-attached storage appliance. You can connect the external hard drive to your computer or to a NAS or other storage device and make a copy. This copy will not stay as current as a mirrored or RAID drive, but you can take it and store it in a different physical building. In that way, if a storm or fire de-

54. *RAID*, Wikipedia (last visited Aug. 31, 2025), https://en.wikipedia.org/wiki/RAID.

stroys your office or if someone breaks in and steals your network file server, you will still have a copy of your client files.

Disaster Recovery

Business continuity is about ensuring your law practice can continue no matter what act of God or other unexpected event occurs. Disaster recovery can sometimes be viewed as a technology on its own or to be focused on technology components. More often, though, it is having a *plan* or process to deal with a disaster. As you make technology selections, think about what would happen if your law firm suffered the most common natural disasters in your area: tornados, hurricanes, flooding, fire. How would you continue to practice law and support your clients? How would you continue to use *this particular piece of technology that you are selecting* in the event of a disaster?

The time to think about this is now, before you have started practice. It does not need to be complicated or expensive. Larger organizations will absolutely spend a lot of money, in some cases creating an entire copy of their physical space and technology at a second location. But as you start out in law practice, you will not need to over-engineer your disaster recovery. You just need to think about what would happen with your choices if a common disaster occurred:

- Cloud-based email with Microsoft 365. How will you have internet access? Will your clients likely have internet or email access to *receive* your emails?
- Cloud-based storage with Microsoft 365 or OneDrive. How will you have internet access or will you be able to use a recent local copy on your computer?
- Cloud-based practice management system. How will you have internet access? What will happen to your critical dates and deadlines?
- External hard drive or cloud backup. How do you access the files, and do you have another device on which to load them?

And so on. In fact, the problems you are likely to run into will occur in spite of your planning. Your laptop computer will fail, or your phone will fall into a toilet. The disaster is often very localized to the lawyer, rather than to a building or a town even. A broken computer can knock your law practice out of commission for a day or more. Do not ignore signs that your computer is not working well—it runs slowly or you get a message from the Windows Self-Monitoring, Analysis, and Reporting Technology (SMART) that your hard drive is failing—but think of it like an ailing child or pet. It is better to spend a bit of time ensuring your technology is working rather than to have it fail and, in addition to needing to be repaired or replaced, losing access to your critical law practice tools. An ounce of prevention can be worth a pound of cure.

Cloud computing systems fail too. You can use other cloud services that monitor major website availability ("Is Microsoft 365 down for everyone or just me?") or the status page for the service itself.[55] You should try to find out what cloud computing infrastructure your service relies on, if you can. For example, you may subscribe to a practice management application in the cloud that itself relies on other cloud computing services for its infrastructure (IaaS) or platform (PaaS). There are two massive cloud infrastructure providers. One is Microsoft, with its Azure platform, and the other is Amazon, with its Amazon Web Services. Both of those providers have status pages. They will not report on the application that *you have licensed*, but they will report their own outages which may explain—or document, if you need to be reimbursed for an outage—how long the outage lasted.[56]

Keep in mind that your duty as a lawyer will be to take reasonable care with your technology. Disaster recovery can become a sinkhole of time and money, like an insurance premium, providing the potential of recovery without considering the likelihood of the risk. Try to keep your disaster recovery plans as simple as possible so that, if the time comes, you are not overwhelmed with complexity in trying to bring your systems back online.

---

55. For example, you can see the current status of Microsoft's cloud products at its status page. https://status.cloud.microsoft/. Google Workspace has a similar resource. https://www.google.com/appsstatus/dashboard/.

56. The Amazon Web Services (AWS) status page. https://health.aws.amazon.com/health/status. Microsoft Azure's status is here: https://azure.status.microsoft/en-us/status. Both show the geographic regions where they operate. An outage in one geographic region may not have any impact on your application if your provider does not operate in that region.

Chapter 12 Exercises

A. Using Exploit-DB and Shodan, see if you can identify a specific class of device with a vulnerability and whether they are visible in Shodan. This will require a free Shodan account.

B. Make a list of all of the devices that connect to the internet in your home or office. Identify the method in which each device is updated; for some, there likely is no update method. If you can, identify what operating system it uses and when it was last updated. Identify any devices that have reached the end of their supported life.

C. Centralize all your passwords in a password manager, and begin using it in preparation for starting to practice.

D. At an organization at which you work or study, learn what their current password manager or two-factor authentication tools are and review their implementation from your user perspective, identifying potential security gaps (can anyone opt out of the password manager or MFA endpoint security? Do they violate NIST guidance by requiring annual password changes? How are single password accounts shared securely so that they can be audited?).

Chapter 13

Practice Management Systems

We have touched on practice management systems here and there as we have laid out the primary technology that you will find in a law practice. It is hard to really convey the power of an integrated practice management system for a lawyer. It embodies practically all of the key productivity tools that you will need for your law practice. In a sense, it is a no-brainer as a one-and-done law practice technology tool. And yet, law practice management software has continued to lag behind other technology adoption by lawyers. This has more to do with how lawyers use technology and less to do with the quality or value of practice management systems.

I will own up to a preference for integrated practice management software. I began working with legal technology in 1992 at a very early practice management company, Future Law, selling a product called Privilege to lawyers and law firms who were just starting to buy the relatively recent portable computer or PC. The software was developed by Ray Bishop, who had been deeply involved in ABA efforts around the economics of law practice and practice management. It reflected how his law practice operated and, as someone who had worked in his law firm for a few years, captured all of the key tools he and his lawyers and staff used.

My role was to provide technical support to our clients who, often as not, were solo lawyers around the United States. A lot of my work involved helping them to configure the application to match how they practiced law. Over the time I worked at Future Law, it became clear that the software, so ideally suited for Ray's firm, did not always reflect how other people worked. The software was highly adaptable though, so it could be tailored to how other lawyers practiced. The challenge was that, to make it highly useful, a lawyer would have to take a lot of time to customize it. On the other hand, if they used a largely turn-key configuration, they would have to adapt their processes to the system. It was an insurmountable challenge for the product.

Although Privilege is gone, this challenge remains with more modern products and is perhaps most readily identifiable when you are searching for software that says it was "designed by lawyers, for lawyers." As this book shows, it is not hard to identify the key law practice technology tools that you will encounter when you graduate from law school. The challenge is figuring out how to match that software to the way that *you* will practice law. Fundamentally, the practice of law is a very individual endeavor. You are responsible as an individual for your professional ethics, your regulatory compliance, and to your clients and colleagues. You may or may not join a law firm but, even there, you will have an individual approach to how you use your technology even as you are part of an organization with hundreds of other law practitioners.

One of the fascinating developments in law practice management software is the emergence of Clio. It is by far the most widely adopted practice management application developed specifically for lawyers, and yet it reflects few of the more typical approaches to law practice technology.[1]

The two founders were not lawyers. They had been asked by a Canadian lawyer regulator to create an application to help lawyers avoid discipline.[2] Fortuitously, cloud computing was starting to make scalable web applications a reality. The lack of a dominant product aimed at solo and small firm lawyers gave Clio a wide opening. It has grown from a Canadian-centric practice management offering to a global phenomenon in legal technology.

One reason I have attributed to their success was that they did not develop their product with their own past law practice experience in mind. Over time, Clio sought user feedback, did development sprints at their customer conferences to build the features lawyers upvoted, and continued to extend functionality. As a cloud-first product, they also got the jump on many of the

1. Keep in mind that, in the 2023 American Bar Association Legal Technology Survey, less than 60% of lawyers had access to practice management software. AM. BAR ASS'N, 2023 LEGAL TECHNOLOGY SURVEY REPORT: LAW OFFICE TECHNOLOGY 32, question 23a-u (2024). This number drops to fewer than 40% of lawyers who actually use it themselves, with only about 11% of lawyers in the largest firms. p. 37(Q23b-d). Microsoft Outlook is the product most lawyers mention for practice management (68%), with Clio in second place (20%) and TimeMatters in third (5%) (also known as PC Law/TimeMatters).

2. Jack Newton and Rian Gavreau met with me and Phil Brown at the Law Society of Ontario (f/k/a Law Society of Upper Canada) early in Clio's existence to discuss whether a product designed for British Columbia lawyers could work in Canada's most populous province. The answer was clearly yes.

legacy products, some of which had been bought by the big legal research platforms (Thomson Reuters owned Elite and ProLaw, LexisNexis had TimeMatters) who may have had the same, traditional limitations on perspective. Some practice management products were unable to adjust to cloud computing and, developed as they were with specific operating systems and requirements in mind, lacked the agility of web browser-based services.

There remains a healthy marketplace for law practice management software. Some products fade away, forcing lawyers to find new integrated systems. A few platforms will remain viable over years, with occasional new entrants. The challenge is that many of these applications will be aimed at the solo or small firm market. While this may be ideal for you, as it will provide you with options when you graduate, it can be difficult for the company selling the product. There are a limited number of lawyers, even when you consider that there are more than 1 million in the United States, to sell their product to. They need to be visible when the lawyer is making their selection for technology. Once the lawyer is locked in, either to a vendor or into processes relying on certain technologies, it can be hard for a new product to overcome that lock-in.

When you are thinking about your law practice and whether practice management software is something you want to adopt, I would focus on two areas. The first is the integrated nature of the software. The second is how you can try it out before you adopt it.

Integration

We have already discussed many of the components of a practice management application individually. The power of practice management software is in their integration. As you consider which application is the most practicable for you, you will want to look at these integrations. If you have a chance, you can dig deeper into the specific functionality, but there is a cost-benefit point where more research will not aid your selection.

This is due to the fact that, no matter how you want to practice law, if you adopt a practice management system, you will be adopting how it *allows you* to practice law. You will most likely have limited options to customize the interface or functionality. I do not consider this inability to customize a bad thing. Many an organization has found themselves in budget overruns and lost time after buying or licensing a product and then trying to force it to adapt to the business' way of working, to processes that themselves may not be coherent and therefore cannot be replicated in a software application. Software customization can be far more costly than adapting one's own processes to the methodology that a software developer built in to their application.

A common feature of cloud computing, and practice management software in the cloud is no exception, is that it tends to be developed within one large feature set. In that way, the developers can continue to iterate and improve and the entire code base benefits all of the product's clients. The more customization an application allows, the more challenging—and costly—maintaining the software will become.

This makes your assessment of practice management while you are a law student ideal. You can learn two things about it and yourself. One, how does it suggest that *you* should practice law? What are the processes that it seems to guide you to follow? You may find that it is exposing processes or practices that you would not have considered if you had just stitched together technology that was already familiar to you. Second, if you find a product you like, you can start to grow accustomed to using those processes before you have to actually apply them to that first prospective client.

The other place that practice management can be powerful is with its integrations with other systems. From the very first products in the 1980s and 1990s, law practice management developers have tended to realize that there were opportunities to build in functionality and then there were places where it made more sense to integrate someone else's existing product. You will notice that no law practice management application has tried to build a word processor to compete with Microsoft Word. I'm not aware of any email clients that are intended to compete with Microsoft Outlook, although this was sometimes a feature of early systems before Microsoft invested more effort into email communication.

This means that, while the internal integrations are powerful and may guide how you practice, so are the external integrations. Practice management software may not support e-billing or document management and retention, or email. It should provide integrations to those external providers—Xero and Intuit for financials, Microsoft products for productivity, and so on—so that you gain the benefit of the integrated approach.

You can see how you may have a chicken-and-egg issue. Do you make your practice management selection first, which may limit the external applications you can use if there is not integration support? Or do you select your key law practice applications—like productivity or accounting or document management—and then find a practice management application that will connect to or support that software?

As a law student or someone who is starting their own law practice, this may be a relatively easy choice. There is not a *right* choice, as each choice comes with its own limitations. At the end of the day, whether you select a practice management application first or last, it will only support the integrations its developers have created. If you are overwhelmed by making choices, then starting with a practice management system as your foundation will make sense. It will limit the next choices you make, potentially simplifying your selection process and constraining your future options.

It would be incorrect to say that the internal features of the practice management system do not matter. The term can be applied loosely by developers, and so you may find that there is some variance of internal functionality from one platform to another. However, it would make sense to prioritize how integrated the platform is internally and the external integrations it offers as much as or more so than solely what the specific features within the practice management system.

Practice management selection should start with the overall applications or resources you need: communications, financial management, file creation, and matter management. Once you have identified products that meet those needs, you can drill down further to see how they provide it: internally or via external connections. This is the opposite of how you might select products where you lack integration, acquiring each new application as you need it.

More than other law practice technologies, your investment in a practice management system should also take into account the viability of the company. A lawyer who started practice at the turn of the century could conceivably have used Microsoft Word and Outlook for the entire time they have been practicing since then. Many lawyers who adopted practice management applications during that time period have had to migrate to new platforms as old ones came to the end of their life during the same time period. An investment in a practice management system will impact how you practice law. If the product fails in the future or is merged into a different product or taken on by a new company, you may find that the way in which you practice is also impacted.

It is one of the areas where even selecting Microsoft might not have been a wise choice. In 2015, Microsoft announced Matter Center, an implementation of their Office 365 platform and using SharePoint in the manner that their internal legal department used it. The product was positioned as a way to bring integration to a number of Microsoft cloud applications in a way that law firms could value. The set of resources can still be found on GitHub, but the marketing disappeared a few years after the initial announcement.[3]

Practice management software is an area where large software developers and legal publishers have not yet been as successful as more focused, dedicated practice management developers. Clio's acquisition of the legal publisher platform vLex Fastcase is perhaps the most notable example of the inverse of this approach, where most of the acquirers were large legal publishers buying practice management systems.[4] Time will tell what the impact is on this broader portfolio and what integrations may be possible now that legal research platforms like vLex have invested so heavily in artificial intelligence.

Adoption

If you have taken experiential classes in law school, there is a good chance you have seen law practice management software in your legal clinics. Law school clinics have been early adopters of practice management, and developers have seen this as an opportunity to expose future lawyers to their products. But legal clinics also work like law firms, and so it makes sense for them to incorporate law practice technology into the experiential learning component.

If you have not been exposed to a practice management system, law school is a great time to give them a trial. The most visible practice management systems will provide some video demos and a free trial period where you can get in and try the system out. As a law student, you may want to be clear up front with the sales team that you are not, in fact, a likely customer at this point. This will save both of you ongoing communication about the product. Keep in mind that a trial period may only be a matter of a week or 10 days. You will want to take on a trial only during a period—perhaps Spring Break or after

3. The Matter Center anchor page—Boosting Productivity for Legal and Business Professionals—can only be found now on the Internet Archive. https://web.archive.org/web/20180311060627/http://www.microsoft.com/en-us/legal/productivity/mattercenter.aspx. The elements of Matter Center can be found on GitHub http://web.archive.org/web/20250625155336/https://github.com/Microsoft/mattercenter.

4. Bob Ambrogi, *In a Mega Deal, Clio Buys vLex for $1 Billion, Merging AI, Research and Practice Management*, LAWSITES (June 30, 2025), https://www.lawnext.com/2025/06/in-a-mega-deal-clio-buys-vlex-for-1-billion-merging-ai-research-and-practice-management.html.

you have completed finals during a semester—when you know you will have relatively few distractions.

Book some time for yourself to incorporate it into your day. Perhaps you can schedule a half hour every morning to open it up and take an action in the system. Upload a document, complete a client record, run a timer or two. Connect one of your external accounts—perhaps your Microsoft OneDrive or Google Drive, something simple and not too complicated—to the system and see how the integration works.

You will want to give yourself some time with each of the practice management applications that you are considering. As a law student, you may have more leisure to engage in this exploration. You can also approach it like a lawyer who is leaving a larger firm to start their own practice. If you know lawyers who are already solo or in small law firms, ask them what they use and why. What are the features they cannot live without and what features do they wish were included? Have they gone without or are they using additional software to fill those gaps? Students who have already graduated ahead of you and lawyers you have met while networking are sure to have opinions about the technology they use, particularly if they have chosen it themselves.

Chapter 13 Exercise

A. Identify five practice management applications that you might want to adopt in your solo law practice. What is one feature or factor that makes each one stand out from the others. Features might include internal functionality or integration. Factors might include where the servers are located, how it handles your data, or even price.

B. The power of practice management applications comes from the way they integrate a great deal of functionality together. Some of them do this internally, building all of the pieces and integrating them. Others do this by creating connections with external applications, the integration relying on that relationship. What are the risks of each approach and which would you be comfortable using when you start practice?

C. Some of the applications you will use for your law practice are free or open source. There are also open-source practice management applications. Would you use one for your law practice? Why or why not?

Chapter 14

Electronic Filing

One of the specialized roles that only a lawyer can provide for someone else is to represent them in court. People can represent themselves in court, but the lawyer is usually the only person who can engage in that representation for another person. When you sent your engagement letter to your client, you may not have been certain at that point whether a lawsuit was the only way to resolve their legal issue. Inevitably, though, one of your client's matters may head towards court. You may refer the matter to someone who litigates in that area, or you may take the case to court yourself. It is now that you will engage with e-filing systems.

When lawyers speak about electronic filing they are, for the most part, talking about filing documents with courts. There are other agencies and administrative bodies that use electronic filing, but the most common application is initiating or responding to a court matter. The technology for e-filing is extremely simple for the lawyer and is largely determined by the court's requirements.[1]

United States federal courts will use the case management and electronic court filing system (CM/ECF) for their filings. When you upload a document into CM/ECF, it will make its way into the court's case management system and, eventually, may end up visible on the docket in the Public Access to Court

1. There is no reason to assume you will ever use e-filing. According to the 2023 American Bar Association Legal Technology Survey report, only about 60% of lawyers indicate their practice is either entirely litigation or split 50/50 with transactional practice areas. AM. BAR ASS'N, 2023 LEGAL TECHNOLOGY SURVEY REPORT: TECHNOLOGY BASICS 7, question 6 (2024). This does not mean you will never use e-filing, but you may find that this is an area you will not need to worry about immediately upon graduating from law school.

Electronic Records (PACER) system. These huge systems are designed by the court, and you do not participate in any selection process to use them. You create an account and use the systems subject to court processes.

Outside of the federal courts, your mileage will vary depending on the court jurisdiction you are in and the resources that court has deployed for e-filing. At the state-court level, it can vary from county to county and courtroom to courtroom. I have seen some courts who use email for their electronic court filing.[2] You comply with their filing system by sending an email with the required attachments. In most cases, though, you are likely to experience some sort of web-based platform that requires you to log in and gives you the ability to upload documents in your client's case. These systems will vary widely, and there is no good way to prepare you for this part of e-filing.[3]

Fortunately, the e-filing process is relatively straightforward. You will use a web browser, a technology selection you have already made. You will also use a portable document format (PDF) creator or editor to generate the documents for the e-filing system.[4] You may have been getting by with a PDF printer like the "Save as PDF" in Microsoft Office applications. You may even have discovered that your web browser acts as a PDF reader and that you can open most PDFs in Microsoft Word. As you prepare to practice, though, you will want to find a PDF editor, an application that allows you to work with and manipulate the portable document format. The PDF editor is the key piece of

---

2. Not surprisingly, companies that already sell productivity software to lawyers are making similar pitches to the courts. Microsoft has a case study on how a court could stitch together multiple Microsoft products to enable a *hybrid courtroom*. *Government Scenario: Enhance Hybrid Courtrooms*, MICROSOFT (last visited May 15, 2025), https://adoption.microsoft.com/en-us/scenario-library/government/enhance-hybrid-courtrooms/ [http://web.archive.org/web/20250515161603/https://adoption.microsoft.com/en-us/scenario-library/government/enhance-hybrid-courtrooms/]. For the most part, though, court operations applications like case management will be designed and supported by a different set of companies from those who are creating applications and services for lawyers.

3. I even asked an e-filing administrator if there was a sandbox where lawyers could practice e-filing, just to see how the process worked. They indicated that there was but only for lawyers who had registered for accounts. Law students are unable to access the test environment.

4. You may not be required to use a PDF creator in every jurisdiction. In some cases, PDFs are optional. Due to the widespread access-to-justice issue in the United States, courts can create flexible options for electronic case filing to enable self-represented parties to use whatever file format they are able to generate. However, due to the PDF's prevalence in legal work, it is a common piece of software, and you will most likely to use it well beyond electronic court filings.

software at this stage, as it provides you with some functionality that you may not otherwise have access to.

Portable Document Format Editor

Although some courts will still refer to PDF as a proprietary document format, it is not. Adobe Systems released it as an open standard in 2008.[5] This confusion will create some uncertainty about whether you can use PDF editors that were not designed by Adobe. In some cases, because the courts themselves use a particular vendor's PDF tools—tools that may have proprietary functionality that is not reflected in the PDF standard—you may find that your experience with a court's form PDF is not optimal unless you use the same software they do.

However, there is no particular reason to use an Adobe application for the creation and maintenance of your own PDF documents. There are a variety of PDF editors—Adobe, Nitro, Foxit, PDF Architect—to choose from. They vary in some functionality, but you will probably find that their pricing and licensing schemes are the most significant information in your selection.[6] This is even more true with a PDF reader, where you will have far more selection than you will find even with PDF editors. However, once you have a PDF editor, it will also act as a PDF reader, and you will not need two applications for this purpose.[7]

---

5. *PDF*, Wikipedia (last visited Aug. 31, 2025), https://en.wikipedia.org/wiki/PDF, and the latest update in 2023: https://www.pdfa-inc.org/product/iso-32000-2-pdf-2-0-bundle-sponsored-access/.

6. While you are a law student, seek out any free access to the Adobe Creative Cloud Suite that your university or law school might provide. This Suite includes the Adobe PDF Editor and will give you an opportunity to play around with it extensively before you start your law practice.

7. Also, you will find that most modern web browsers will automatically show a PDF within the web browser window. Even though you may be prompted to add one, you do not need to have a proprietary Adobe Reader or Foxit browser extension to read and interact with PDFs in your web browser.

PDFs in the Law Practice

The PDF is probably the second most common document format—after the Microsoft Word .doc or .docx file—in the law practice. Like Microsoft products, some of the specific functionality that lawyers need has been built into PDF editors. If you are in a law firm, you may find that they have already made the selection of PDF editor for you. However, if you are shopping around, it will be these law-specific uses that will matter most in your selection.

Bates Numbering

One of the most obscure uses of a PDF editor, perhaps unique to the legal profession, will be the application of Bates Numbers to a filing. There will be times when you are uploading a collection of related documents that create a single case file submission. These may be a mixture of documents you have authored in Microsoft Word, then converted to PDF, as well as documents that you have scanned into a PDF format or received from somewhere as a PDF. Each document may have page numbers or it may have no way of identifying each page. For this reason, it is not uncommon to find courts requiring that the entire filing be Bates stamped.

A man in New York created the Bates Stamp. It originally was a metal stamp that, each time you stamped a page, incremented up one number. In this way, you could set the stamp device to "1" and, as you stamped each page, it would go up one number. Even if the stack of pages contained multiple documents, each with a "page 1" and so on, the Bates numbers would be sequential from the first page in the stack to the last.

A Bates numbering function in a PDF editor works the same way. You assemble your stack of PDF files—no matter what their source—and place them in the order you will use them or want the court to review them. You apply the Bates numbering, and it will create a new, consolidated PDF with the numbering on each page. Once each page is numbered, it will be easier to refer to a particular page in your packet without having to describe the document beyond its Bates number.

Redaction

There are two ways to redact documents that you are going to submit to a court or send to someone outside your firm. One is the old-fashioned, and yet still reliable, way and one is more modern. The old-fashioned way is to use a permanent black marker on a piece of paper. So many files are born digitally these days that you may not have a paper original of a document you are going to share as a PDF and need to redact. Print off a copy and use the marker to blot out the information that you do not want to share. Once you have completed your redaction, scan the redacted page back into a PDF file, and you can share it with some confidence that the information you blotted out is unreadable.

This is a lot of work. However, the thing about marker on paper is that you can understand how it works. The black marker ink is attached to the paper. It obscures the information underneath it because it is *part* of the document now. In digital redaction, lawyers have sometimes mistaken obscuring information with redacting it.[8] That is because, unlike an ink marker, they are placing their obscuring marks *on top of* the document.[9] If you redact a document by doing that—for example, placing a black box over the text but leaving the text in the document—you are merely obscuring the visibility of the information. The text remains a part of the document, and you risk someone being able to access it. In this way, your failure to properly redact the document may end up with you inadvertently disclosing information.

When you use a PDF editor with a redaction function, it removes the text or other document elements from the document. If you received a PDF document from a client or in relation to a client matter, you will want to make sure you redact a *copy* of the original document. Otherwise you will permanently obscure the original.

Once you have a copy of your original, the actual redaction process is simple. You highlight the areas to redact and initiate the redaction function. Once you save the PDF, it will no longer contain the information you were seeking to protect.

---

8. Herbert B. Dixon, Jr., *Embarrassing Redaction Failures*, Judge's J., Spring 2019, https://www.americanbar.org/groups/judicial/resources/judges-journal/archive/embarrassing-redaction-failures/.

9. In some cases, the information that was meant to be redacted was recoverable, visible by merely highlighting the obscured area and cutting and pasting the selection in a new document. Since the text existed below the obscuring document element, a cut-and-paste maneuver was able to select it.

Optical Character Recognition

Although much of law practice uses digital documents—things that were *born* digital—you will still need to work with paper. You may inherit old wills or other documents that were created by your client or others without a computer or phone. They may be born digital documents that have been saved to paper where the digital copy is inaccessible. Governments and health professionals still produce a significant amount of paper when they provide information, the latter even going so far as sometimes requiring a fax machine.

A scanner used to be a common technology peripheral in law firms. A printer and a fax machine would create paper copies and the scanner would convert the paper into a digital file. The scanner creates an image of the document, though, and it may not be a machine-readable file. You can look at it and read it with your eyes, but your computer will not be able to understand what it contains.

Some scanners would include optical character recognition (OCR) software so that, once you had scanned a document, it could be converted into machine-readable text. Once it is machine-readable, your Windows computer or other search tools could index it and make it searchable. You would also be able to select portions of it to cut and paste into your documents, email, or practice management system.

Practice Pointer

Unsure whether you are dealing with a PDF that needs to undergo optical character recognition? Drag your mouse across it in your PDF editor or reader and see if you can select any discrete text or information. If you cannot, it is very likely a photo of a document.

Scanners are less necessary than they once were. Many business printers are multi-function devices. They provide the ability to make a copy, to print a document from a device, or to scan a print document and turn it into a digital one. Similarly, mobile apps like Microsoft Lens (not to be confused with Google Lens, the identification help search tool) can capture multi-page documents like a scanner.[10] They can save them as images or combine them into a PDF or even a Microsoft Word document. They perform the OCR process in the same way that more substantial apps and hardware did in the past.

If you receive a document that has already been converted into a PDF and is an image, you can still convert it using OCR. PDF editors will usually have the ability to read—and sometimes will warn you the PDF you have opened is an image and ask you to undergo the OCR process—an image and convert it into text. Again, just as with redaction, OCR a copy of the original document, not the original digital version.

There are hundreds of simple OCR tools, many free. For example, you can upload an image or PDF to Google Drive. If you then attempt to open it in Google Docs, the app will automatically go through an OCR process, rendering a copy of the imaged text below the image. You may find that some OCR tools are faster than others, particularly if you have a large number of pages.

Another distinguishing feature between OCR tools is their ability to recognize the text correctly. The clearer the scanned image, the better the recognized output will match the original's text. However, OCR is a technology that, like AI, is going to give you an answer whether it is correct or not. It is common to have OCR generate a word with misspellings or replace letters with other keyboard characters so that it achieves *a* word, even if it is not the correct word. An OCR application, when it sees columns of text, may still attempt to interpret the document from left to right, top to bottom, jumbling the two columns of text into a single column.

The quality of the OCR of your software will be a selection criterion. Once you have selected whatever tool you are using for OCR, you will want to get accustomed to its strengths and weaknesses. Your PDF editor will most likely support OCR, but it may not always get the output correct. You may find that, particularly for shorter documents, it is easier for you or your staff to re-type the portion of information you need than to go through an OCR process that requires substantial cleanup of the text afterwards.

10. The app, available for Android and iPhones, used to be called Microsoft Office Lens but is now just referred to as Microsoft Lens. If you are logged into a Microsoft account, it can upload documents you image within the app to your OneDrive storage.

Digital Signatures

The rise of digital documents has meant the increased need for digital signatures. While some documents still require a so-called *wet* signature, or one made with ink, it is common to have a legal matter resolved entirely with digital signatures. Some lawyers will use a document signing platform to manage this process. PDF readers and editors tend to also have the ability to support digital signatures, although not all signatures are the same.

The digital signature type that may be the most familiar to you is the mere application of a picture of a signature to a document. You can accomplish this in any Microsoft Word document using the Microsoft Signature Line option under the Insert tab on the Ribbon or even by pasting in an image. In common PDF tools, you can add either an image of a wet ink signature, created and scanned in advance, or you can type your signature name and it will be rendered in a stereotypical handwriting font.

There is also the option in many PDF tools to create an actual digital signature. It is less a representation of your ink signature and more of a digital piece of code added to the document. If you use Adobe Acrobat's editor, under the "use a certificate" function, you can sign the document with a digital certificate. This will place information about the digital certificate that identifies you, as well as date and time, into the document.

Your use of digital signatures within PDFs will vary widely on the use case and the audience. If you are trying to get a client to sign a document, you may prefer to use a platform that they can log into and not have them fiddle with a signature function or software. You may also need to have them sign a document that is subject to specific requirements about how the signature is applied and by whom. As a baseline, having a PDF editor with some ability to save a signature and to have others apply a signature is a reasonable selection requirement. The lack of a consistent approach within the legal system to how all legal documents should be signed means that a particular digital signature approach should not drive your selection process.

E-Filing Output: Online Dockets

The United States federal court system known as PACER (Public Access to Court Electronic Records) has been mentioned before, including as a legal research tool. Online case management systems run by the courts or by their third-party cloud providers will store documents created by the court administration and by the parties.[11] These online systems are sometimes available to the public or parties via the internet.[12]

As you will already have gathered from your 1L legal research experience, as you dig deeper into a jurisdiction, the smaller courts and bodies have fewer resources and are less likely to have their information published online. Just as you would find a dearth of trial court opinions in many state legal research case law databases, you may find online dockets and electronic access only in larger cities or more populous counties. If you need something from an offline docket, there are services that will send a courier to retrieve a document held by a court. Some courts lack the resources to publish their court filings online while others embrace *security through obscurity*. Although the case files are public records, they are kept off the internet—or only made available to lawyers licensed to practice before the court—in order to limit their dissemination.

Even if your practice does not require you to use e-filing from the front end, knowing about what it has to offer on the back end, in the docket, can be a practice advantage. You can find out about cases going on in your jurisdiction or practice area. You can research a prospective client to see what other litigation or cases they have been involved in. Lawyers file a variety of procedural documents through e-filing, and some of these motions and briefs may be good exemplars that you can convert into your own templates or re-use in your own practice. Keep your ears open when you are interact-

11. These case management providers are creating and licensing products for courts. These products are different from lawyer practice management applications, although sometimes the label "case management system" is applied to the software lawyers use. In most cases, a company selling practice management software to lawyers is not also selling a case management application to courts.

12. This varies widely and is depending on the resources of a jurisdiction. Some legal publishers sell docket access, but there remain large gaps in digitally accessible dockets around the United States. In some cases, legal publishers are paying for someone to go to a court to retrieve a document, digitizing it, and then adding it to their docket collection. It is not being pulled directly from the court's digital case management system.

ing with colleagues because these sorts of strong precedents may be shared around when someone finds a really good example, particularly if it has led to a successful outcome.

Chapter 14 Exercise

A. Create a PACER account (they are free to any member of the public; you can skip providing a payment method when prompted). Watch your local news and find a case that is currently in front of a federal court. See if you can find the docket and review a few of the documents filed in the case. Make a list of the important metadata around the case: who are the parties, lawyers, and judges? What is the issue? What did the court decide (if it has reached a decision or issued an order)? Keep in mind that you can search PACER and access up to $30 worth of documents per quarter for free.

B. Prepare a PDF from Microsoft Word, and redact it using a PDF editor, either one licensed for you by your law school or an open source app. Then print off the Word document and capture an image of it using a mobile app, scanner, or multi-function copier. Attempt to redact the image of the document. What differences do you experience in trying to achieve the same result?

Chapter 15

Litigation

Litigation is a choice when dealing with a client matter. Your new client may have been seeking relief from the very beginning that required a court or you may have only determined that a lawsuit was necessary after some initial research and investigation. Not all cases reach a litigation stage, though, and not all lawyers engage in litigation.[1] If, however, you have completed your electronic filing on behalf of a client and initiated or responded to a lawsuit, it is time to think about this very specific area of technology.

Technology used by litigators tends to do one of two things: support tasks that the lawyer must lead, like assisting in the presentation of evidence in court, or support productivity, like reducing the time spent reviewing deposition transcripts. They are split chronologically as well: those that are used before trial and those that are used as part of the trial itself.

1. While we see a lot of trials on television and in the media, they represent a very small portion of legal outcomes for lawyer clients. About 90% of criminal defendants in federal cases will plead guilty before trial. John Gramlich, *Fewer Than 1% of Federal Criminal Defendants Were Acquitted in 2022*, Pew Research Center (June 14, 2023), https://www.pewresearch.org/short-reads/2023/06/14/fewer-than-1-of-defendants-in-federal-criminal-cases-were-acquitted-in-2022/ [https://web.archive.org/web/20250723102551/https://www.pewresearch.org/short-reads/2023/06/14/fewer-than-1-of-defendants-in-federal-criminal-cases-were-acquitted-in-2022/]. It is harder to pin down civil outcomes. In U.S. district courts, only 0.4% of cases reached trial in 2024. United States Courts, *Table C-4—U.S. District Courts—Civil Statistical Tables for the Federal Judiciary*, U.S. Courts (December 31, 2024), https://www.uscourts.gov/sites/default/files/2025-03/stfj_c4_1231.2024.xlsx. [http://web.archive.org/web/20250614064004/https://www.uscourts.gov/sites/default/files/2025-03/stfj_c4_1231.2024.xlsx].

Pre-Trial Technology

A Word About Legal Holds

It will come as no surprise by now that some aspects of legal technology are less about the technology you use and more about a process and perhaps technology that other people use. Legal holds are one of those areas. When you file a lawsuit or receive a complaint that one has been filed against your client, you may need to initiate a request for information related to that legal issue. This might include documents that were created or emails or texts that were sent that relate to the matter. In order to comply with the request, your client will need a way to freeze and preserve all of the information they currently have in relation to this new pending matter. You may have discussed spoliation or the destruction of relevant evidence in class in law school. The legal hold is a method of preventing spoliation.

It is most likely that you do not have access to or control over those documents. Your client or other parties related to the legal issue will. You will want to learn how they retain their email, how they store their documents and who has access, and so on. Some organizations may use a product like Microsoft SharePoint where there are tools built into the platform that support litigation holds.[2]

When might you be required to initiate a legal hold on materials you control? When you are a party to a lawsuit or are part of a group—like a board of directors or a public governance board—that is itself a party. It is worth thinking about how you would manage a legal hold on your own documents and emails, but it is far more likely you would need to help a client initiate a hold.

Many of your clients will lack the technology know-how or tools to self-preserve the information you will need to represent them effectively.[3] You may

2. Microsoft SharePoint (*eDiscovery and In-place Holds in SharePoint Server*, Microsoft (Feb. 21, 2023), https://learn.microsoft.com/en-us/SharePoint/governance/ediscovery-and-in-place-holds-in-sharepoint-server [http://web.archive.org/web/20241013012249/https://learn.microsoft.com/en-us/SharePoint/governance/ediscovery-and-in-place-holds-in-sharepoint-server]) and Microsoft Exchange email servers (*Place a Mailbox on Litigation Hold*, Microsoft (Apr. 30, 2025), https://learn.microsoft.com/en-us/exchange/policy-and-compliance/holds/litigation-holds [http://web.archive.org/web/20250516112118/https://learn.microsoft.com/en-us/exchange/policy-and-compliance/holds/litigation-holds]) support the creation of holds on content they store.

3. They will reflect the legal profession, in fact. According to the 2023 American Bar Association Legal Technology Survey Report, Technology Basics & Security volume, less than 50% of lawyers in firms with between 1 and 99 had a policy to deal with record holds

not be certain how to help them. The point to take away here is that there are technology areas that you will not be able to control and will have to work with choices that others make about their use of technology. There will not always be an off-the-shelf or simple technology solution when managing information related to a litigation matter.

E-Discovery

The next stage in the litigation process that may require technology is the discovery phase. You will most likely be filing motions during this time period—motions to dismiss, motions for summary judgment—but if you have to gather additional information, you will gather it during the discovery phase.

You may make a request for documents or other evidence. The documents will arrive as paper or digital files (also known as "electronically stored information" or ESI in e-discovery parlance), and you will need to decide how you want to process them. If the information is voluminous, you will want to consider using an outside service provider to help you to wrangle the digital media so that it is accessible.

Litigation support software is something you can license directly but, unless you are engaged in regular or ongoing litigation, you may not need to. Like so many other areas of practice technology, litigation support is delivered through the cloud, and you can license it when you need it and then drop it when you have finished. Alternatively, like with accounting software, you may find that you do not want to license it directly at all. Instead, you would hire the expertise—and there are many national and local ediscovery consultants and organizations to choose from almost anywhere there is a courtroom—who can provide you with access to the systems that they use and license.[4]

It is a key area that a lawyer might consider entirely outsourcing. The ability to organize and manage a large body of documents—and the variety of formats and types, especially email or texts that may not be easy to extract

within the law firm itself. AM. BAR ASS'N, 2023 LEGAL TECHNOLOGY SURVEY REPORT: TECHNOLOGY BASICS 63, question 55 (2024).

4. No surprise, there is a Microsoft e-discovery platform called Purview. http://web.archive.org/web/20250630173357/https://learn.microsoft.com/en-us/purview/edisc. Like so many e-discovery applications, it creates a level of complexity that many lawyers will not be able to manage on their own. It also requires Microsoft systems that, while common in the legal profession, may be more hit or miss when dealing with the typical clients of solo and small law firm practices. The existence of technology does not mean that it will be able to be brought to bear against every client's matter, nor should it.

and make viewable—is something that goes beyond the day-to-day skill set needed to practice law. Some lawyers and some law firms may specialize in these areas, but that very specialization will drive their selection of products and approaches.

Similarly, there is a great deal of opportunity for lawyers to mistakenly damage the discovered information if it is ESI. We touched on document metadata earlier in this book and the need to use it wisely. You may have removed metadata in documents you were sending out to clients or opposing counsel or the court. But you may have been using metadata to better describe the document, beyond its contents. Your clients and other parties may also use metadata that way, and when you receive discoverable information, it will have that metadata still attached to the document or email.

This can be really helpful because, just as metadata can help you to sort and manage information you create, it can be used to sort and manage other people's data. The difficulty is that, unlike metadata in your own documents, you do not want the metadata received within discovery to change. The metadata can provide you with information about when a document or email was created or sent, by whom, and what changes were made or responses received. If you are not careful, opening a document can overwrite this metadata and create evidentiary problems.

There are guidelines that can help you to navigate discovery and e-discovery. One place you might look are the Sedona Conference Principles on e-discovery, which summarize much of the wisdom that has accumulated over the years.[5] For example, digital discovery can *technically* allow retrieval of masses of information that may or not be related to the legal issue. In order to determine relevance, someone or some tool will need to make an assessment. But before even seeking out that large body of digital data, the question should be asked: do we need to? For example:

> Notwithstanding the presence of such [electronically stored information or] ESI on the device, it may not be necessary to image the device if the costs, burdens, and other issues associated with imag-

5. The Sedona Conference, *The Sedona Principles, Third Edition: Best Practices, Recommendations & Principles for Addressing Electronic Document Production*, 19 Sedona Conf. J. 1 (2018), https://thesedonaconference.org/sites/default/files/publications/The%20Sedona%20Principles%20Third%20Edition.19TSCJ1.pdf [http://web.archive.org/web/20250526075911/https://thesedonaconference.org/sites/default/files/publications/The%20Sedona%20Principles%20Third%20Edition.19TSCJ1.pdf#page=17.21].

> ing the device outweigh the benefits of retrieving unique, relevant ESI from the device. Indeed, wholesale text message retention is regularly disproportionate for both sides of the litigation, e.g., in a wage and hour class action where employees use text messaging on their personal devices for work.[6]

When you think about discovery, think about how much information you will need to gather and, while the opposing party or court may force you to tailor your requests for production, there is a technological value to doing so as well. The more data you gather, the more time and money you will need to sort through it to figure out how to use it.

Interrogatories and Depositions

Lawyers can seek written answers through documents known as interrogatories and verbal answers through depositions. Both take on a question-and-answer mode and are a way of gathering information before going to trial. You create the initial components of both processes the same way—using a word processor, most likely—but the outputs may benefit from the application of additional technology.

> **Practice Pointer**
>
> You do not need to develop interrogatories from scratch as a new lawyer. Legal publishers and others have collected interrogatories into databases where you can download a copy as a template and customize it in Microsoft Word according to your needs. This can be a useful starting point when you are unsure how to phrase a question you want to ask or if you want to see how someone else has dealt with developing particular legal elements.

When you receive the answers to interrogatories or the transcripts of the depositions, you will need to review them. You can do this by reading them but, especially with depositions, the transcripts will be long and not necessarily as linear as interrogatory answers. For example, in a deposition, since the

6. *Id.* at 63.

questions are not provided in advance, you might have added a question or doubled-back to a previous one. This means that information that is related can be spread across the transcript.

Deposition summarization used to be something that staff would have to complete for a lawyer's review, either by reviewing the audio or the transcript prepared by the court reporter that attended the deposition. This has largely been eliminated by the use of real-time transcription by court reporters, which can be done both in-person and through virtual tools. Real-time transcription can provide the lawyer with a document that is machine-readable—so it can be keyword searchable but also marked up with highlighting or cut-and-pasted into a brief—while the deposition is occurring. Perhaps as importantly, it can provide the lawyer with an opportunity to review what the deponent has said before the deposition has been brought to a close or to refer back to prior statements.

Just as with legal holds and e-discovery, real-time transcription and the tools surrounding deposition support are more likely services that you should hire rather than technology you should acquire. As we see more artificial intelligence options develop and mature, generative AI may provide an opportunity for more efficient summarization of answers to interrogatories and deposition transcripts in real-time.

Trial Preparation Tools

There are a number of small utilities that have been designed for lawyers to use to prepare trials. These can help to develop information to support the story you will be telling—or attempting to extract—during trial. For example, you may want to be clear about a timeline of events and create a chronology. This document or tool can link to the evidence and documents you have collected prior to trial, giving you an easy reference that you can then use both for trial preparation and during a trial.

One hoary technology that remains is the trial notebook. Originally, it was a large binder (perhaps more than one) that contained all of the information required for trial: copies of exhibits, copies of cases and other supporting documentation, questions that you would pose to witnesses, information about parties and expert witnesses. The notebook concept remains and can be replicated in tools like Microsoft OneNote.[7]

Some law-specific apps exist like LexisNexis' CaseMap+ and LitSoftware's TrialPad that will bring a more law-oriented approach to the trial binder. TrialPad in particular has had a long run as a tool for solos, since it can be managed on an iPad tablet. Like any technology you use to prepare for trial, you will want to practice with it so that, if a trial comes around, you are comfortable balancing your role as the lawyer and also managing your technology. Immediately before a trial is not the first time to pick up a new technology.

Trial Technology

If all else fails and you are unable to resolve the matter prior to trial through a successful motion or settlement, you will want to think through what technology you will need at trial. These will tend to be supportive tools because, in a courtroom, the judge and the lawyers play specific roles that cannot be delegated to technology. You may be limited by what the court will allow you to use in the case as well.

More commonly, you may find a great deal of variation in the types of technology that can be deployed for a trial within a courthouse as well as variances between the courtrooms within that building. Even technology you take for granted such as internet access may not be available to you. Courthouses can be physically older structures that may or may not support wireless connectivity for courtroom participants. The building may inhibit the reach of your phone to send and receive data in a way that is reliable enough to support trial presentations. Be aware of the limitations of your physical trial location and consider backups—like trial materials stored on portable storage or devices—just in case you do not have access to the internet or other resources you were planning to rely on.

This lack of technology support can be even more true when it comes to technology that many law schools have implemented in their trial advocacy

7. In fact, an early template created by Microsoft in OneNote was for the legal community and comprised a simple trial notebook. While this has long since disappeared, the OneNote look and feel resembles a traditional paper file organizer. Similarly, PowerPoint and Word can be used to create simple timelines and chronologies, and you can link from the document to supporting files.

or moot court programs and classrooms. You may be accustomed to every classroom in your law school having a projector and attached computer for presentation purposes. Some schools will have document cameras to allow digital displays of paper evidence. These common law school technologies may or may not be available in the courtroom in which you ply your craft. This is another reason to consider, as you prepare for court, not only the information and arguments you will make on behalf of your client, but how you will deliver them. If you are regularly in courtrooms, you may want to invest in common courtroom technologies to save on having to rent them repeatedly. Alternatively, you can hire a courtroom audio-visual consultant to help you with the hardware you need to provide your client with the best representation you can.

Evidence Management

One area that a lawyer may need technology and assistance with is evidence management. This will depend on how much evidence you have gathered prior to trial and how much of it will be used within your case and what formats you plan to present it in. There are strategic and litigation best practices that, like the e-discovery principles, can lean towards the notion that less is more. Either way, you will need a way to quickly retrieve and display electronic evidence.

It is common to hire a consultant to assist with evidence management or to have a staff person manage this function. Your digital documents will have been coded and prepared in advance for quick recall. You will have created an exhibits list so that you, the court, and the opposing party will all know what you are referring to. In a complicated case, you may prefer to have someone in the courtroom with you to retrieve and ensure the correct exhibit is presented while you are giving your presentation.

There may also be an app for that. Some of the trial preparation tools—specifically TrialPad—are portable enough that you can use them for your examination during trial and also have quick access to other parts of your trial binder. This is an area where the technology exists, and you will need to determine whether you are comfortable applying it during the pressurized experience of a trial.

Trial Presentation

It will come as no surprise that the leading trial presentation tool is Microsoft PowerPoint. This is not because it excels as a presentation tool for trials but, I expect, because everyone going to trial will probably have a copy of it. If your trial requires a relatively simple presentation of information in a mostly linear fashion, PowerPoint or Apple's KeyNote are easy-to-access tools that will provide the basic functionality to get your story across.

Keep in mind that they may be familiar tools, but they were designed to perform a particular function. If you are going to use presentation tools, use them to make a presentation and not as a document camera or merely as a way to throw a bunch of information on a screen. Think about how you will present your information to get the visual benefit that presentation software offers. Then practice so that you are able to move through your presentation fluidly. You do not want to use a presentation application to present a document full of text. When you think about how you are going to present the details of your case, use the features of the presentation software to make your story as compelling as possible.

In some cases, you will have more complicated information that you want to present. Perhaps you have video testimony and you want to be able to switch between videos, rather than being limited to a linear presentation of their content. In this case, you will want to look at other trial presentation applications and, again, possibly hire the consultants who use those on a regular basis and have greater expertise than you do.

Perhaps more than any other part of law practice, you will find a wide variety of niche applications available to the litigator. In some cases, they will suggest a solution to a problem you did not realize you had. At the same time, a trial is a complicated event, and you have an important role to play. Your use of technology should be balanced with that role so that you are able to be as adaptable and agile as possible to the unforeseen events that may arise. You may find that it is easier to go without trial technology unless you have a compelling reason to use it.

Chapter 15 Exercise

A. Create a timeline using Microsoft PowerPoint that puts the important time-related elements in order. Prepare the slides so that, if shown during a trial to participants who may not have seen it (like a jury), it will be visually clear and appealing. Write a reflection on the challenges on making information legible and design choices you may have used related to color or shapes or alignment to try to help tell your story.

Chapter 16

File Retention and Closed Matters

We have already discussed document management, and you may wonder what else could possibly be said about it. File retention goes beyond documents, though, and should be a key part of how you manage your case files. This is particularly crucial when you reach the end of a matter and are closing the file. As discussed above, this may come as soon as you have completed a conflicts check and sent a non-engagement letter to the prospective client.

You will need to ensure that all of the related objects belonging to the client's matter—emails, texts, phone logs and perhaps digital voice mail, documents, digital evidence provided including photos or videos—are stored together. You will need to be able to distinguish what belongs to you and what belongs to them. Every client's closed file will need to be retained for some period of time, whether it relates to a potential statute of limitations (for example, your legal malpractice insurer may require you to keep files during the period in which you might be sued by a former client) or for professional ethics reasons. There are specific areas of law—like wills and trusts—where the very nature of the client matter will require the file to be retained, perhaps indefinitely.

The first thing you will want to do—and you can do this while in law school—is to plan out your file retention policy. Your legal malpractice insurer may want you to have one, or give you a discount for one, so there is no time like the present to start to think about it. When you start to practice, this policy will provide you, your insurer, your regulator, and your clients with a guideline for how long you intend to keep client files. The benefit of creating this policy at the very start of your law practice is that you can start to build your technology around that policy. Law firms who develop their file retention policy after the fact may find that their file storage systems or email servers do not have the capabilities necessary to allow compliance with the policy.

We touched on metadata above: applying labels or tags to emails or calendar appointments or other objects you create in relation to a case. We also discussed how to create files and folders or tags so that you can quickly find and retrieve documents and other information stored on your law firm's systems. All of these organization processes come into play at the end of the matter as well. Those steps you took at the beginning to make yourself efficient? They should also help to speed up the steps you will need to take when you close the file.

Records Management and Preservation

One of the technologies that solo and small firm lawyers can use to level the playing field is Microsoft SharePoint. Unlike a typical file storage system, made up of folders and files but otherwise not really managed, SharePoint can support workflows that help you to ensure documents are kept even after they are no longer needed.[1] Document management systems will usually do this as well.

Even if you end up working in a small law firm or going solo, you are likely to come into contact with Microsoft SharePoint. It is a common file storage resource in the legal world, especially now that we are seeing the individual OneDrive accounts blending with the SharePoint server environment.[2] As with most systems, you can use the surface features for the easiest tasks.

1. Microsoft Windows servers do support the use of something called group policies that can aid in file retention and management. However, group policies are more likely to be found in an environment where there are enough devices—and IT staff—that they are needed to solve a greater level of complexity than exists in most solo and small firm law practices. For more on group policies: *Group Policy Overview for Windows Server*, Microsoft (June 16, 2025), https://learn.microsoft.com/en-us/windows-server/identity/ad-ds/manage/group-policy/group-policy-overview [https://web.archive.org/web/20250618065427/https://learn.microsoft.com/en-us/windows-server/identity/ad-ds/manage/group-policy/group-policy-overview].

2. *Overview of Microsoft OneDrive in SharePoint Server*, Microsoft (Jan. 19, 2023), https://learn.microsoft.com/en-us/sharepoint/sites/onedrive-for-business-overview [https://web.archive.org/web/20250411175950/https://learn.microsoft.com/en-us/sharepoint/sites/onedrive-for-business-overview].

It is a simple matter to create a folder and files on SharePoint. The power is really under the hood, where you can start to manage the metadata to make information findable. It is also where you will find workflow tools that can be applied to your retention needs.

The concept known as a legal hold is covered above, but many of the tools that work to make that effective will be used again for your long-term file management and retention. You will want to have tools that you can use to stop the accidental or intentional deletion of your client files until it is appropriate. Your systems should have the ability to indicate what type of content a document is (the two largest types may be your own work product, things you own and will re-use on other cases, and things that belong to the client alone).

These content management systems will aid you in your preservation. But, as with so much of the technology—perhaps all technology—that you will use in your law practice, it requires you to have thought through how you want to use it. It is one thing to know that you can automate processes. It is another to know what those processes are.

One place to start is with something like SharePoint's retention labels. They are a concept that can be easy to grasp and link your initial creation of metadata—who is the client, who is the document author, what is the document's title, and so on—with the document's end-of-life. If you are thinking about how you will manage that document when the client matter is closed, then you will be prepared to gather the correct information when you are in the middle of intake for the then-prospective client.

It works a little bit like the macros and other automation techniques above. You or your technical support can set up the retention rules in SharePoint.[3] For example, with documents where someone has set the metadata field for Status to "Closed" and where the document metadata Type is set to "Client," you can have SharePoint automatically apply a retention period. For documents where the Status is "Closed" but the title includes "Draft," you might automatically set those to be deleted after a certain period of time, on the assumption neither you nor your client needs or is entitled to iterations on documents you create for them.

The automation piece is key. Unless you have staff to help you, you will need to look for ways to automate a lot of these processes. Otherwise, you may find

---

3. *Use Retention Labels to Manage the Lifecycle of Documents Stored in SharePoint*, MICROSOFT (Dec. 3, 2024), https://learn.microsoft.com/en-us/purview/auto-apply-retention-labels-scenario [http://web.archive.org/web/20250108104921/https://learn.microsoft.com/en-us/purview/auto-apply-retention-labels-scenario].

that documents disappear before they are supposed to, swept up in a periodic but perhaps unplanned clean up of a storage drive.

Again, looking back to the beginning of this book and thinking about using technology to practice law, file retention and closing files is another ideal place for a checklist. Just as you will use checklists when you are determining whether to take on a client, you want to be sure that you have taken all of the necessary steps at the end of the client's matter. Not only will this ensure that you are taking the steps you need to for professional reasons, but it allows you to close the matter cleanly for your client. They can have a smooth conclusion to their own matter and feel good about referring their friends or their own clients to you.

The checklist will also do something that technology will not do on its own. A lot of records retention discussions focus on the technology and what it is able to do. But where do the objects come from that are put into the systems that manage them? I doubt there is a system that can automatically extract and manage every type of record—texts, email, attachments, documents, and spreadsheets—unless those things are gathered or made available to it. Imagine if your client gives you a CD with a video file on it. Or you have downloaded a recorded phone call or a security camera video from the internet. Where will you put those and how will you manage them so that, when the case is closed, those objects gathered for the case outside of the typical document creation processes of law practice are still retained correctly?

The first place where law practice technology can come into play with the end of a client matter is to organize and retain what you are able to. Especially in the modern law practice, a great deal of the information you are creating or managing for a client will be in a digital format. The things that are either in an unusual format—like an audio or video file—or that are physical and do not exist in a digital format will make up a much smaller number of items in most cases. If you focus on what you can manage, and get that sorted out, then you can deal with the edge cases. Again, you are about to head out into the practice of law, a career that might span five decades. There is no telling what that balance of paper and digital information will look like even 10 years from now, let alone 50.

If you are able to use a document management system, investigate its ability to retain and allow you to manage your documents once the file is closed. It may be that a system, like SharePoint, is able to handle the entire lifecycle of your documents. Once you have a solution for your documents, you can consider other types of file formats.

The file format issue is perhaps the most complex one, and it is one where a lawyer may just throw their hands up in the air and decide that paper is the best format for a client's closed file. This is because file formats change. In the span of the careers of most senior partners at law firms, they will have seen documents created in multiple products like Corel WordPerfect and Microsoft Word as well as multiple file types, like Microsoft .doc and .docx. It is conceivable that the file formats that your law practice uses in your first year after law school will be either different, if they exist at all, or created with different products by the time you are ready to retire. There are lawyers practicing today who started before the availability of the personal computer and the ability to retain client files digitally for the lifetime of their practice. These will be challenges that you will be helping to trailblaze.

Closed File Storage

Another issue is the storage problem. This may be easier to grasp as you are likely to have already experienced a storage challenge. Perhaps you saved too many videos on your phone and its storage was filled. Or you used a cloud service like Google Drive or Apple iCloud and filled the initial, free storage, to the point at which it started warning you that you would need to buy more space. You can imagine that, over the lifetime of a law practice, you will store a huge amount of data. All of the storage media on which it sits will need to be paid for, either by you purchasing and hosting your own media or paying someone else to store the data for you.

One way to manage the storage is to think about it living in one of three buckets. The first is the storage you need for your day-to-day law practice. The second is the storage you need for client matters that have recently closed. Those are the ones that you may be retaining forever but, in reality, you may only be subject to being named as a defendant in a legal malpractice case (or be subject to a disciplinary complaint) for a shorter period of years. This might be a six- or seven-year time frame. The third is the long-term storage, perhaps for the life of your client or your own life.[4]

4. If you are more curious about this, the archival profession has a standardized approach to handling these different stages of digital object lifecycles, using terms like DIPs and AIPs. The idea is that you maintain different copies for different purposes. The AIP version would be archival, untouched and secured against change. The DIP version of the same document would be a replica of the original and could be shared or altered to make

The day-to-day storage is something that you will budget for and manage each year. You can change cloud providers or switch from cloud to local media storage, move from flat files and folders to integrated systems and back again. These are your live files.

They may not be very distinguishable from that second bucket, those closed matters that may remain in the same content management or storage system as your open case files. If they do remain in proximity to your open files, you will want to ensure they are distinguished in some way. This could be as simple as placing them in a folder tree that is separated from the open matters. For example, you might have a computer storage system where the folder structure looks like this:

- 🗁 Client Files
  - 🗁 Open Matters
    - 🗁 ul-Haq Accounting – business creation
    - 🗁 Franklin, Ben – stamp collection
  - 🗁 Closed Matters
    - 🗁 Franklin, Ben – employment claim (government)

In this situation, it would be a simple matter to move a folder containing all of the items from the Ben Franklin stamp collection matter, once it is closed, into the Closed Matters folder (where other cases Ben has brought to you have been stored).

This sort of approach creates a visual structure that is obvious to someone who looks at it, both in what goes where but also where they may be if they are browsing. Similarly, a folder structure like this would allow you to set retention strategies on the closed matters without impacting the open ones. Even something as straight-forward as ensuring that, once a folder is dropped in the Closed Matters area, it is automatically altered to be read-only so that it can't be deleted before the end of its life.[5]

---

it accessible. *Open Archival Information System*, Wikipedia (last visited Aug. 31, 2025), https://en.wikipedia.org/wiki/Open_Archival_Information_System.

5. Every file on every system has a set of attributes that describe how it can be used. Each person interacting with a file can read it (R), write to it (W), or execute it (E). The latter files tend to be the apps themselves. Most lawyers will not edit or need to work on executable files. But everything else we make tends to be Read and Write accessible. This allows the creation, editing, and deletion of files. If you make a file read-only, you can allow people to view it without allowing them to modify or delete it.

A content management or document management system like Microsoft SharePoint or NetDocuments can apply that sort of protection automatically. You can also go into the file properties of each document you create in a Microsoft product and protect it, blocking the ability for others to edit it, although this is time consuming at scale. Or you might open up Windows Explorer and navigate to the folder in which all of the client files live, right-click on the folder properties, and make the folder and files read-only at the file level.

There are many ways to achieve the same outcomes if your goal is to preserve files against deletion or alteration. It is worth emphasizing too that most of these do not require any specific technology. You do not need a content management system to do these things for you, although it probably can. Records management-capable applications will provide the tools so that you can automate some of these functions, but you can also have a checklist that reflects your closing file process and perform the steps manually.

Closed File Accessibility

Another way to manage the long-term retention is to remove the files entirely from your working systems. It is commonplace for a company to download and place digital files onto a portable medium, like a CD or DVD disc or a USB storage drive. You might take this approach with your client matters, immediately exporting them to a portable device and giving them to your client to retain for themselves. Alternatively, if they are stored on a fixed medium—like a CD-R as opposed to a CD-RW (read/write)—you could store these discs yourself in a safe, off-site, long-term storage facility.

This brings us back around to the file format issue, though. There is another medium that remains common in law firms for backup and storage and that is the digital tape. Like the CD and USB drive, it is an external storage medium that can keep a large copy of data and be removed from your law practice. It is often used as a backup medium because it can store so much data in such a compact device. It can also be used when you are off-loading closed files from your law practice although, unless the matter is large, it may be costly and inefficient in comparison to smaller portable media.

The downside is that, over the years, tape design and science has changed. Tapes you buy at the beginning of your law practice may become obsolete, just as we saw with lawyers who used floppy diskettes. Eventually, those floppy diskettes were replaced and the drives that were required to read them were no longer available. If you had not invested time or money in ensuring that the data on those drives was migrated forward to a newer medium, that data was for all practical purposes lost.

Similarly, if you are storing documents or other digital objects for a period of years, you need to make sure that not only is the media on which they are stored accessible, that the files themselves can be opened and accessed. It is one thing to give someone a set of digital files. If they decide to access them five or ten years later, and they are able to see the files in their folders but no longer have an app that will open them, that data is lost to them. When you consider how long a lawyer practices, there is a good chance that there will be changes in storage media that mean that those off-loaded early career client matters become inaccessible as you become a seasoned practitioner.

There are file format types that are designed for long-term preservation. These include the PDF/A portable document (archival) format. It can improve the likelihood that the documents that you are retaining for yourself or for your client are accessible into the future. The PDF format is a highly stable format, and so readers for it should continue to be available, and the PDF/A version is designed specifically to ensure that it can be accessed by the widest number of PDF readers. The downside is that, in saving a file to the PDF/A format, you will lose some functionality in the document itself—for example, hyperlinks to external cases or statutes in a brief will be flattened so the links no longer work—and you will also lose the metadata that is in the original document. If you are keeping these files for potential future litigation purposes, like being sued by a client for legal malpractice, you may not want to alter the original files that provide evidence about the work you did. Like so many issues with law practice technology, you will need to balance your technology solution with your professional obligations.

There is not a good technological answer to this problem. It will mean that, periodically, your law practice will need to assess the accessibility of its long-term storage files. Ideally, you will want to keep the number of files and objects you are storing long-term to an absolute minimum. If you can, create that CD or external storage drive—put your branding on it to help with referrals—and offload what you can to the client themselves. In that way, you can keep only the minimum of what you need for your own purposes. Much of your work product can be folded back into your day-to-day law practice: re-using briefs, motions, and other precedents and know-how. This eliminates it from this aging file format issue.

You may decide to off-load or store documents in their native formats at the risk of losing access to those files if the app that is required to open them is no longer available. On the other hand, you might off-load your closed files to your clients in the PDF format—on the reasonable likelihood that they are even less likely to have the originating apps needed over the long term to open the documents you provide them in the native formats—to improve the likelihood that they will be able to access them on their own.

Do not exclude paper from your closed file approach either. It may seem like the opposite of a technology solution, but paper is one of our oldest technologies. One of the reasons it has lasted so long is that the tools needed to recover information from it—our eyeballs or their equivalent—have continued to exist. If the key documents in a client matter can be reduced to paper, it may be the best long-term storage solution although it comes with its own costs and burdens.[6] Paper does not eliminate all long-term storage concerns. You will still need to consider where you will store it, and the cost is likely to be substantially more than offline digital storage. It will be susceptible to the same acts of God—fires, floods, tornados—and paper as a medium can deteriorate over time. But it should remain an option for your closed files.

Chapter 16 Exercise

A. Identify a computer file that you own that is at least seven years old. Knowing what you know after reading this chapter, how might you store it, or name it, or otherwise manage it for longevity? How are you ensuring that it will always be accessible?

6. Seriously, if you consider paper, plan for the cost of storing it properly. Periodically, a story will appear in the news where some garage or farm outbuilding has blown down and confidential lawyer files are blowing around a small village or town. You do not want to be that lawyer. Paper storage comes with a cost, and it will grow—the storage and the cost—over the lifetime of your law practice.

Chapter 17

Special Technology Situations

There are some areas of law practice technology that we do not think about until it is too late. These are not areas of law practice nor are they really the business of law. They have more to do with areas where your professional obligations as a lawyer run into technology challenges that are unusual. In particular, how do you maintain control over your law practice information when you no longer have control over your technology.

Crossing International Borders

The shift in law firms to largely digital law practices means that lawyers are carrying more of their client information—or access to it—with them when they are away from the office. We often think of this in terms of going down the street to the bank or courthouse or to client offices or to our homes. But what happens when you travel to a point at which your technology is accessible by a state actor, like a police officer or a border control guard?

In the past, this was probably mostly a concern of lawyers who either lived near a border or who crossed borders in order to practice, working with an international client base. More recently, lawyers have been stopped and had their devices checked or taken even when they were not traveling for work. A trip to a vacation spot outside the United States might result in a lawyer being stopped and asked to provide access to their personal device on their return.

This can create a challenge for the lawyer who has not contemplated the issue before they travel. While there is governmental guidance for United States lawyers, it requires preparation so that, if they or their devices are detained, they are not likely to disclose client or private information.[1]

One element of this is that the preparation probably only needs to focus on the information that is resident on your device. Anything that you connect to remotely should be outside the scope of any border search.

> Officers may not intentionally use the device to access information that is solely stored remotely. To avoid retrieving or accessing information stored remotely and not otherwise present on the device, Officers will either request that the traveler disable connectivity to any network (e.g., by placing the device in airplane mode), or ... Officers will themselves disable network connectivity.[2]

There is a reasonableness issue here as well as trust. There is a good chance they will try to make a copy of your device, keeping the copy while returning the device itself to you. You are taking the state security agents at their word that they will not access remote information. This is complicated, though, when apps like Microsoft Outlook or Google Gmail store your email or your contacts on your phone. A device in airplane mode or otherwise offline is likely to have synchronized information about your email and communications and possibly other details—you might pay your law firm expenses with an app that records who you met with and when and how much it cost, for example—that you would not want to disclose.

There is an entire section of the United States Customs and Border Patrol directive dealing with lawyer-client privileged information. On the one hand, this is a positive recognition of the sensitivity of certain information. It also

---

1. The primary guidance is from the United States Custom and Border Patrol in 2018 in CBP Directive No. 3340-049A. U.S. Customs and Border Prot., Dep't of Homeland Sec., CBP Directive no. 3340-049A, Border Search of Electronic Devices (2018), https://www.cbp.gov/sites/default/files/assets/documents/2018-Jan/CBP-Directive-3340-049A-Border-Search-of-Electronic-Media-Compliant.pdf [http://web.archive.org/web/20250630222717/https://www.cbp.gov/sites/default/files/assets/documents/2018-Jan/CBP-Directive-3340-049A-Border-Search-of-Electronic-Media-Compliant.pdf].

2. *Id.*, § 5.1.2. Additionally, they are instructed to "take care to ensure, throughout the course of a border search, that they do not take actions that would make any changes to the contents of the device."

requires the lawyer to have engaged in a substantial amount of preparation and endure disruption to invoke this section. This would include:

- Asserting privilege upon being requested for device access (§ 5.2.1)
- Knowing with some specificity what is or is not privileged and indicating that, preferably in writing (§ 5.2.1.1) so you can assist the CBP officer in identifying the privileged information
- Prior to a review of privileged information—you are identifying it, you are not excluding it from the search—a Filter team will be created to ensure the privileged information is segregated. (§ 5.2.1.2)
- Once the review is complete, your data will be destroyed except that a copy may be retained. (§ 5.2.1.3)

In other words, if you assert a claim of lawyer-client privilege, you will lose control of your device while this assertion is reviewed and someone accesses your device files. Alternatively, you can refuse to provide a PIN or password and potentially lose access to the device in any event, possibly permanently.[3] Lawyers who are not U.S. citizens should be wary of refusing access to their devices since this can impact their ability to re-enter the United States.

The centrality of our phones to our daily lives, let alone to how you will practice law, makes the potential disruption around a border device search untenable. Unless you are willing to part with the device, you will want to avoid taking any device that has important information with you through the United States border. The assertion of lawyer-client privilege will not necessarily result in the protection of your client information, but it will almost certainly result in your temporary loss of access to your device.

Lawyers who are going to cross a border should leave behind their devices with client data on them. This may be as simple as just planning ahead and using a personal phone that is separate from your work phone. You would need to keep contacts and calendars and other client data isolated from your personal phone. In that situation, you can provide the border guard with access to your secured personal device without any concern about what they access or that it might include confidential client information.

This assumes you are willing to forego your own privacy rights, separate from protecting your clients, by providing access to your personal device. If

3. United States citizens can refuse to provide a PIN or password and will be allowed to re-enter the United States. Individuals who are not citizens may also refuse to provide a PIN or password but may find that they are refused entry. *Id.*, § 5.2.1.3.

you are not willing, you will want to take a device through the border only if it is entirely clean of your personal information as well as of client data. People often refer to these devices as burner phones, and they are conceived of as entirely disposable. In some cases, they are called clean devices in the case of more expensive technology like laptops. In either case, the device carries nothing about you or your law practice on it.

It has become much easier to manage this thanks to cloud computing. If you have selected cloud-based systems for your email or for your law practice management system, then these can be reached with any web browser. All you need to know is your username and your password and you can access them anywhere, from any device.

You can use a device like a Chromebook or an inexpensive phone (or even an old phone that can be used on Wi-Fi networks) that has a web browser installed. You can create a burner email account to allow you to log in and set up the phone or laptop. But you would not install any additional software or otherwise personalize the device. Once you were preparing to cross the border, you would use the factory reset or, in the case of a Chromebook its powerwash feature, to return the device to its default condition.

The problem with this approach may already have suggested itself: if you are using strong passwords and multi-factor authentication, how does that work on a clean or burner device? You will still need to memorize your password manager password, so if that is web accessible, that will provide you with access to all of your other passwords. Any multi-factor authentication with text messages or SMS, though, will not reach you. If you use an authenticator app or passkeys that are tied to your physical device, those will not be usable either if you use a burner phone. You will want to have a way to use multi-factor via email or some online system—some password managers like Bitwarden support 2FA within the password management profile—that is device neutral. When you enable multi-factor authentication on an account, you are often given a list of backup codes to use in case you are unable to generate or receive a texted code. If you have stored these somewhere on the cloud, whether in a password manager or not, they can be an alternate way to get around not having your authenticator device on you.

In some cases, you can swap your own SIM card from your primary phone, the one with the private and client information on it and put it in the burner phone. In that way, you can receive SMS multi-factor codes (and phone calls and texts from clients and your law office) while you are traveling. You will just want to remember to pop the SIM out and wipe the device before returning to the border.

You can see that, to prepare to cross a border, you do not really need new or specialized technology. An old phone and a cheap laptop can be all you really need. What you really need to do is spend time planning how you will use the technology. The devices can run the same operating systems and even be the same make and models as your primary work technology. In fact, the more similar the hardware and operating systems are they are, the better they will be able to support your work if you are out of the country and need to keep up with your law practice. The primary difference is that you want to ensure that, if your device is accessed or detained, you do not expose client confidential information, your own private information, or experience a law practice business disruption because you have lost access to your device.

Selling Your Practice

It may be hard to fathom at this point, before law school has even ended, that there will come a time when you will stop practicing law voluntarily. In fact, many lawyers find that the practice of law is not how they want to spend their lives, and they make a career change that may or may not involve their law degree. If you are at a law firm when the time comes for you to take down your shingle, you may be able to avoid this step entirely.[4]

If you are a solo, though, you will want to be thinking about how you can move your physical and digital client files to another lawyer so that your clients do not lose their representation. Similarly, you may be holding onto some client files—like wills—that have not yet been resolved. It is important to consider this, perhaps as part of your file retention and client matter closing strategy.

There are rules to guide lawyers when they are bringing their practice to a close. They contain no surprises, and they are focused on ensuring that

4. If you have not heard the term before, it is common for a lawyer to be said to be "hanging out their shingle" when they start to practice law. *Hang Out One's Shingle*, MERRIAM-WEBSTER (last visited Aug. 31, 2025), https://www.merriam-webster.com/dictionary/hang%20out%20one's%20shingle.

a client's representation is not put at a disadvantage for reasons outside of their control:

> (d) Upon termination of representation, a lawyer shall take steps to the extent reasonably practicable to protect a client's interests, such as giving reasonable notice to the client, allowing time for employment of other counsel, surrendering papers and property to which the client is entitled and refunding any advance payment of fee or expense that has not been earned or incurred. The lawyer may retain papers relating to the client to the extent permitted by other law.[5]

As you can see, there are a number of steps, all of which take planning. You will need to communicate with your clients to let them know about the change. You may have sold your law practice to another lawyer, who can assume the client's matters, or the clients can move on to other lawyers. You need to have maintained accurate financial accounting and trust funds to ensure that monies managed by you but belonging to others will be returned to them. Unless you have not been actively taking clients for a number of years, there's a good chance that the final matters you resolved for your clients—or even the ones that were in progress—will have documents you need to retain and manage even after you have left practice.

The thing to keep in mind is that, while you have left the practice of law, it will not have left you. For some years after you have left—and some lawyers return to practice after doing something else for a number of years—you may have to maintain some of the technology infrastructure that you built out for your law practice. Things like custom integrations and vendor lock-in may continue to be concerns even though your clients have moved on to other lawyers.

Anything but Microsoft

It is clear by now that Microsoft has deep roots in the legal profession and, to some degree, constrains its law practice technology growth. If you decide not to use Microsoft products, you will probably run into complications while practicing law. A court filing system may balk at your documents, or, if you have opted out of Microsoft Windows itself, you may find a lack of applica-

5. A.B.A. Model Rules of Professional Conduct, r. 1.16 (Am. Bar Ass'n 2025).

tions or compatibility issues. These are not insurmountable, and, with a bit of planning, you can adapt entirely to a Microsoft-free law practice.

There are plenty of options to avoid Microsoft products if that is your preference. Ever since the first Macintosh computer was released by Apple, lawyers have extolled the value of these sleeker, often more thoughtfully designed, systems. Macs remain persistently available in the legal profession, even if they are never widely adopted or even see significant growth.[6] This stagnation relates only to computer systems. The Apple iPhone dominates the legal profession's mobile devices in the same way that Microsoft does on the computer.[7]

Android runs only 20% of the phones for the legal profession but it shares a technology base—Linux—with other operating systems that lawyers could use. Linux, like Android, is open-source and so is free-to-acquire and operate on your own. There is a wide variety of free and commercial software that runs on Linux, with many comparable products to those found on Windows and Mac OS systems. Also, like every modern computer, you can use a web browser to access the internet and cloud computing and any application you license there.

At first impression, you might blanche at taking a partial or full open-source approach. But it is worth keeping in mind if only to let your technology selection and planning maintain as large a horizon as possible. Most lawyers already use a wide variety of open-source applications—Google Chrome and Microsoft Edge are based on open-source Chromium, Android is open-source, as is Firefox, and Mediawiki, the app that runs Wikipedia—in their day-to-day law practice. Even our legal research, while it often centers around commercial products, tends to rely on public domain information that is (or could be) freely accessible.

---

6. About 11% of respondents to the ABA's 2023 Legal Technology Survey indicated they used a Macintosh OS operating system. This number is substantially higher—16% —among solos and drops to about 5% in some of the larger law firms. This reflects the sole practitioner's ability to make technology choices without worrying about office interoperability AM. BAR ASS'N, 2023 LEGAL TECHNOLOGY SURVEY REPORT: LAW OFFICE TECHNOLOGY 13, question 12 (2024).

7. Nearly 78% of respondents—and over 85% in all law firms with more than 50 lawyers—use the iPhone for work-related tasks. Android is a distant second with 20% of respondents. Solos are more likely to be on Android devices than large law firm lawyers. AM. BAR ASS'N, 2023 LEGAL TECHNOLOGY SURVEY REPORT: LIFE & PRACTICE 25, question 25 (2024).

Open-source applications lie on a continuum, then, that many lawyers have already started along. In most cases, they have traveled as far along that road as they need or are able to. But you may find that one of the Linux distributions (or flavors), like Ubuntu or Mint, fits your needs better than Microsoft Windows. Even small things like having more flexibility in how you customize your desktop—for example, Microsoft has removed the Windows 10 feature that you could move your task bar to the top of your screen, a limitation that you could overcome on Linux—may make a Linux operating system more appealing. As Microsoft moves towards an advertising-driven approach on its consumer technology, you may find that you are having to make a choice between a more expensive Microsoft license and an ostensibly free but ad-driven alternative in order to keep Windows. Similarly, the increasing integration of artificial intelligence by Microsoft embedding its CoPilot product in the operating system may cause you to want to look at other, AI-free options.

The choices for lawyers to mix-and-match commercial software have never been greater than they are now. Both Apple Mac OS and Linux distributions have software called Windows emulators available. Products like CodeWeaver's CrossOver create an environment where you can install a Windows version of an application—if there is not one native to the Mac or Linux operating system you want to use—and run it as though it were on Windows. For example, you might select Ubuntu Linux for your operating system and, with CrossOver, install Microsoft Word, Excel, and PowerPoint. Your web browser could still be Google Chrome, and you would be running the same applications as the vast majority of lawyers practicing in the United States, if not the most common operating system.

This assumes you want to run the same software as most lawyers. If you are only concerned with creating the same output formats as most lawyers, your options broaden significantly. There is a mature office suite of tools known as LibreOffice that provides very similar functionality to Microsoft Office and has been around almost as long. There is no trace of it being designed for lawyers, so things like a Table of Authorities button will be missing. The functionality to build a Table of Authorities is there, though, and, while there will be a learning curve, it may not be any steeper than the one you face with gaining expertise with Microsoft products.

Beyond the interface, there is a great deal of uniformity. You can print to PDF and generate PDFs just as you can on Windows computers. The PDFs are standards-compliant and can be used both for e-filing and for your long-term client file retention. You can save and open files in Microsoft's Word, Excel, and PowerPoint file formats in LibreOffice.[8]

There may be some internal formatting challenges—different fonts, differing support for certain features—but, for professional responsibility reasons, you are unlikely to be sending editable documents to many people outside of your law firm; ideally you would send things in a fixed format like PDF, both to ensure the document is not changed and that it does not carry metadata.

If you need to work on a shared document, you may want to upload it to Microsoft OneDrive or Google Drive so that you can access and edit the document with your colleagues. This would be the more efficient approach even if you were on Microsoft Windows and had the same Microsoft Office suite as your collaborators. It is unlikely, in the legal profession, that the person receiving a document created with an Office Open XML compatible application will be unable to open it, no matter what operating system it came from.

The flexibility on desktop or device software is growing but does not compare with the options available on the cloud. You may not realize it, but Google's Chromebooks are based on a Linux distribution of the Chromium operating system (which is different from the Chromium web browser). While the Chromebook operating system is proprietary, the approach they advocate for can be replicated with any Windows, Mac, or Linux operating system: the web browser as the interface with the world.

Web-based applications do not, for the most part, care what operating system you are running. They are far more likely to care about the web browser you are using to interact with their app. While some people have installed Microsoft Edge on Linux, it is the one web browser that probably, like Safari for Apple devices, is not intended to run on other operating systems. Linux, like those other operating systems, has web browsers that were designed just for it, but you will also find Linux versions of Google Chrome (and Chromium) as well as Mozilla's Firefox and other open-source web browsers.

The web-browser-as-central-technology means that any cloud-based applications—law practice management systems, accounting apps, social media, email and calendar, even Microsoft 365 on the web—are accessible from any

8. For a long time, Microsoft Office documents were created in a proprietary format. In 2005 and shortly after, Microsoft sponsored the creation of the Office Open XML format. The format is now a standard and is supported widely, available in Microsoft Office (the X at the end of each format file ending—docx, pptx, xslx—indicates it's an XML-based file format), Google Docs, LibreOffice, and Corel WordPerfect, among others. *Office Open XML*, WIKIPEDIA (last visited Aug. 31, 2025), https://en.wikipedia.org/wiki/Office_Open_XML.

non-Microsoft Windows device with an internet connection just as well as they are from a Windows-based one. Similarly, lawyers will find their interfaces with courts and their research access with legal publishers to primarily occur via a web browser. It can level the playing field when it comes to choice for a lawyer's practice technology.

It goes without saying that most lawyers will not end up working on a Linux-based computer. It remains an unfamiliar technology to most law students even as it has matured and is adopted by large organizations outside of the legal profession. The constraining effect of Microsoft Office and Windows on lawyers means that other operating systems, including Apple's MacOS, will remain relatively scarce in law firms. This does not mean you should not consider the option. Even if you decide it is easier to go with Microsoft products, that there is less *friction* in conforming with the majority of the legal profession, it is worth remembering this large, mature technology exists and is an option for law practice.

Dying

As the saying goes, we can avoid everything but death and taxes. Hopefully, you will have left your law practice behind and enjoyed retirement or an alternate career path before death finds you. It can be wishful thinking, though, to assume that you will be able to manage the conclusion of your law practice, let alone your life. Unfortunately, it is common for lawyers to die without planning what will happen to their law practice. Even when a lawyer is in a law firm, a death can throw client matters into confusion while people try to get a grasp on what needs to be done.

A place to start is to ensure that, in your day-to-day law practice, you are keeping your systems current. Your contacts should be in your contact manager, not on pieces of paper lying on your desk. Your emails should be accessible and, hopefully, organized in your email client. Your calendar should be up to date and critical dates flagged so that neither you nor others miss a statute of limitations or filing date. You may not be thinking about other people finding information that belongs to you, but the better organized your information is, the more likely someone coming along after you will be able to benefit from your planning.

The Model Rules place the obligation on a lawyer to have some continuity, but Rule 1.3 only lays out, in the comments, what due diligence *may require* of a sole practitioner. Primarily, it is identifying a lawyer who will be able to continue the work:

> [5] To prevent neglect of client matters in the event of a sole practitioner's death or disability, the duty of diligence may require that each sole practitioner prepare a plan, in conformity with applicable rules, that designates another competent lawyer to review client files, notify each client of the lawyer's death or disability, and determine whether there is a need for immediate protective action. Cf. Rule 28 of the American Bar Association Model Rules for Lawyer Disciplinary Enforcement (providing for court appointment of a lawyer to inventory files and take other protective action in absence of a plan providing for another lawyer to protect the interests of the clients of a deceased or disabled lawyer).[9]

It does not provide any mechanism for how that lawyer will gain access to client files, whether in paper or digital formats. Someone might look under a flowerpot for a door key, but that is trickier—and should be—when dealing with online systems: usernames, passwords, multi-factors. If a court has to appoint a lawyer to inventory files, that only creates additional delay while also not resolving the access issue.

In the recent past, if a lawyer died, they often had paper files that needed to be managed. While this was difficult, because paper files might be voluminous and, in their own way, might have been tricky to organize, at least they were accessible. Someone could go into an office or storage facility and see the paper files, identifying what needed to be worked on and what needed to be sent to another lawyer or back to the client.

This is less easy with digital systems unless you have taken the time to plan. It is common for a person to die or become incapacitated and for their online accounts to continue without them.[10] Monthly Amazon kitchen supply orders will continue to be shipped and automated payments for Netflix and online services may continue. Unless the form of payment is declined or needs to be

9. A.B.A. Model Rules of Professional Conduct, r. 1.3, cmt. 5 (Am. Bar Ass'n 2025).

10. I use the term incapacitated because it is not only death that may bring a sudden stop to your law practice. You might be injured and unable to practice for a long period of time. Some lawyers commit crimes and are jailed and unable or unwilling to assist in the transfer of their clients' matters. You may feel invincible as you finish law school and get ready to practice, but there are a wide variety of ways your law practice could come to a short, sharp stop without death being the reason.

renewed, there may be no way for the publishers and platforms to know that anything has changed on your end of the transaction. No one will be able to manage your personal and professional systems unless you have planned for this access in advance.

This can be incredibly important for a lawyer, not just because of the client's needs for continued representation. A lawyer who has put their trust in cloud computing may have access to their practice management service or website domain name or email only so long as they make their monthly or annual payments. Most online technology subscriptions will have a period after which, if a payment is no longer made, the account is deleted without recourse. If you were to be incapacitated, if anything happened to the payments for the services that hold your client and law practice data, you might end up losing all of that information. It could be an unrecoverable loss.

In the past, a lawyer might avoid this issue by keeping their client and professional information off the cloud. An on-premises-centric environment would mean that, subject to electricity, most systems would keep running in perpetuity. Even in a power outage, the data and systems would remain. Microsoft Windows computers could, in the past, contain a password that was empty or blank.[11] That option no longer exists and, in most cases, a Windows computer will require a password, PIN, or passkey in order to gain access. A lawyer using a professional version of Windows may also have encrypted their hard drive, using Microsoft's default Bitlocker encryption, which would mean that, even if someone knew how to remove the hard drive storage from the computer, they may still face challenges accessing the files the drive holds.

You might think that a death or even a person who has been given a Power of Attorney might be enough for someone else to assume access to your online accounts. In fact, without a username and password and, increasingly, access to the multi-factor authentication device, there is no quick way to gain access to someone else's accounts. Even if you have authorized someone to have that access, it could take weeks or months, if it ever happens, for them to be given access by the platform owner. Your clients may not be able to wait for that resolution.

This can happen even if you have not been incapacitated. If you use a multi-factor authentication app on a phone that falls into a swimming pool, you may be unable to validate your identity. Unless you have thought about

11. To be clear, the password slot did not contain anything. I once set up a faculty computer over a summer and let them know their password was blank. They typed in "blank" repeatedly without success.

backup email accounts or phone numbers (although how many people have multiple phone numbers) in advance of losing access and been diligent about keeping a copy of your offline authentication codes, you could easily lose access to client matters without any extraordinary circumstances. Our access to our digital lives is incredibly brittle and needs regular attention.

This is why you should plan for this possibility from the start. Now, as you are preparing to go into law practice, be thinking about how you will leave law practice. For your sake, for your clients' sake, and, frankly, for the sake of the people who will have to take care of you or your estate, it is better to plan now than later. Fortunately, many of the plans are things you should be doing anyway as part of practicing ethically with technology as a lawyer.

The best place to start is with your passwords. If there was any reason to be reluctant to use biometrics like your face or your fingerprint, becoming incapacitated or dying may be the best reason to avoid them. Unlike your finger or face, you can leave your password for someone else to use. If you think back to the chapter on security, there are three access-related items that you really need to memorize to run a modern law practice:

- The password to access your computer (your Windows PIN or password)
- The password to access your password manager (your primary password)
- The password or PIN for your phone

Those three items will provide you with access to all of the other resources that you use for your personal life and your law practice. Your computer PIN or password will give access to everything on that device, including documents and applications. Your password manager should have information about what accounts you have because you will have a unique password for each account, they should each have an entry. Your password manager is an ideal place to store your security questions and answers—especially if you decide to create unique answers for every question—and can also store the URL that people would need to use to access the site. Your phone or device PIN will allow someone to get on the device that may contain your multi-factor authentication app, or passkeys, or receive SMS texts with codes so that they can log in to your accounts.

You should revisit every site on which you have multi-factor authentication set up. The first thing you should do is ensure there is a backup method—an email account, an alternative phone number, perhaps belonging to the lawyer you have designated to step in if you experience an emergency—to validate your access to your account. Then find the backup codes that most providers create when you turn on multi-factor authentication. If you find that they are only created when MFA is turned on, you may want to turn MFA off and turn it back on again—going through the complete setup a second time—in order to generate that code or, often, set of 10 codes.

Once you have the MFA backup codes, you can store those in an offline place. Since they are alternatives to using your mobile device to receive a code or create a code with an app, you should still protect them. But they do not change, and you can print them off and store them with other critical documents.

Some sites will also provide you with a method to designate a successor. This remains relatively rare, but you should investigate and configure it on those platforms where it is an option. I would not go so far as to say this was a requirement for lawyers, just because it would substantially limit the technology available for law practice. Also, it is never the only option to secure an account, but you might consider it a plus factor when making a technology selection.

Google users on free and paid Workspace accounts will have access to Google's Inactive Account Manager.[12] This allows you to designate an individual in advance to assume control of your account. By default, it assumes that you are alive but have forgotten about your Google account. It will send you emails and text messages to the last known email addresses and phone numbers listed on your account.

More importantly, though, it allows you to add up to 10 other people to be notified if the condition you set is triggered. By default, the condition is failure to access the account for 18 months. This may work for a personal account, but it is far too long a window for a lawyer. You might set the condition to a few weeks or a month. Realistically, even if you take a holiday, you are likely to be accessing your law firm email within a four- or five-week period. This may feel short but, if your other access methods have failed, the longer you wait to allow notifications to go out, the more likely something in a client matter will fall through the widening crack.

---

12. *Inactive Account Manager*, GOOGLE ACCOUNT (last visited Aug. 31, 2025), https://myaccount.google.com/inactive.

Since technology does not care who provides the authentication, if you store your three key pieces of information—Windows, password manager, and phone PIN—somewhere safe and ensure someone else knows where to find it, you can make the issue of access during your incapacitation much simpler. A trusted person with those items can gain access and help to ensure your clients are not left in the lurch.

Beyond passwords, there are other ways to access digital files when a lawyer is incapacitated. They are all more complicated, though, than merely getting the same access that *you have* when you log in with a username, password, and multiple factors. For example, it is usually possible to remove a hard drive from a device or create a copy of it. This tactic, often used in e-discovery for evidentiary purposes, can yield access to files and data.

This makes the data accessible, but it does not necessarily make it usable. If, when you were using the data, you used a special application—like a practice management system or an accounting application—on your PC, then that software may be required to use the data. If someone removes the hard drive storage from your computer and attempts to use that data, they would need to install the same software that you had. This is not necessarily difficult, but it may be time-consuming. A lawyer selected by you or appointed by the court may not know how to remove a drive, let alone attach it to a new computer and access its contents. If this situation were to happen, it would likely result in financial expenses and the need to hire technical expertise.

Alternatively, you may have been diligent about creating a backup of your law firm's data. Even then, a backup will need to be restored to the systems from which it came. It is not usually accessible on its own—unless it consists of discrete files, for example, documents uploaded to a Microsoft OneDrive or SharePoint account—and so the existence of the data does not guarantee it is usable.

As a matter of finding the most expeditious path, putting your successor or colleague or family in your own shoes is the best option. As you plan for how you will practice efficiently and securely, think about how you will make those tools—particularly the password manager and your computer—available in an emergency.

Chapter 17 Exercises

A. Install Libre Office. Create a Table of Authorities using a multiple-index strategy.

B. Devise a strategy for collecting and maintaining authentication codes for each online account you use. Create a checklist that describes the steps you will take each time you create or update your online accounts to ensure that you are gathering the necessary information in the event of your incapacitation.

Index